MW00563473

Search for the Guru

Prequel to
Adventures of a Western Mystic: Apprentice to the Masters

By
Peter Mt. Shasta

Church of the Seven Rays
P. O. Box 1103
Mount Shasta, California 96067
U.S.A.

Copyright 2013, 2014 by Peter Mt. Shasta. All rights reserved.

No part of this book may be reproduced, stored in a retrieval system, or be transmitted by any means without the written permission of the author.

ISBN: 978–0982807385 (Revised Edition, March, 2014)

ISBN: 978–0982807392 (LSI Edition, May, 2014)

Library of Congress Control Number: 2014901140

By the same author:

"I AM" the Open Door
(Pearl Publishing, 1978)

Adventures of a Western Mystic: Apprentice to the Masters
(Church of the Seven Rays, 2010)

"I AM" Affirmations and the Secret of their Effective Use
(Church of the Seven Rays, 2012)

Website: www.PeterMtShasta.com

Cover: Peter Mt. Shasta, 1972, after first trip to India

Dedication

To the people of India, keepers of the Dharma.

Contents

Prayer to the Divine Guru:

Asatoma Sadgamaya
Tamasoma Jyotirgamaya
Mrtyorma Amritamgamaya.

From untruth lead us to truth,
From darkness lead us to light,
From death lead us to immortality.

—Brihadarayaka Upanishad

In Gratitude

I would like to thank the following for their invaluable editorial assistance: Karen Carty, Sandee Collings, Iris Credo, Ashish and Runa Gupta, Caroline Hopper, Prasannakshi Karnamadakala, Kellie Jean Lewis, Carl Marsak, Daye Proffit, Aaron Rose, Sai Santosh Bangalore, Miles and Deepti Wilkinson, and others who wish to remain anonymous. Their dedicated efforts have greatly enhanced the final outcome.

Note

Who am I? What am I? Why am I here? These are the eternal questions I began trying to answer in childhood, a quest that eventually led to the Far East. In both India and America I met great saints, yogis and sages who spurred me toward realization. I have written here of that adventure in hopes that it will benefit others. Some events may have inadvertently been placed in a different sequence than they actually occurred. Also, some names have been changed.

This autobiography covers the period from birth to my return from India in 1973. For the account of subsequent adventures please read the sequel (written prior to this book), *Adventures of a Western Mystic: Apprentice to the Masters.*

Preface

Who Needs a Guru?

In the quest for wisdom, it is traditional to seek out someone further along the path, someone who has already mastered what you seek. In India this principle and practice is embodied in the search for a Guru. Guru is a Sanskrit word that is a combination of *gu*, meaning darkness or ignorance, and *ru*, meaning light or wisdom; hence, the Guru is a teacher who leads one from ignorance to wisdom, from darkness to light.

This person may or may not have certain powers known as *siddhis*, which can be attained through concentration; but these powers do not necessarily indicate the teacher has attained enlightenment. Among the impressive powers that can be attained are: knowledge of past lifetimes, psychic ability to know what others are thinking and doing, the ability to manipulate external circumstances such as teleporting objects, healing the sick and mastery of the physical body. As the great yogi Ramakrishna said, these powers are simply phenomena, and to strive after them is not only a waste of time, but actually an obstacle to spiritual realization. A true Guru does not usually demonstrate what powers they may have, knowing that to do so may only distract from the true path. By far, one of the greatest powers is the ability to appear as an ordinary person and yet to walk as a Master, unrecognized in the world.

To have a relationship with a Guru is so important in India and Tibet that more emphasis is placed on the Guru than God, as the Guru is the personification of God in daily life. The Guru is not only your innermost, spiritual friend, but also the one who serves as your guide in the ocean of delusion. Even those spiritual traditions that promote spontaneous realization, such as *Dzogchen* or *Zen*, give detailed instruction for which it is first absolutely essential to *search for a Guru*.

CHAPTER 1

Descent

At one time I knew who I was. Then I forgot—or rather, was forced to forget. Remembering who I am has been a slow process. Before this life I was in a body of light beyond the Earth, and I knew the Source. I was part of a family of interdependent beings linked in consciousness. Out of this field of awareness two white-robed beings appeared, whom I sensed wished to communicate something of importance.

"It's time," one said.

"Time?"

"Time to return."

"Return where?"

"To Earth," the other said.

"But, I don't want to go back."

"You must. Don't you remember? You were shown the plan and you agreed...."

"No, I don't remember. What plan?"

Their tolerance for questions ceased and I felt myself in the grip of a will I was unable to resist.

"Now, forget who you are," they commanded.

"No, I will not forget!"

"Forget!" they ordered again.

I felt consciousness slipping away as I was pushed toward Earth. The planet was enveloped in a brown haze, which I realized was generated by selfishness, and I felt a repugnance. Below I saw areas of darkness shot through by red flashes generated by violent anger, and I realized with horror that I was descending into a world of deadly conflict. I tried to break free from these Masters forcing me downward but they continued to push me lower, and into the awaiting fetus in my mother's womb, still commanding, "Forget...forget...forget...."

It was 1944, toward the end of the Second World War. I was born on an Army base in Florida while my father was stationed on the island of

Guam in the South Pacific. In less than a year atomic bombs would be dropped on Japan, resulting in the end of that war, although the struggles of humanity would continue.

Through the bars of the cage-like crib I saw the dimly lit room. I was cold and wet and felt the pain of hunger. I cried but no one came, for mothers had been taught that their freedom lay in ignoring the cries of their infants—that they needed to conform to a preset schedule of feeding and sleeping. Thus, I grew up in emotional isolation, feeling abandoned—that I had done something wrong. How could I ever earn the love of my mother?

After what seemed an eternity a woman entered the room—the woman who had been a vehicle for my return to Earth, and I saw with a shock that in many past lifetimes she was the same soul that had caused my death. Now she was atoning for that harm by giving me life. I was relieved to see that she did not recognize me, that she saw only a baby whose helpless inability to speak she equated with lack of comprehension.

During childhood I saw people who had no understanding of life and their role in it, and who lied to themselves and others because of that inability. I marveled at what seemed to be a mutual agreement to believe each others' lies. When I tried to awaken them and point out their self-deception they became angry, so I gradually allowed that ability to see their inner natures atrophy. I tried to become what they called a "normal human being," accepting illusions as reality. I observed how people acted, and mimicked what worked, creating an ego that enabled me to function in the world.

Chapter 2

"I'm a Swami"

That ego may have partially dissolved at bath time, for as the waves sloshed over my naked body in the tub, I felt more in touch with my real Self. As I dried off the first thing I always did was to wrap a towel around my head in the shape of a turban, which I instinctively knew how to arrange. I would then sit on the bath mat, cross my legs in *padmasana* and feel a great peace fill my being.[1]

"What are you doing in there?" my mother would ask, knocking on the bathroom door.

"Oh, nothing."

"Then open the door."

"What is that?" my mother would ask, looking at the towel on my head.

"What I'm supposed to wear," I said with certainty.

"Why is that?"

"Because, I am a *swami!*"[2]

"A swami, what's that?"

I didn't know, but was certain that it was what I wanted to be.

It never occurred to me that it was unusual for an American kid to want to be a swami rather than a train engineer, fireman, or baseball player like my friends. All I knew was that while wearing a turban I felt self-reliant and free of uncertainty.[3]

I used to awaken at five o'clock in the morning full of energy and ready to start the day; however, my mother forbade me to waken her until at least seven. Filled with boredom, I would be desperate for something to

---

1   *Padmasana:* a yogic, cross-legged, sitting posture in which the spine is kept straight to allow greater flow of the life force upward through all the spiritual centers (*chakras*).

2   *Swami:* a renunciate initiated into a particular religious order.

3   Many years later a Master known as the Mahachohan came in a dream and revealed a past lifetime in which I had been a swami in the mountains of northern India and taught many people to meditate.

do, and would sit on the edge of my bed scanning the toys on the shelf and the books in the bookcase. I could rarely find something that would interest me for more than a few minutes. My attention would be drawn to the tree outside the window, waiting for its leaves to be illuminated by the rising sun, then back to the clock hanging on the wall, where the second hand slowly inched around the dial.

Then one morning as I was sitting there in the semi-darkness a being in white appeared. Nothing like this had ever happened but his appearance seemed perfectly natural. I listened intently to what he had to say.

"I have come to help you pass the time," he said, obviously aware of my frustration. Without wasting any time he said, "Listen to the sound in your head. As you focus on the sound it will change. Just listen to what you hear and time will disappear." Then he was gone.

I had heard these sounds, but fearing they might be a sign of insanity or some incurable disease, had tried to ignore them. Now this mysterious being had implied that not only were they all right, but they were something of benefit. When I did as he said, I was fascinated that the sound would often begin as a hum like that of an electronic device, then change to the sound of crickets on a warm summer night or even the chirping of birds. Sometimes when I opened my eyes I would discover that the sun had risen, and I was actually hearing the birds in the branches of the tree outside the window. I would be overjoyed that two hours had elapsed and I felt a sense of peace and serenity to start the day.[4]

In later years I would not need to focus on the sounds but would

---

4   *Nada Yoga:* union with the Source through sound, described in the Vedic text, the *Nada Brahma*. Consciousness manifests as both light and sound; this yoga focuses on the audible aspect. Some of these sounds may originate from the flow of blood through the blood vessels in the head, which stimulates the inner and middle ear. They may also be produced by bioelectric currents. By focusing attention on these sensitive parts of the ear, the blood flow can be altered to produce different sounds (as in biofeedback therapy). Whatever the source, focusing on them, like focusing on the breath or the use of a mantra, stills the mind to allow the realization of expanded awareness. Eventually, as awareness expands the sound of *Om* can be heard, the sound which pre-exists the creation of the material universe.

automatically go inward to access that place of serenity within myself without realizing what I was doing, not knowing this was called meditation. I would come home from school, throw my books on the desk, sit on the edge of the bed, and go into this inner place. When my mother asked, "What were you doing sitting on the edge of your bed staring into space?" I did not know how to answer, for I was not aware that I was doing anything.

When she consulted the school psychologist he asked, "He's not hurting anything is he?"

"No."

"Well, then, you might as well let him continue."

The only unfortunate consequence was that sometimes I would go into this state of transcendence at the most inopportune times. Once it happened in the middle of a baseball game Saturday morning when I was playing the right outfield position. I had not realized that the innings had changed. What was hurtful was that my team did not call me in until it was my turn at bat.

In school, sometimes I would look up to find everyone staring at me.

"Where were you?"

"What do you mean?" I would ask, embarrassed, the blood rushing to my ears.

"You were gone!"

CHAPTER 3

Childhood

An immense Persian rug covered our living room floor, and my earliest memories of childhood are associated with that rug. I spent hours looking at its elaborate patterns and tracing out their designs with my finger. Its pattern was a garden, with four avenues approaching the center, where there was a fountain. The avenues represented the four elements—earth, water, air and fire—and the fountain was Divinity at the center of life. I longed for such order and certainty, but in vain. No one seemed to know the purpose of life or even if it had a purpose.[5]

My mother divorced my father when I was about two. When he came home from the South Pacific after the Second World War, they discovered they had little in common. She wanted a life in high society and to travel the world, while he wanted to be a schoolteacher. She detested religion as superstition, and although my mother's father had founded a synagogue, I grew up knowing nothing about Judaism. I did not know that having a mother who was of Jewish descent meant that I was also considered Jewish. We left Florida and moved in with my grandmother in her big house on a hill in Scarsdale, New York, since on his teacher's salary my father could only afford a pittance in child support.

My radiant, white-haired grandmother, Hannah, generously bestowed the love I rarely felt from my mother, who was always pressuring me to act like a gentleman and "make something of yourself." That meant becoming wealthy in some respectable profession—becoming a doctor, lawyer, banker, or engineer.

Hannah used to invite me upstairs to listen to the Metropolitan Opera every Sunday afternoon on WQXR, the most popular classical music

---

5   Societies such as the Native American that live closer to the earth listen to the elders, who explain the purpose of life, often through story or song. There are series of progressive initiations into the mysteries of human existence. In the modern age, elders are often abandoned or isolated in group homes.

radio station in the state. She had her own living room, which contained a magnificent cherry-wood, Steinway piano. I used to sit at her feet on the ornate, Chinese silk carpet while she played the various leitmotifs of the Wagnerian operas so I would recognize them during the performance. There was a separate music for each theme, among them: Woton, King of the Gods; Rhine maidens and their gold; the dwarf, Alberich, who stole their gold and forged a ring to rule the world; the dragon, Fafner, who guarded the ring; Siegfried, the hero; Brunhilde, his lover; the sacred fire, guarded by the fire god, Loge; and the Valkyrie who carried the slain heroes to the heaven of Valhalla.[6]

Wagner's entire four opera Ring Cycle was broadcast live on WQXR from New York City. It seemed miraculous that from my grandmother's upstairs window I could see the Empire State Building twenty-five miles away, knowing that the opera we were listening to was being was being performed live there. It was all a part of the mystical atmosphere created those Sunday afternoons, just the two of us listening to the tale of how even the Gods, questing for ever greater power, were condemned to lose their dominion and fall to Earth as mortals—finding their ultimate redemption only through love.

That same struggle for power existed even between these two women with whom I lived. My mother sought control through domination and will, a power against which I rebelled; yet for my grandmother, who emanated love, wisdom, and compassion, I would gladly have done anything. Even in the Germanic legend of the Opera the power of the spear possessed by the God Wotan came from the agreement of those over whom he ruled. When he betrayed those agreements and acted solely to satisfy himself, the magic power of the spear was broken and his power unraveled.

My grandmother explained with a sparkle in her eye how with the aid of the *Tarnkappe*, a helmet that made Siegfried invisible, he slew the dragon, Fafner and drank his blood. Then he could understand the birds, which told him how to escape those plotting against him and

---

6   The Ring of the Nibelung (*Der Ring des Nibelungen*), by Richard Wagner (1813–1883). The Ring is composed of four operas: The Rhine Gold (*Das Rheingold*), The Valkyrie (*Die Valküre*), Siegfried (*Siegfried*), and Twilight of the Gods (*Götterdämmerung*).

achieve victory. In the fading afternoon light she told me how this was symbolic of the need for every man to subdue the dragon of his lower nature to become a Master. As she explained this philosophy, a gentle light emanated from her face, which even in her advanced age gave her a serene, unearthly beauty.

You need to feel love from at least one person during the first years of life to grow up healthy, many psychologists say, and I received that love from my grandmother. I used to ponder over her name because it was the same spelled forward or backward (a palindrome), and I felt it had a kind of magic, that only a perfected being could have a name like that. Decades later she appeared in the vision of my inner eye and conveyed that helping me in childhood had been her last earthly assignment prior to her ascension.

Divorce in those days was uncommon. Not having a father at home was a constant embarrassment. I felt that I was being punished undeservedly for some unknown sin, and I felt that shame acutely. One day while riding in a car with several friends, one of them asked, "What does your father do?"

Petrified, I stopped breathing, and then finally blurted out, "I don't have a father!"

After a silence during which I cringed with shame, they changed the subject. It wasn't until I reached college that I discovered that many of my classmates had similar wounds. Society was continuing to be seduced by the Hollywood delusion that love at first sight was a basis for marriage. Then, when the romance wore off, people looked for someone new. They were as ignorant of the purpose of marriage as they were the purpose of life.

On occasion my father visited, and we went on outings together— long walks which would always start with our cutting a branch from a fallen tree in the woods across the street.

"A man should always have a good stick when he goes for a hike," he said. "You never know when you might need to protect yourself from a wild animal."

I thought the chance of encountering anything wilder than a stray dog in Scarsdale, a tame suburb of New York, was pretty slim.

Later on when my sixth grade teacher said that President

Teddy Roosevelt characterized his foreign policy as "Speak softly and carry a big stick," I thought of those sticks that my father and I had brandished on our walks. I learned years later when studying the Tarot (a deck of cards using symbolism derived from the Kabbalah) that the stick on which the Hermit leaned, depicted in one of the cards, was his faith in God—a belief it took me a long time to develop.

When I was about seven my grandmother, Hannah, died. Then things worsened with my mother. She had no idea how to raise a child. She had been raised by a series of governesses, a new one almost every year, and then sent off at the age of fourteen to a military-like boarding school in Germany. It was easy to get immigrant Irish girls "fresh off the boat" in those days, who would work for room and board and a little spending money. They would do the housework and take care of the children. At the end of the day my mother would be kissed goodnight by her mother. With a frequently changing mother figure, it was understandable that the emotional bonding necessary to be a parent was absent. I rarely remember a hug from her except on special occasions like when I went off to summer camp. Her main focus seemed to be in teaching me how to behave properly in every situation and to make sure I got grades sufficient for admission to college.

My grades were not so good, though, for I realized that most of the teachers didn't really know the truth and couldn't see the point in trying to remember what they were saying. They were teaching words from a textbook, which had the effect of anesthesia. I didn't see the point in studying. It was like being fed from a can when you craved fresh food from the garden. I never felt that shiver of truth, so in class I would sit near the window and play with the tiny red mites that came inside and crawled on the sill. They made their home in the old, ivy-covered, brick walls. It was the same school my mother had attended. At the beginning of class I would coax one of those little red dots with legs onto a sheet of paper and draw a maze around it with a ballpoint pen. Due to some toxic chemical in the ink they wouldn't cross the lines, and I would see if they could find their way out by the end of class. This was far more interesting than any "facts" the teacher wanted us to memorize. Education seemed to be more about indoctrination than about teaching one to think.

One exception to the boredom of school was my first grade teacher, Mrs. Robinson, an inquisitive, kindly, white-haired lady who loved what she taught. She used to take everyone who got permission from their parents on nature walks on weekends. These outings were magical; they had to be to get twenty kids out of bed before sunrise on Saturday morning.

I remember her pointing out a spider web on tall weeds, drops of dew clinging to each joint in the web. The sun's rays hit the drops and they sparkled like diamonds, each one emitting rainbows, and these diamonds were free. In the midst of the web a big spider basked in her abundance. Feeling our attention, she began to do rapid push-ups, vibrating the web to scare us from her treasure. On our return a few hours later the dew was gone, as was the spider—perhaps eaten by one of the many red-winged blackbirds.

Another exception was Euclidian geometry class, where a theorem could be proved as being true, e.g., "Things equal to the same thing are equal to each other." There was a beautiful finality in writing at the bottom of the page of a theorem's proof "Q.E.D."—*quod erat demonstrandum* (Greek: The proof is demonstrated). It was frustrating that life outside geometry class was not so logical. I was frustrated by the pressure to become something, but what? No choices seemed appealing. Later I discovered there were places in the world, indigenous societies, where people grew up feeling they were an integral part of a meaningful community, where life had a purpose.

To escape this pressure I decided to run away from home. I was about nine, younger than when the Indian mystic Ramana Maharshi ran away to Mount Arunachala.[7] I didn't know that in India both culture and climate supported the wandering mystics known as *sadhus*, dropouts from materialism and the pressures of family obligations. One could survive on the donations of society. I didn't see any reason to stay home, for I didn't like the life toward which I was heading, as if down a dark tunnel.

---

7   Ramana Maharshi (1879–1950), the Indian mystic, ran away from home at the age of sixteen. He had felt the sensation of imminent death only to discover the transcendent self, the true "I" that exists independent of death. He became known later in life for teaching the path of self-inquiry, asking those who came to him, "Who are you?

25

I packed a canteen, Boy Scout knife, sleeping bag, and a few changes of clothes in a backpack and headed out one evening after dinner, sneaking out the back door unobserved. There was no point in going too far that first night, so I built a camp in the woods behind the neighbor's house. I unrolled my sleeping bag on a bed of dry leaves.

As I lay there looking up at the stars, I felt freedom for the first time, and that my destiny was my own. If there had been a tradition of *sannyasa* in the US as there was in India, I would most likely have joined a group of *sadhus* and wandered off to practice *tapas* (meditations and austerities) in some holy place.[8] However, the longer I lay there the more I realized that my plan was doomed, that I would be apprehended soon and returned home to my mother, who would never forgive herself if I disappeared. Despite the frustration, I sensed that in some way I was responsible for her, that there was something we needed to work out together.

Ants had begun to crawl into my sleeping bag. I felt the roughness of the leaves as I rolled over and thought of the warm, soft bed in my room only a few hundred yards the other side of the neighbor's hedge. Maybe I should spend the night in my own bed, I rationalized, and get an early start before sunrise. I returned home without my mother realizing I had been gone.

I woke to her shout, "Breakfast is ready!"

Famished, I rushed downstairs. I can always leave home some other day, I told myself, a day that did not come for another nine years.

---

8   *Sannyas:* the last of the four stages of Hindu life known as *ashramas*. In this stage, generally after the age of fifty, one leaves the family, renounces attachment to material existence, and seeks liberation. This is different from an *ashram*, a residence for spiritual practitioners. A male renunciate is a *sannyasin*, a female is a *sannyasini*. A *sadhu* or a female *sadhvi* is a renunciate of any age who has been initiated by a Guru and lives according to strict rules such as renunciation of possessions, not touching money, not staying in one place for more than three days, begging for food, being celibate, and performing certain prescribed spiritual practices. As it is considered good karma to give to those on the spiritual path, some beggars dress as renunciates as a means of livelihood. In modern India this path of renunciation is regarded with some skepticism.

CHAPTER 4

A Boy and His Dog

My mother gave me a dog when I was around ten, and we soon became inseparable. He was a mongrel, and at my mother's parties his huge tail frequently cleared the coffee table of wine glasses with one flip—so I named him Flipsy.

I was an only child and he became my best friend. Since my grandmother had died, he was the only one I loved. Every day when I came home from school he would jump on me, and we would roll on the ground playing. I craved this contact since my mother hardly ever expressed herself with a touch; she had read an article in the *Readers Digest* that said women shouldn't touch their sons or they would become gay.

Within six months Flipsy had grown into a big, adventuresome dog who liked to roam the town while I was away at school. My mother would frequently be angry when I came home because he had dug up somebody's garden a mile away. Tying him up was out of the question as he howled pitifully.

When one day my mother announced we had to have a serious talk I knew something terrible was going to happen. She had that pained look on her face that meant she was going to say something hurtful, and I cringed. What had I done wrong?

"This is going to hurt me a lot more than it does you, but I need to discuss what we are going to do with Flipsy."

There was no discussion, only her logic that we needed to get rid of Flipsy because he was causing too many problems. The reason he roamed, she said, was because we didn't have enough space for him. He would be happier on a farm where there was plenty of room.

"You don't want him to be unhappy do you?"

I knew that her mind was made up and there was no point arguing. By the time we reached the county Humane Society shelter, however, giving him away seemed unbearable. The man at the shelter forced him into a fenced-in four foot by ten foot enclosure outside and as I looked into his eyes through the wire mesh I heard him communicating silently,

"What have I done wrong? I have tried to be good. I love you. Please don't abandon me."

"Just walk away," my mother said. "Don't look back. Just ignore him; it will be much easier that way."

I did as she said, and turned my back on my best friend, walking down the driveway toward the parking lot as his incessant howling ripped at my heart. When I got home I threw myself onto my bed and cried. I did not forgive my mother for giving away Flipsy until after her death. I realize now how that wound began my awakening to compassion.

Years later in meditation, whenever that pain arose, along with the blame I felt toward my mother, I used *Vipassana* to observe those emotions until they dissolved into emptiness.[9]

No wonder it is so easy for the Church to convince people they are sinners who should fear God, because the abuses of childhood make people feel like sinners.[10] In other cultures, such as the Tibetan, children grow

---

9   *Vipassana:* unlike other meditation practices encouraging escape from the world, focuses on cutting through the illusions of life—which leads to mastery in the world. It is practiced with the eyes open and uses the observation of the in-breath and out-breath to quiet the mind. For concise instruction read *"I AM" Affirmations and the Secret of their Effective Use* by Peter Mt. Shasta (Church of the Seven Rays, 2012). Free meditation instruction of this type is also given at Shambhala Meditation Centers: www.Shambhala.org.

10 The Christian church, based on the interpretations of *Genesis* by Irenaeus and St. Augustine (later by Luther and Calvin), teaches that it was Adam and Eve's disobedience to God (eating a forbidden apple) that was the original sin—causing ensuing generations to be born with sin, and which can only be alleviated through baptism. Other Christian faiths believe that it was not disobedience that was the Original Sin, but concupiscence (sexual desire). Both interpretations portray God as fallible, if not perverse, in creating humanity solely for the purpose of damnation. Either way, the concept of Original Sin, that we are born evil and must achieve goodness, permeates western culture. Neither Judaism nor Islam accept that doctrine, believing that we are born innocent and have a right to be happy and enjoy life.

up feeling loved, independent of any expected behavior or achievement. Even after being driven from their homes, imprisoned and tortured by the Communist Chinese, most of them still feel within themselves a *basic goodness* that cannot be taken away.[11]

---

11   His Holiness, the Dalai Lama was shocked when he came to the West in the 1970s and found people so emotionally wounded that they could not even understand the concept of basic goodness. When he told people to tune in to their mother's love, he was devastated to hear how few had felt that love. Women are being educated to believe that being a mother is less important than having a career, and the effect on society of children growing up without the nurturing of their mothers has been emotionally and spiritually devastating.

CHAPTER 5

America and the Culture of Death

Like other little boys, I was given a pistol as one of my first toys. The first one was wood, soon replaced by a squirt gun, then a plastic one that made noise. This was replaced by a cap gun that used a roll of paper caps containing real gunpowder. It didn't shoot projectiles but it was metal, looked like a real six-shooter, and gave off real smoke. These were used in almost all our games, which were invariably Cowboys and Indians, Cops and Robbers and War. Ultimately, the high point of all these games was getting shot and dying as convincingly as possible. If my playmate was so unfortunate as not to have a gun, I would lend him one of mine or he would simply point his finger and shout, "Bang, bang, you're dead!"

Lying in the grass with my eyes gradually closing, I would try to imagine dying. What would I miss about life? I watched the ants going unconcernedly about their business, climbing up and down the stalks oblivious of my death, and I realized that I would miss them. I would miss even the emerald color of the lawn. I had to let go of everything, but at least I was dying with the satisfaction that I was a real man, that I had died doing my duty. That was always protecting my home, family, and country from the enemy.[12] Of course, I never questioned who the "enemy" was as that was implicit in the version of history that permeated our culture.[13]

Consciously causing the death of another living being occurred when I was twelve. I had wanted a BB gun from the time I had first seen a picture of a Daisy Air Rifle in *Boy's Life* magazine. One day when I was with my mother and we walked past a store that had one of these rifles displayed in the window, I managed to persuade her to make the purchase. She gave a lecture about not pointing it at anyone and always treating it as

---

12   The need of the male to prepare for death in the line of duty may explain why most of the patriarchal spiritual paths begin with the contemplation of one's own death and the afterlife. The matriarchal paths instead tend to focus on love, nurturing, and harmony with Nature.

13   "History is written by the victors," attributed to Winston Churchill.

though loaded. Once it was put in my hands, I went outside feeling like Davy Crockett, whose life and death stand at the Alamo my friends and I had watched many times on television. I headed out, pretending that it was up to me to bring home game for dinner, and promptly shot a robin that was pecking for worms in the back yard lawn.

The bird quivered, and as I stooped over we looked into each other's eyes. I stood appalled as its eyes glazed over and the bird finally lay still. I had not realized that it would suffer, that death was not clean and painless like in the movies. This was no longer a game from which you could get up and walk away.

Trembling with remorse, I decided to give the bird a proper funeral. I got a shovel from the tool shed and gently scooped the soft, limp body onto the metal blade. I carried the bird in front of me, horrified at the corpse of what a minute before had been a carefree creature harming no one. I was going to bury it in the woods across the street, that were at the bottom of the hill on which we lived, feeling that it would be happier there. As I walked down the steep grassy hill, suddenly it was as though someone tripped me, and my feet shot up in the air. At the same moment the shovel catapulted the corpse into the sky. I watched in horror for a moment as the dead bird hovered with its wings spread, awaiting its fall onto my face. Breathless and gasping for air, I watched it land with a thud beside me, its cold, gray eyes staring lifelessly into mine. Struggling to breathe, I was sure I was dying as well—immediate punishment for what I had done. Gradually, as air once again began to enter my lungs, I swore that unless there was some very obvious purpose, I would never kill another living creature. Years later that resolve would be tested during the Vietnam War.

Another experience with death occurred in ninth grade biology class. I had been given a microscope. Soon the teacher, Mr. Ricci, came by and placed a drop of water containing a single paramecium on the slide. I had to make a sketch of the single-celled organism, which, under the magnification of the microscope, filled my entire field of vision. After we had completed the sketch we were to subject the creature to a number of tests. The more I watched it swimming around, waving its arm-like cilia, the more attached to it I became. The cheerful creature had essentially the same organs as I, but so small they were called organelles. It breathed in oxygen and exhaled carbon dioxide, ate food, and excreted waste and even seemed to have certain goals and objectives. Following Mr. Ricci's instructions, I subjected it to light and dark, warmth and cold, and made notes on how it behaved. As the end of the class approached I hurriedly performed the last test, to impart a drop of methyl alcohol to the slide. Instantly a thousand tiny hairs shot out from its sides to protect itself, which was impossible—and it died.

I was devastated, as though I had just killed a friend. I was so upset that Mr. Ricci had not told us we were going to kill the creature that after the bell rang I walked down the hall toward the principal's office to report what had happened. Approaching the office, I rehearsed the complaint in my mind, realizing that when I told the principal we had killed paramecia he would probably laugh and say something like, "You killed a thousand such organisms on your way to school."

Nonetheless, the scale of the death did not seem important. Under the microscope the creature had seemed large. Working together we had shared a rapport. It had trusted me with its life. Like me, it sought to avoid suffering and to seek happiness.

CHAPTER 6

The Suburbs

I grew up in Scarsdale, a suburb of New York City that was home to many high-powered executives, owners of multi-national corporations, and high government officials—people used to getting their way. Saturday mornings I played baseball with the son of the Secretary of State, who insisted on being the pitcher and who would throw a temper tantrum if he didn't like the umpire's call. The Secretary of Defense was my assistant in our church youth group. He was a former president of Ford and later became President of the World Bank. No wonder he always seemed so stressed. Years later he confessed in his memoirs that his decision to involve the U.S. in the Vietnam War was a mistake—a decision that caused the deaths of over two million people. Even though I saw these government and corporate elite going to church and supposedly praying for peace, few seemed to live according to their beliefs, and I concluded that their real religion was self-interest. After church the congregation would go next door for tea and cookies, although at home many were alcoholics.

I wondered, "Do any of them ever inquire into the meaning of life?"

Despite our Jewish ancestry, both my mother and grandmother attended the Unitarian Church every Sunday, where they heard talks on such diverse subjects as recent discoveries about the Great Pyramid and the reproductive cycle of the amoeba, all of which appealed to my scientific nature. Despite the fact that Unitarianism disavows belief in religious dogma, they still sang Christian hymns, and the children went to Sunday school where we discussed Bible stories. Although I was skeptical about an all-knowing God and even more doubtful that he had a single Son who was one with Him, I found the life of Jesus moving. Whoever he was, he was an inspiration, and I aspired to be like him. Often a silence would fill the room, and I would feel a presence that almost moved me to tears—a presence that I would realize later was the one on whom our attention was focused.[14]

---

14   In Mathew 18:20 Jesus said, "Where two or more are gathered together in my name, there I am in the midst of them."

I found it interesting that one rainy spring the weather was terrible for months on end, but it would clear up on Sunday and there would be a blue sky, a phenomenon I kept track of for at least eight weeks. This observation led me to formulate a hypothesis that our environment is influenced by human emotion. All those people thinking about God, singing and listening to beautiful music, or simply anticipating a game of golf, planting flowers in the garden, or having a family picnic, generated enough good energy to disperse the clouds so the sun could shine.

In high school when I discovered that most of my friends as well as some girls I liked were Presbyterian, I joined their youth group, which met every Sunday evening. Even though most were like me and had no firm belief in God, we liked to get together and speculate under the watchful eye of the minister. I found it hard to imagine that Jesus or His Father, with whom he was one, had personally created Heaven and Earth. I could also not imagine that a loving God would condemn to Hell for eternity those who had been born prior to Jesus' birth.

I began to see a difference between God and religion, especially when I discovered that "Presbyterian" came from the Greek, meaning "old man." Jesus taught spiritual truth and never said to start a religion. Most religion did seem to be thought up by old men, especially as there was never any mention of the feminine aspect of God. There was only the Father, Son, and Holy Ghost! What about the Daughter and Mother?

One night someone got up the courage to ask the pastor, "What proof do you have of God's existence?"

"I don't have proof," the pastor replied, "You just arrive at some point in your life where you believe."

His moment of faith had come during the Korean War when, as an Air Force squadron leader, he'd seen plane after plane shot down, but he had returned safely, his plane unscathed. I didn't get up the courage to ask how he had gone from believing in God to believing in Presbyterianism.

Gradually the church elders began to put pressure on my mother to join the church, which I think was motivated less by concerns for her spiritual salvation than their desire to improve the church's cash flow. My mother and I agreed to become Presbyterians as long as the oath-taking ceremony was private and we wouldn't be required to get up in front of the congregation. The minister agreed and when the day came he led us to the sacristy in the back of the church to participate in a private ceremony around the baptismal font. After swearing to the Apostle's Creed we were anointed with holy water.[15]

This was a ready-made belief system to which members had to swear allegiance. So, this was the meaning of religious "faith?" You were supposed to believe what you were told, regardless of any understanding or direct experience. I was shocked that I hadn't even been given a copy of the creed to read before the swearing in.

Hearing that Jesus had to sit at the right hand of His Father for eternity was a frustrating prospect, since I felt bored when I had to sit anywhere for longer than half an hour. The Creed ended with a series of theological concepts beyond my comprehension, such as how a virgin could conceive a child, how God could will that being to be crucified and how that crucifixion was supposed benefit humanity. Nonetheless, when the moment came and the pastor said, "Do you so swear?" I said, "I do," feeling I had just taken an oath I would later regret.

We found an empty pew, and the regular Sunday morning service began. The opening hymn ended and the organ fell silent. The minister rose and stood before the congregation. I was shocked when he said, "Peggy and Peter, please come to the front of the church so that the congregation can welcome you as new members."

"You liar!" I thought, "A few minutes ago you just swore to us that our conversion to Presbyterianism would be private." As I rose I wanted to shout, "This minister is a liar, and if his own beliefs are correct he is surely going to Hell!"

No one had ever lied to me so blatantly. However, I was too embarrassed to say a word. I had not been a Presbyterian for ten minutes and already I regretted the process. I vowed never to agree to anything I did not understand from the beginning. I would quit right after the service, I thought, but a cute girl from school, Holly, came up and gave me a hug.

"I hope you're coming on our weekend ski retreat," she said, blushing.

---

15 The Apostles' Creed was supposedly written by the twelve apostle, but the first written record of it occurs around 390 AD, which makes that collaboration impossible.

As I looked into her unabashed blue eyes, I decided that being a member of the church might not be so bad after all.

The religious leaders of the church did not seem to have the answers to life's great questions, such as *Why am I here?* Even later in college I found that the western philosophers did not know the purpose of life either. They were like the proverbial "blind man in a dark room looking for a black cat that is not there" and about which they loved to argue.[16] At least Socrates refreshingly admitted, "I know that I know nothing," yet went on to inspire self-inquiry. His student, Plato, went on to speak of the soul's emergence from the dark cave of ignorance into the wisdom of the sun; but did not teach a method for escaping the cave.[17] Only much later in the teachings of the Far East did I discover those who had actually emerged into the light and had direct perception of truth—and who could teach methods enabling anyone to have that same experience. I vowed to someday escape this dream life among the sleeping Lotus-eaters and find those who were awake—the *Buddhas*.[18]

My best friend Bob and I sensed that there were other realities beyond the suburbs—an awakening that might be possible—at which the Beatniks hinted. On weekends we put on black turtleneck sweaters and caught a train into New York City to Grand Central Station. We'd buy a pack of cigarettes from a vending machine and take the Lexington Avenue subway down to Bleecker Street in Greenwich Village. We made the rounds of all the cool places, like the Bitter End and Café Wha, where Bob Dylan and many others got their start. The manic life of the Welsh poet Dylan Thomas became a sort of unconscious ideal for many poets, musicians, and artists since burning the candle at both ends seemed to facilitate transcendence of the mundane. Many of these talented artists died young in that effort, transcending life itself, like Janis Joplin,

---

16 "The hardest thing of all is to find a black cat in a dark room, especially if there is no cat." Originally attributed to Confucius.

17 *The Republic*, Plato (c. 428–348 BCE). See the allegory of the cave.

18 In *The Odyssey*, Odysseus tells of a land where people ate the fruit of the Lotus, which made them forget everything and never want to leave. *Buddha:* Awakened One (Sanskrit)..

Jim Morrison, and Jimi Hendrix, possibly without attaining victory over the lower self.

· There are old poets and drunk poets, but there are no old, drunk poets, so at some point the artist—in fact everyone—needs to decide if they really want to conquer their demons or give in to them and drown in an ocean of self-pity. Bruce Lee also died young but consciously struggled to overcome the demons, some of which he felt he had inherited from his ancestors.[19]

One night, as Bob and I were walking down Christopher Street in the West Village, I was galvanized by the cover of a book I saw illuminated by a spotlight in a dark store window: *Introduction to Zen Buddhism*, by D. T. Suzuki, with an Introduction by C. G. Jung. Zen seemed to be the quintessence, the very soul of the Beat Movement. The store was closed, but beneath the book was a review in which it said, "You already know the sound of two hands clapping; what is the sound of one hand clapping? Solve this *koan* and achieve *satori*, becoming conscious of consciousness itself."[20]

I could not solve the riddle but it definitely got me thinking about enlightenment and if it was actually something I could attain. As we continued walking I asked Bob, "What do you think the koan means?"

Without thinking, he gave a spontaneous Beat answer that was probably close to the true meaning, "Like wow!"

---

19 An excellent dramatic portrayal of this struggle is in the film *Dragon: The Bruce Lee Story* (Universal Pictures, 1993). Psychologist Bert Hellinger (Baden, Germany, 1925) developed Family Constellation work to help people get in touch with and heal often unconscious family trauma. Hellinger was influenced by his time spent with the Zulus in South Africa, who regard the ancestors as a living and vital part of daily life.

20 *Koan:* (Japanese) paradoxical statement or riddle that cannot be solved using conventional reason, and which, meditated upon, can spur one to realize the true nature of reality, *Satori* (enlightenment). Two hands represent duality; one hand, the realization of oneness.

CHAPTER 7

Becoming a Rocket Scientist

Throughout childhood I dreamed of escape from Earth and began to think that I needed to build my own space ship.[21] I used to build rockets in the basement and launch them at night in a bright flash from the back yard, which alarmed the neighbors, who would call the fire department. I had an intuitive grasp of technology and when I visited the Nike-Hercules missile base near our home I shocked the officer with knowledge pertaining to top-secret information.[22] He wanted to know where I had gotten the classified material and when I said, "I figured it out myself," he looked at me with skepticism; but since I was only ten, he said he wouldn't interrogate me. However, he gave my mother his card and asked her to stay in touch.

"We have need of kids like you in the military," he said, "but first you need to go to college."

College, not enlightenment, had been held out from childhood as the doorway to ultimate happiness. I had to get good grades in high school so I could get into a good college, so I could go to graduate school, so I could get a good job with a good company, so I could get a good wife, have beautiful children, and live in suburbia. That was the future that my mother had envisioned and was making plans for me to attain—depressing, but I didn't know anything else.

---

21   One of my high school classmates, Jeffrey Hoffman, did become an astronaut.

22   These missile bases located around the country were supposed to protect the U.S. from the Soviet attack, which the populace was led to anticipate as imminent. In 1969, Clark Clifford, Secretary of Defense under President Lyndon Johnson, whom my mother occasionally invited to cocktail parties, had these missile bases deactivated. At one of these parties I learned, to my surprise, that despite the much-publicized conflict with Communism, the Russian Revolution had been financed on Wall Street. All through the Cold War, the Chase Manhattan Bank had an office in Moscow.

To escape the pressure, Bob and I got drunk behind the neighbor's garage. It wasn't satori, but it did yield a brief escape from my mother's control—and the belief that drunkenness was now a milestone I had passed on the road to manhood.

One day my mother and I had a rare visit from a distant, elderly aunt and uncle, Olga and Harold. He had been a brilliant thoracic surgeon and eventually had become quite wealthy. In fact, they owned a lake in Connecticut on which they had built a stone mansion surrounded by pine trees. I had learned to swim there when I was two years old. Our whole family gathered there once a year for Thanksgiving dinner, a dreaded occasion characterized by constant bickering. They also had an apartment in New York City where they spent the winters, taking in Broadway plays while they escaped the snow that frequently closed their quarter mile driveway. On their way back home, they arrived unexpectedly at our house one day.

"And so what hobbies do you have, Peter?" Olga asked after the initial pleasantries.

"I build rockets!"

"What kind of rockets?"

Immediately I went to the basement and brought up the latest missile, which I showed off proudly. I didn't tell them that occasionally they exploded. A recent blast, which my mother had chosen to ignore, had demolished a lot of the test tubes and flasks in the laboratory. Strangely, I had been unscathed. The debris had formed a perfect semi-circle around me. I did not read about the protective Tube of Light that came from the Higher Self for another twelve years.

Olga and Harold were duly impressed by my knowledge and enthusiasm, and a few weeks later I received a letter from their attorney containing a stock certificate for ten shares of International Business Machines. He explained that my aunt and uncle had directed him to convey a similar stock certificate every birthday to pay for college. Since my mother kindly paid my tuition, when I later traveled to the East those accumulated certificates paid for expenses.

Arriving at Syracuse University in upstate New York in the fall of 1962, I was shocked when I went to buy the engineering books and found they were math from beginning to end. I was gripped by the feeling that I had made a terrible mistake. There were no pictures of rockets or instructions on how to build them, only pages of calculus. It was too late, as now I was committed to the study of engineering, and there was nothing I could do. Not only was there no mention of space ships, in the first class our assignment was to think of cheaper ways to make a washing machine—not what I had gone to college to learn. What made it worse was that while I was back in the dorm struggling over calculus problems, down the hall a friend who was an art major was sketching nudes as he listened to the soothing sound of Modern Jazz Quartet. I became so depressed by the direction my life had taken that by the middle of the semester I felt suicidal.

Engineering students were also required to take a humanities class. My class was in comparative religion, taught by Gabriel Vahanian, author of *The Death of God,* and we discussed his premise. It is not that God does not exist, he said, but that He has become irrelevant. If God existed, wouldn't He have struck this man down by now, I reasoned? Being a scientist, I decided to challenge God and perform an experiment to find out,

Does God exist?

If He does exist, does He care about me?

If He cares, why is He letting me suffer?

I sought out a place where I could be alone. Some friends and I had rented the attic of an old house as a getaway—a sort of retreat. It was still empty save for an old easy chair, into which I flopped, and I pulled out the Boy Scout knife I had carried in my pocket since childhood. I put the nicked, discolored blade against the veins of my left wrist.

"OK, God, if you hear me, now is the time to prove yourself."

There was no reply, so I pressed the blade harder, "God, do you hear me? This is your last chance."

Focusing my will for the stroke across the veins, suddenly my consciousness was above the chair, looking down at the movie of my death. I saw in my mind the blood running down my wrists and thought *what a waste of a perfectly good body.* I saw my friends finding my body and calling the police, then the dean phoning my mother, and her grief.

She was devastated, but at last would be forced to release her control.

However, I was not dead or lost in darkness. There was an "I" that was still observing, and I realized that my human self might be making a mistake. Lingering on the edge of a cliff, the curiosity of what might yet happen stalled the jump.

"What if I remain, but do nothing? What if I stop trying, and simply be? Life without the compulsion to do something—how revolutionary! I can let go of everything—*not* go to class, *not* complete assignments—go where I want. What is the worst that can happen, get kicked out of school? Then I can hitchhike to the docks in New York, and sign on a freighter as crew and see the world. There are options. There are always options—but I was usually too preoccupied to see them. I'll keep the knife in my pocket and kill myself any time I choose."

A sense of power flooded through me as I realized that I was no longer a victim. "My life is my own—I am free! I am the creator of my own destiny. Now I will live moment by moment and see what happens."

I put the knife back in my pocket, feeling as though the burden I had carried since childhood was gone. It was not for another two years that I would read the famous line by the French philosopher, Albert Camus,

There is but one truly serious philosophical problem, and that is suicide. Judging whether life is or is not worth living amounts to answering the fundamental question of philosophy.[23]

Next morning, strangely, I felt like going to class. I would not go out of obligation but rather simple curiosity. I felt as invisible as a dream, now that I was simply an observer. I felt euphoric; for the first time I could remember I had no obligations or agenda. As I looked around at these people, I seemed to see them for the first time, and I realized that I was not like them. I didn't care about getting a job, getting ahead, or living what they called the good life. I realized I did not want to be an engineer. The whole life for which I had been prepared from childhood seemed to be crumbling. *But if I am not that, then what am I?*

---

23 *An Absurd Reasoning*, Albert Camus (1913–1960), French, Nobel Prize winning philosopher and author.

Walking past a building on the edge of campus the next day, I saw a sign that said "Counseling." I had walked by that building many times but had ignored it, assuming that counseling was for crazy people, not normal people like me.

Seeming to be propelled by an invisible energy, I entered the office, and when a man asked why I was there I said I didn't know what to do with my life. Smiling at the answer that he probably heard many times a day, he handed me a thick packet and sent me to a table in the corner to complete a questionnaire. When I came back the next day for the evaluation he said, "What on earth were you doing in engineering? You are an artist, a mystic!"

Next semester, I transferred into the college of Liberal Arts and began to study philosophy and literature. Life improved as I discovered the writings of others who had also grappled with the meaning of life. Although God had not answered my questions directly, the fact that I was still alive was an answer of sorts. I noticed one day in philosophy class that the girl who sat next to me had lacerated wrists. By the end of that first year a number of students who struggled with the same questions as I were no longer alive.

Regretfully, most of the philosophers we studied seemed to know little about real life, and used a lot of words to hide their confusion. The truth is simple, I later realized; those who understand their subject can express themselves clearly and in few words. I was mystified at the popularity of Descartes, who tried to use logic to prove the existence of God based on a lump of clay, and whose most famous statement was, "I think, therefore I am." It would have been more accurate to say, "I am, therefore I think." Then, *How do I control what I think,* and finally, *How do I transcend thinking and arrive at direct perception of Self?* [24] The true philosophers of the day, who spoke directly to the experience of the times, were musicians like Bob Dylan, the Beatles, and the Moody Blues.

I was jarred out of that ivory tower existence one day while sitting in

---

24 This argument, *cogito ergo sum,* was stated by the French thinker, René Descartes, who tried to apply mathematical theory to life. Although he claimed that the pineal gland was the seat of the soul, it seems that he never found the yogic methods of the Far East that activate that gland. Hence, he never seemed to get beyond the rational mind.

the library. A television was turned on, which I had never heard happen in the library before. An electric announcement pierced the crypt-like calm and I felt the world was about to change in some irretrievable way. Perhaps it was like the moment before a tsunami, when the water draws back into sea. There is a calm, an eerie stillness, before the ocean rushes onto the shore and sweeps away everything.

The fateful words filled the room, "I regret to inform you that President Kennedy has been shot in Dallas and is not expected to live." It was November 22nd, 1963. The American Camelot had been brought down by those with whom Kennedy would not cooperate. I went back to my dorm room and was shocked by the words of my roommate, who was grandson of Averell Harriman, former Governor of New York and at one time reputed to be the wealthiest man in the US.[25]

"Why would anyone want to kill him?" I asked.

"I guess he got in the way," he replied, a knowing smirk on his lips.

There were forces in the world, I realized then, about which I knew nothing, and college education had not shone any light in these areas.

On graduation day a few years later, walking away from the commencement ceremony in my cap and gown, I realized that the diploma I held was a worthless piece of paper. It would not bring me the life I wanted. I had wasted four years learning useless information, and still did not understand the meaning of life or my purpose. My mother could not have taught me, for she did not know herself. Nor had the schools I had attended implied any meaning beyond the pursuit of pleasure, status, and wealth. Sadly, there were no elders to seek out as in other cultures, who could be consulted for their wisdom; for they either had senile dementia or had been relegated to old people's homes.

---

25 W. Averell Harriman (1891–1986) was one of the principals of the Wall Street banking firm Brown Brothers, Harriman and Co., which helped manage German financial interests during the Second World War. He was U.S. Ambassador at Large under President Lyndon Johnson, who implicated him in the assassination of Vietnamese President Diem and his brother at the beginning of the Vietnam War. A Soviet agent who defected to the US claimed that Harriman was working covertly with the Soviets, allegations that were denied by the CIA. In 1969 he was awarded the Presidential Medal of Freedom.

A university is supposed to teach you about the universe—to prepare you for life. Apart from a few exceptional professors who had taught me to think for myself, I still did not know the answers to the questions *What is life, and what is its meaning? What is happiness, and how is it attained?* I stuck my diploma in the bottom drawer of a desk and went on retreat, vowing to become a hermit and find the answers myself.

CHAPTER 8

Escaping Vietnam

After a summer of seclusion I realized that even though I had not found any meaning to life and had no desire to do anything in the world, I needed to make myself useful—to prove that I was finally a man. I felt I needed to justify all the money my mother had spent on sending me to college. With a degree in literature and philosophy, about the only job I could get was teaching, so in the fall of 1967 I went to work as a high school teacher in the English Department at Oakwood Friends School in Poughkeepsie, New York. It was a private Quaker school where there were some exceptional students, one of them being Bonnie Raitt, who went on to become a Grammy Award winning songwriter, singer, and anti-war activist. I was only a few years older than the students and a few became friends who eventually showed up at my farm after graduation. However, I didn't find being there satisfying, especially since there was turmoil in the administration of the ostensibly Quaker school. We would sit at meeting every day and anyone who felt inspired could get up and speak, but the real issues remained unsaid. Students feared reprisals from faculty and the faculty didn't want to appear vulnerable to the students or each other. The Quaker principles were practiced in name only.

I did not renew my contract for the next year, even though this risked cancellation of deferment from the military draft. It was the height of the Vietnam War, but during the warm summer amid the verdant, rolling hills of New York's Hudson Valley, the jungles of Vietnam seemed far away.

One morning I was shocked to receive the dreaded letter from the Draft Board: "You are hereby ordered to report for induction into the Armed Forces of the United States." I shuddered as I remembered my friends who had been killed, come home with psychological problems, or become drug addicts. At that time I was a pacifist, a belief I shared with the Quakers. If confronted, I would have laid down my life, concluding that my time had come, rather than kill another human being. It was not for another twenty years, when I had a child, that I realized there was a time and place to fight for what was yours to protect. However, this was a civil war in a foreign country and no threat to the United States. Furthermore, since Congress had never declared war, our military involvement in a foreign country was illegal. If inducted and sent to Vietnam, I vowed to throw down my gun and refuse to fire.

I rose at five a.m. to take the train to Mount Vernon, where my Draft Board was located. By eight o'clock we were on the bus into New York City to the Selective Service headquarters on Whitehall Street. Along with hundreds of other "selectees" wearing only underwear, we were herded from room to room. I thought how strange it was that Robert McNamara, the man who engineered this war, had sat in front of me in church listening to sermons on peace and how we should love one another. There didn't seem to be much that I could do about that hypocrisy now; earlier I could have burned my draft card and gone to jail. Now that I had put my body in the hands of the government I didn't seem to have much choice except to refuse to fight—which would result in a military jail. I only knew that I could not shoot another human being who had done me no harm.

Months earlier I had participated in a war protest march on Washington. I had piled onto one of the dozens of buses that left from lower Manhattan and converged with thousands of other protesters in front of the White House. We walked down Constitution Avenue to the Lincoln Memorial where, as the sun set into the Potomac River, we put our arms around each other and sang "Give Peace a Chance." The Fifth Dimension then sang their soul-stirring song, "Age of Aquarius," about the dawning of the New Age.

A flock of white doves was released, and as they soared over the heads of the crowd they were illuminated by the last rays of the setting sun. It was a transcendent moment in which I felt universal love. We felt united in a common purpose—to bring an end to the war—and I felt, for the first time, a love of humanity, that we were really all one family. We may have been naïve, however, Nixon and Kissinger said later that these popular uprisings did pressure them to hasten the war's end.

All day long our draft group was shunted from one room to another, questioned and examined by an assortment of doctors, psychiatrists, and bureaucrats, whose purpose seemed as much to break down our sense of dignity as to determine if we were fit for duty—until finally we were allowed to get dressed, and all three hundred of us were brought together in a large room on the ground floor.

A gruff man in a uniform addressed us, and announced when and where we were to report for active duty. That meant being shipped off to Vietnam to shoot and be shot at. However, first he read the names of those the service had decided to reject. Second on the list he read my name, and I rose in shock. I stumbled to the front where he handed my papers to me and said I was dismissed. Because of the gout that had plagued me on and off the past couple of years they didn't want me—I was one of three not accepted.

Outside I breathed the fresh air, savoring the freedom like a condemned man suddenly granted a stay of execution. Across the street I ran into the guy who had been dismissed before me and as we looked into each other's eyes there was an unspoken recognition—that out of the three hundred who had been marched into the building at sunrise only the two of us and one other had been graced with release—while the others in the building were going to be shipped half way around the world to possibly be wounded or killed.

As the day waned, the sinking sun became a bloody globe spreading into the Hudson River. In silence, we stood and watched the sunset. Observing the breath passing in and out of my lungs, which I had always taken for granted, now caused me to become acutely aware of the preciousness of human existence.

"Have a great life," he said.

"Yes, you too," I replied, waving goodbye, wondering what he would do with his freedom, where his path would take him, and if we would ever meet again.

CHAPTER 9

The Porsche and the Lord of Death

That summer I truly sought to become a hermit and bought a five-acre farm from two kindly Italian spinsters, Lucia and Ida Machiaroli. They considered Mother Earth sacred, not to be profited from, so they sold it to me at the price they paid for it thirty years before. There was a white, two-story frame house with two barns on an isolated hilltop overlooking the Hudson River, and a view of the Catskill Mountains in the distance. A hand water pump in the front yard and another in the counter beside the kitchen sink supplied delicious water from the well whenever the power went off, and there was a wood stove in the living room. Up the road was Olana, the former hilltop mansion of the mystic Frederick Church (1826–1900), famous for his paintings and his place in the Hudson River School. He had traveled the world and seen the vision of America as the place where East and West would fuse and produce a new culture that would unify humanity. His paintings were filled with mystical light infusing pastoral landscapes.

This farm was the perfect place to write. Other writer friends lived not far away, Peter Kane Dufault, who later ran for Congress, and the poet Halsey Davis, who looked for all the world like Walt Whitman. When I didn't feel inspired I would make a pot of coffee. If that didn't invoke the Muse I would uncork a bottle of wine.

I was working on a novel that drew on my experience one summer staying with the former wife of a Hollywood movie director on the Spanish Island of Ibiza. She had a beautiful, whitewashed *finca* (estate) in the hills above Santa Eulalia, that overlooked the azure Mediterranean. It was about the nature of good and evil, the struggle in which I found myself that summer when friends of the Rolling Stones came to visit. One morning I woke up in a field, not remembering how I had gotten there, and barely able to rise to my feet. I was only twenty-one at the time and realized that if I kept partying at that rate I would not live very long. That was when I gave up drinking.

As I wrote, the story kept expanding as my concept of reality changed until I realized that I would never finish the book, and burned it in a 55-gallon oil drum in the back yard. I turned to poetry instead as it captured the moment, something I could finish before the next vision arrived. When the Muse was ignoring me I took my old Porsche out of the barn and went for a spin down the lonely, winding roads of Columbia County.

One day I went out to the barn to go for a drive and, climbing behind the wheel, was startled by an apparition. Sitting beside me in the passenger seat was the terrifying being whose picture I had seen on the Tarot card known as Death, the grim reaper. He wore a black robe, and the scythe he used to harvest souls was slung over his shoulder.

"Get out!" I shouted, but he seemed unconcerned. Feeling an icy chill, I shouted again, "Get out!"

With a thin smile on his face he nodded and said, "Few are happy to see me, so your words don't offend me. However, your time is up. I have come to take you, but can still give you a little more time to get ready." Then he disappeared. Shivering, I got out of the car and stood in the sun.

It was only a trick of the mind, I thought, a daydream. I had seen the grim reaper in paintings and on the Tarot card, so maybe I had projected it from my subconscious? I was a poet; after all weren't poets supposed to have visions? I would use the apparition in a poem, I decided, trying to banish the shock of the visitation.[26] Forcing myself to get back into the car, I drove into town to get supplies.

Excitedly, I prepared to give my first public poetry reading. Halsey and I had been invited to give a poetry reading at a private school in Poughkeepsie. The performance went well. We were given a hearty applause and I was sure that it was the start of my career as a poet. I saw myself following in the steps of Walt Whitman, William Blake, and my then favorite, the Russian poet, Vladimir Mayakovski. Afterward Halsey, his wife, Anne, and I went back to their home near Clinton Corners and celebrated our sudden fame with a few shots of Cognac. I hardly ever drank hard stuff and it went to my head. We talked on and on, discussing

---

26 Apparitions or visions can be projected by a Master, or can appear spontaneously in one's own consciousness. Also, astral entities, disembodied spirits, and thought forms can appear in whatever form they choose, even appearing as a Master, in order to lead one astray.

the genius of each other's poems and soon it was after midnight.

"You can spend the night here," Anne offered.

"No thanks, I'll be fine. In the Porsche it'll only be a twenty minute drive home."

Confident of the road-hugging reputation of this precision German machine, and sure that the road would be deserted at this hour, I revved up the engine to a high whine and departed in a spray of gravel. Since the salesman had told me when I bought the car, "You can't spin out a Porsche no matter what you do," I trusted the legend and the invincibility of youth. Banishing the thought of a meeting with destiny, I whirled down the country road unconcerned.

The sign showed a hairpin turn so I down-shifted into second gear and accelerated into the turn like a racecar driver. I didn't see the sand on the road left from the previous winter and suddenly the car spun out of control. The rear of the car, containing the engine, spun around, and I shot backward off the road. Before I knew, the car had spun off a cliff. It was pitch dark, yet in the center of that darkness was a ruby light. I had read in the *Tibetan Book of the Dead* that when you die you see a red light you are supposed to follow, so I concluded that I was dead and in the *bardo*.[27] I stared into the light, waiting for it to lead to a higher world, but I remained in the car.

Finally, I realized that it was only the power light on the dashboard. I opened the door, not realizing that the back of the Porsche was over the edge of a cliff, supported in the branches of a tree, and I stepped into space. Dropping to the ground with a breath-jarring jolt, I was again unhurt. In shock, I scrambled up the cliff onto the road and began running. I didn't know where I was going, only that I was running from Death, the unwelcome presence. He had once again intruded unexpectedly. The cold night air stabbed my chest. I ran through the night, running as fast as I could down the country road.

Soon I came to a town where I saw a light—one solitary light illumining the darkness. I ran up to the porch and banged on the door. Miraculously

---

27 *Bardo:* (Tibetan) transitional state, originally between death and rebirth. However, later Buddhist teachings consider sleep, meditation, and other types of experience also as bardos.

it opened and I beheld a Madonna-like woman standing in the doorway in a white gown, an infant held against her breast.

"Was anyone hurt?" she asked, seeming to know of the accident before I could say a word.

"No, there was no one else," I stammered, beginning to realize that if she could see me I must be alive. It seemed she had been waiting for my knock.

"It was my baby that woke me," she said. "Would you like to use the phone?"

Soon I was talking to Halsey,

"Where are you?" he asked, surprised.

"Linlithgo," the woman said, which I repeated to Halsey.

"But, that's only two miles from here. I'll be right there."

Soon Halsey arrived and I thanked the saintly woman with the courage to open the door to a stranger in the dark of night.

The next morning the tow-truck driver and I stood and watched as his winch pulled the car back onto the road. It had remained suspended in the tree all night. Now it emerged from the edge of the ravine without a scratch.

"You had a brush with death," the driver said, looking at me wide-eyed. "It's only by the grace of God you are alive."

Or, was it simply luck, I wondered?

I remembered now the apparition of Death. I had seen the grim reaper and heard his threat but had not seen God. Why would God have saved me when there were millions he seemed to be ignoring? I had not prayed to God for protection, yet I seemed to have been snatched from the very clutches of the Lord of Death to continue the game of life.

CHAPTER 10

My Would-Be Commune

The very idea of preparing vigorously for a 60-year career in the suit-and-tie world, followed by a few years of retirement, then a terminal illness caused by pollutants did not appeal at all to quite a number of young Americans....[28]

—Ed Sanders

I didn't want to start a commune, simply to be alone and write poetry, but people kept coming to visit. It never became big like the Hog Farm,[29] but all kinds of people dropped in and some stayed for varying lengths of time. The problem was that no one really wanted to work—the downfall of most communes. Former Harvard professor Timothy Leary lived in Millbrook, about a three-quarter hour drive south, and he invited a lot of people to come and experiment with LSD. I sat next to him one evening at a poetry reading at Vassar College but he seemed to be in a drugged daze that made conversation impossible. That removed all desire to visit him. If I had I would most likely have met Richard Alpert there before

---

28 *Scrapbook of a Taos Hippie: Tribal Tales from the Heart of a Cultural Revolution*, by Iris Keltz's (Cinco Putos Press, 2000). From the Introduction by Ed Sanders.

29 The Hog Farm Commune, started by Wavy Gravy, provided a free food kitchen and security at the Woodstock Festival. When asked how he was going to control such a large crowd he said that instead of setting up a police force he would organize a "Please Force" ("Please do this and don't do that"). He was also instrumental in setting up the Seva Foundation (Sanskrit: Service) with Ram Dass and Dr. Larry Brilliant, which eventually helped restore sight to over three million people in Asia and Africa. I met Wavy at the commune in New Mexico and much later in Mt. Shasta, and attended his political rally for President outside the Democratic Convention at Madison Square Garden, New York, August 1980.

he became Ram Dass.[30] I would also have met, Dr. Ramamurti Mishra, the Guru I was soon to meet, who also used to drop in at Millbrook. While in the middle of an LSD experiment he once got a phone call from Bellevue Hospital requesting him to perform brain surgery. He was enlightened enough to be able to drive into New York City and perform the operation successfully with no one the wiser.[31]

There were a lot of crazy people walking around in those days who seemed empowered by the prevalent permissiveness, which was summed up as, "Do your own thing." The guideline for action seemed to be, "If it feels good do it." Expressing whatever you were feeling was considered cool, no matter how offensive or inappropriate. Judgment was suspended and life was viewed like one big acid trip, a movie to be watched.[32] Judgments were a bummer; and whatever happened no matter how shocking was far out!

Leary expressed his philosophy as, "Turn on, tune in and drop out," but for most that was put into practice by merely turning on (taking whatever drug was offered); tuning in was then impossible, and dropping out was inevitable. Burning out was also a possibility, especially among those who used speed (amphetamine).[33]

---

30   A few years later I was sitting on a balcony with Ram Dass in India when he read aloud a letter he had just received from Leary after his release from prison. Leary said that he regretted not pursuing the spiritual path as Ram Dass had, and that he realized too late that drugs were not the answer. Ram Dass seemed to feel a deep sadness for his former colleague, who tried to reduce the quest for God to the consumption of a pill. Leary later admitted that the CIA had supplied him with LSD as part of their mind modification experiments.

31   Neem Karoli Baba once took a dose of LSD from Ram Dass large enough for five people, but seemed to remain unaffected.

32   Learning to see life as a dream is a valid spiritual practice. In Tibetan Dream Yoga one learns to become conscious in the dream state and see all phenomena as illusory as the rainbow; then one learns to manifest the same consciousness in the daily, waking state. See *The Tibetan Yogas of Dream and Sleep* by Tenzin Wangyal Rinpoche (Snow Lion, 1998).

33   According to Dr. Ramamurti Mishra, use of psychoactive drugs, especially synthetic drugs, burns up the *Yuan Qi*, the life force with which we are born, and also depletes the *Wei Qi*, the energy supporting

It was hard to distinguish those who just looked a bit crazy from those who really were.[34] One of the genuinely crazy ones appeared at a café in Woodstock and after hearing me talk about my farm, asked if he could come and visit. He said he had just been with Swami Muktananda in India so I invited him back to the farm. He didn't mention until later that Muktananda had kicked him out of his ashram and that when he had returned to New York his parents had committed him to Bellevue Hospital. He had been released from the psychiatric ward the previous day and hitchhiked straight to Woodstock. After a week of increasing eccentricity during which he repeatedly rearranged the furniture, conducted rituals in the living room with lit candles during the night and finally became violent, I had to ask him to leave.

Then there was a girl who showed up with her four month old baby, whose family was a founding member of the Bilderberg Group.[35] They had kicked her out of the house for having an "illegitimate" child, and she was living on welfare to survive. I had fixed up the barn with a sink and wood burning stove and she and her baby stayed there with the other outcasts I had rescued. Naively I had thought that if I could get them off the streets and transplant them to the country their lives would improve, not realizing they would bring their problems with them—which then became my problems.

Most of the people I knew in the 60s and 70s seemed estranged from their parents, who didn't understand their kids' frustration with the status quo. Not having been raised during the Depression and to seek security and material well being at all costs, we suffered under the weight of materialism, and longed for the freedom of the spirit. The older generation did not

---

immune response. He also stated that marijuana hinders meditation, and that its tars remain in the body for many years.

34 Ramakrishna said, "If you're going to be crazy, it's better to be crazy from chasing after spiritual than material things."

35 The Bilderberg Group: a secretive association of international, political and financial leaders, including members of central banks, which originally met at the Bilderberg Hotel in the Netherlands, and whose meetings are by invitation only. They reportedly plan global policies they wish to implement.

understand the frustration that led to rebellion, long hair, opposition to the Vietnam War and the use of drugs—which were all part of the desire to a bring about a more life-enhancing reality, life in harmony with the universe. We sought what I believe Jesus meant by the *life more abundant.*[36] The plea of parents was, "Why can't you just find your niche?" We didn't want a niche. We didn't care about normal—because normal sucked. We wanted freedom to be ourselves. We wanted to belong to a real community that embodied meaningful values—and to live in a world where people loved and respected each other.[37]

Tompkins Square, New York City. Chanting still goes on where Swami Prabhupada began chanting the Maha Mantra.

---

36   John 10:10, "I came that they may have life, and have it more abundantly."
37   Tibetan Lama, Trungpa Rinpoche, later presented a similar vision that he called Shambhala.

CHAPTER 11

The East Village

Winter on the farm during the long, cold months, looking out the frosted windows at the windswept fields of dead weeds, finally inspired me to move to New York City. Some hippie actors from the Open Theater wanted to move to the country, so in the summer of 1971 we agreed to trade places, their use of the farm for my occupancy of their fifth floor railroad flat on Avenue B on the Lower East Side.[38] They didn't tell me that the next-door neighbor was a drug dealer and that I would come home at night to find junkies injecting heroin into their veins in the stairwell.

It was called a railroad flat because it had four narrow rooms in a row like a train, for which I paid forty-seven dollars a month. It was just south of Tompkins Square Park, a war zone of drug dealers, muggers, and cat burglars—called that because they came down the fire escape like cats. It was here that Krishna Consciousness was introduced to the West by a monk, Swami Bhaktivedanta Prabhupada, who had come from India at the request of his Guru.[39] Not knowing anything about the West, he had sat under a tree in the park chanting the Maha Mantra:

Hare Krishna, Hare Krishna, Krishna Krishna, Hare Hare,
Hare Rama, Hare Rama, Rama Rama, Hare Hare.

Allen Ginsburg, the Beat poet, lived nearby and came and chanted

---

38   The Open Theatre: an experimental theatre group in New York City directed by Joseph Chaikin and Peter Feldman, which gave actors free range to express their imaginations in unique ways.

39   The International Society for Krishna Consciousness was founded in New York City in 1966. The movement is an offshoot of Vaishnavism, which worships God as Vishnu. Rama is the seventh incarnation (Avatar) of Vishnu, and Krishna the eighth, the form chosen for worship by Sri Prabhupada. He felt that "God" was too general a name, and that "Krishna" was more specific for the purpose of devotional worship.

with him, so small crowds began to chant the ancient mantra, which spread like wildfire through the hippie community. Ginsburg began chanting the mantra at poetry readings, helping transplant this seed of higher consciousness in the West—from where it took root around the world. Soon it appeared in the Broadway musical *Hair*, then in George Harrison's *My Sweet Lord*. The simple joy of singing and dancing to this Sanskrit mantra, which invoked God in the form of Avatars, Rama and Krishna, was manna to the souls of the spiritually starved children descended from the Puritans.[40]

The dedication of this one monk in Tompkins Square to chant this mantra daily sparked an awakening of the world to the beauty of the ancient spiritual teachings of the East. I little dreamed that I would soon be participating in this merging of the East and West, and that on my way to India I would stay at George Harrison's house, which he had donated to the Krishna movement.

Although it was reassuring as a poet to have Ginsburg living nearby on 10th Street, life in the East Village was a struggle for survival. Walking down the street, I had to look over my shoulder, for I never knew when I'd be hit up by a junkie looking for a fix or held at knifepoint.

---

40 *Avatar:* a human incarnation born with all the aspects of Divinity, who comes to Earth on a mission to assist humanity. According to Sathya Sai Baba, Rama was an Avatar who came about 20,000 years ago in Ayodhya. He gives an account of Rama's life in the amazing book *Ram Katha Rasavahini*. Krishna, a later *Avatar,* was born about 5,800 years ago in Vrindavan, India. His life is described in the *Bhagavata Purana* and *Mahabharata,* where the sage Narada says to Sri Vyasadeva, "It is personally experienced by me that those who are always full of cares and anxieties, due to desiring contact of the senses with their objects, can cross the ocean of darkness on a most suitable boat—the constant chanting of the transcendental activities of the Personality of Godhead" (through chanting the names of God). The vibration of Sanskrit has a harmonizing effect on the spiritual/emotional centers known as *chakras;* and the focused chanting of these names of God energizes and raises the frequency of these centers. However, the chanting of a mantra can itself become dogma once it has outlived its usefulness.

George Harrison of the Beatles with members of the Hare Krishna movement

One hot summer night as I walked up B Street to go to a movie, I passed Tompkins Square Park and felt the chill of fear. I looked back over my shoulder and saw three black teenagers crossing the street behind me and walking hurriedly in my direction. Not wanting to be prejudiced and run just because they were black, I ignored what my body was trying to tell me and kept walking. Suddenly my entire body was lifted from the ground and carried under the marquee of an abandoned theatre. A gun barrel was thrust into my ribs and the blade of a knife was flashed in my face. I felt the prick of its blade against my throat as the third assailant rifled my pockets and shouted, "Don't struggle, man; if you do, you're dead."

Knowing that there was nothing I could do, I relaxed against the wall without fear and watched the scene unfold as though watching a movie. They took the few bills that I had, threw my empty wallet on the ground, and ran. I was left in shock.

Up the street a young Hispanic man in an undershirt, sitting on the steps of his building, shouted, "Hey, did those guys rip you off?"

"Yes, they did," I stammered.

"I have a gun; if you had shouted I would have blown them away, man."

"Thanks," I said, meekly, and headed back to my apartment a block away. By the time I entered the door a deep rage had welled up within, not so much about the loss of the few ten-dollar bills, but at being violated.

"I will get my own gun," I vowed, "so that will never happen again."

However, I decided to throw the coins for the *I Ching*, the famous Chinese book of prophecy. Miraculously, the paragraph I was directed to by the fall of the coins said in essence, "Those who take up the sword die by the sword. The wise man instead confronts the anger within himself rather than seeking revenge."

It was not the answer I wanted at the moment, but was the one that kept me alive during the remainder of my stay in New York. Several more times I was held at knifepoint, but eventually, when the anger was gone, I could look the attacker in the eye with love and they could no longer take anything.

Out the window I looked onto the roof of the school across the street where during recess kids sniffed glue and smoked joints. My building was rent controlled, which meant that in the winter the landlord turned off the heat to save money, saying the furnace was broken, and the tenants froze. When my fingers became too stiff to write I would cross Tompkins Square to the public library where it was warm and hang out there, writing poetry to the comforting sound of clanking radiators.

I later read these poems at Fordham University at the Lincoln Center, a reading that came about through a bizarre sequence of events. I had thrown a party at my flat and only three people had shown up, one of them being Holly, the girl with piercing blue eyes from my church youth group I'd had a crush on during high school. I had never gotten up the courage to ask her out and now she was married to the famous filmmaker Jonas Mekas, and affiliated with the University.[41] After the reading they

---

41   Jonas Mekas was also a movie critic for the *Village Voice*. He made avant-garde films such as *Report from Millbrook*, about Timothy Leary's arrest on drug charges by later Watergate co-conspirator, G. Gordon Liddy; *Hare Krishna*, showing the Beatles chanting the Maha

gave me a small honorarium that I used to buy a bouquet of roses. I gave them out to people in Central Park and on the way home in the subway, telling people, "Give it away to someone else." It seemed that money made from poetry should be spent creating beauty.

At night the streets blossomed with danger. Leaving the Fillmore East one night after a Jethro Tull concert, a beautiful East Indian girl introduced herself as Sushila and asked if I would be her bodyguard and escort her home. I hesitated when she told me she lived on East Second Street, an area even more dangerous than my neighborhood, but she was the first Indian woman I had met and her limpid eyes beckoned with a mystery I could not refuse.

Had she been American I would have known she wanted more than an escort, but since I had heard that Indian culture does not allow contact outside marriage I was uncertain. Our walk was thankfully uneventful and at her door she shook my hand. We exchanged phone numbers and agreed to go out sometime for tea.

Next morning I was awakened by a phone call from a man with an Indian accent who introduced himself as Sushila's brother. He thanked me for escorting his sister home and then said that if I ever tried to see her again he would kill me; nothing personal, just a matter of protecting family honor.

"Hey, this is America," I said angrily, "I will do what I want."

After a few days reflection, however, I saw the wisdom of heeding his request and never tried to see the girl again.

Although Ginsburg, Kerouac, and the other Beat writers had dabbled in Buddhism, none of them except Ginsburg had really practiced it seriously—which is obvious by the self-cherishing addiction to suffering that suffuses most of their work.[42] Few of them made an effort to cut

---

Mantra with Maharishi Mahesh Yogi; and *Happy Birthday to John,* starring Allen Ginsburg, John Lennon, Yoko Ono, Ringo Starr, and Andy Warhol.

42 "Beat" originally meant "beaten down, downtrodden"; however Kerouac and other writers of the post Second World War era saw suffering as necessary to break out of the grip of materialism. For

through that clinging to the anxieties of the personal self except Ginsburg, whose major initiation into the nature of mind came through the Tibetan Lama, Chögyam Trungpa Rinpoche, whom he accepted as his Guru. They met in 1971 when they had both hailed the same taxi, and discovered they had both wanted to meet each other. Trungpa Rinpoche was an unconventional and highly controversial teacher with whom I later had transformative encounters.[43]

---

them it was the first step to spiritual awakening, much in the same way as the Beatitudes say, "Blessed are the poor in spirit, for theirs is the kingdom of God." Kerouac coined the phrase "Beat Generation" in 1948. He despised the term "Beatnik," coined by *San Francisco Chronicle* columnist Herb Caen, which he saw as derogatory. The later term, "hippie," was also used by the media in a derogatory sense to describe the younger generation who were trying to imitate the older Beats—who tried to be "hip" by merely letting their hair grow, wearing colorful clothes, and acting without regard for consequences. However, the term has African roots, meaning "one with open eyes, one who knows." Very few hippies used the term, preferring "freak"— invoking another unfortunate, negative self-image. Both the Beats and Hippies had the common drive to be non-conformists to the rigid belief systems based on ignorance and greed, which had given rise to one war after another—the Vietnam War being the most current at that time.

43 "In the early 70s, Ginsburg found Tibetan Buddhist Lama, Chögyam Trungpa, One of the first things that Trungpa asked him was, 'Do you even know what you're doing when you're chanting mantras in front of these huge audiences?' Trungpa warned Allen that he was getting his audiences high—but then what? He was leaving them high and dry. Trungpa had his own problems, but he stressed to Allen the importance of having a stable, regular meditation practice. 'You're not looking to get high, you're not looking to avoid getting low, you're just putting your ass in a chair and breathing, and watching what's happening—and whatever's happening is the meditation.' That turns out to be of more lasting benefit than grasping after states of transcendence and bliss." ("The Plot to Turn On the World: The Leary/Ginsburg Acid Conspiracy," Steve Silberman; www.PLOS.org, April, 2011)Trungpa Rinpoche wrote: *Meditation in Action, Cutting Through*

Allen Ginsburg, beat poet, with Tibetan Buddhist Lama, Trungpa Rinpoche

Ginsburg eventually realized that even though devotional chanting could lead to bliss, it could also be like a drug that encouraged self-avoidance. No matter how high you get you still have to come back to conventional reality, deal with who you are, and cut through your emotional attachments and aversions. Self-observation, on the contrary, grants liberation in the present moment.[44]

Ginsburg was one of those people who was so outrageous that he made it safe for others to risk being only slightly outrageous, and express what they had to say no matter how unconventional or confrontational. Every society needs someone like that, a gadfly like Socrates.

Dylan Thomas eventually drank himself to death across town at the Whitehorse Tavern on 11th Street, where later Bob Dylan, Jim Morrison, Hunter S. Thompson, and others would hang out. A few blocks away

---

Spiritual Materialism, and *Shambhala: The Sacred Path of the Warrior.*

44 This meditative practice is called *Shamatha* (tranquility), which leads to *Vipassana* (insight). It is taught worldwide by Shambhala International. Concise instruction is in *"I Am" Affirmations and the Secret of their Effective Use* by Peter Mt. Shasta (Church of the Seven Rays, 2012).

Swami Satchidananda taught how to develop inspiration naturally, without booze and drugs, through the science of yoga—the means to union with Divinity.[45]

Swami Satchidananda, founder of Integral Yoga

45   Swami Satchidananda studied with Ramana Maharshi and later with Swami Sivananda, whose ashram I would later visit in Rishikesh. He was invited to the US in 1966 by artist Peter Max, and in 1969 gave the opening prayer at the Woodstock Festival. He went on to develop Integral Yoga, with centers around the world, and founded Yogaville, a spiritual community in Virginia.

*Swami Satchidananda giving the opening prayer
at the 1969 Woodstock Music Festival*

CHAPTER 12

Yoga

A t the end of a day writing poetry I used to hang out at night at the Broadway Central Bar, where Walt Whitman used to drink a century before, seeking the same source of inspiration he must have found there.[46] A few years later the bar was crushed when the hotel above collapsed, killing the patrons. It wasn't my time yet, but the long late-night hours spent carousing made me lethargic and dissipated my inspiration. When a friend suggested taking up yoga, I laughed because all the poets I knew, like Ginsburg, were self-destructive neurotics, and having seen my friend standing on his head breathing like a bellows, I could not see myself doing the same. This was before yoga was marketed to the masses on television and yoga studios sprouted up in shopping malls. To my way of thinking, yoga seemed more of a girl thing.

I was willing to experiment, though, so when I ran into a girl who was going to teach a class at the Free University on 14th Street, I decided to give it a try. She said to skip food before class, and as I walked across town I worked up a huge appetite, fantasizing the breakfast I would eat later—a meal that never took place.

From the first move, tensing and relaxing all the muscles and visualizing light streaming through my body, I felt the tingling of a never-before-felt energy and realized the truth of what before had only been words: *I am more than the body!*

I had believed only in what I could touch. Now I felt an invisible life force called *prana*, and wanted to know what was happening. After class, charged with this prana, I seemed to glide more than walk down to Weiser's, the largest metaphysical bookstore in the City. I walked in the door and as I noticed old and rare books stacked to the ceiling felt that I was entering an ancient temple.

"What's the best book you have on yoga?" I asked the owl-like clerk

---

46 When I showed Walt Whitman's long poem, *Leaves of Grass,* to a yogi in India, he said, "He was a great *Siddha* (enlightened being).

perched on a ladder with a load of books in his arm. He descended the
ladder and with a knowing look handed me a large, hardbound copy of
Vivekananda: A Biography, by Swami Nikhilananda.

"I think this is what you're looking for," he smiled, and when he placed
it in my hands I felt a shiver. Despite its drab brown cover it seemed to
vibrate with truth, and I rushed home to devour its message. Vivekananda
gave the perfect introduction to eastern wisdom because, like many
Indians in the Post-Industrial Revolution era, he was raised to abandon
the mysticism of his native land and emulate the scientific ways of the
West. All that changed when he met his Guru, Sri Ramakrishna, known
as the God-Man of India. It seemed that his words were destined for my
eyes; I felt that I was entering a new world. This wisdom is what my soul
had been seeking, words which prior to experiencing the energy triggered
by yoga would have meant nothing. In my most inspired flights of poetic
vision I had only glimpsed a transcendent reality that Vivekananda said
could be permanently attained through an easily learned method of self-
discipline. I wondered why I had waited so long to open this inner door.[47]

If prana was actually the energy of God, as Ramakrishna said, I
wanted to feel its presence all the time, and within every cell of my body.[48]
When the class at the Free University ended a month later I craved to go
deeper into yoga and began attending classes with Swami Satchidananda.
He seemed to be a real yogi, whose sparkling eyes and overall radiance
were an inspiration. Though his classes focused mostly on physical, hatha
yoga, I found that as my body relaxed my mind became still, allowing the
circulating energy to open the door of awareness.[49]

---

47 When a visitor asked Ramakrishna why he could see God and they
    could not, he replied, "I see God because every minute my attention
    is on God. You see matter because all day your attention is on matter.
    When your attention is on God as much as it is now on matter, then
    you too will to see God."
48 In 1977 this universal life force, which could be directed with the mind
    to achieve any purpose, would be popularized as the Force in the film
    Star Wars by George Lucas.
49 There are many forms of yoga in addition to the popular *hatha yoga*.

When he entered the yoga studio one afternoon and found people lying on their backs on their yoga mats, Swami joked that *Savasana* (corpse pose) was everyone's favorite position. Even though he had to wake a few people, he was happy that in downtown New York people could relax at all. His message caught on and soon posters of Swami Satchidananda sitting cross-legged, radiating a glowing smile, began appearing all over the country. Yoga studios and the new phenomenon of health food stores began springing up in shopping malls from Brooklyn to Beverly Hills.

I did not become a yogi overnight. I was torn between rising early to stretch every fiber of my being and fill my body with light, or sleeping late, writing poetry, and going out on the town at night—two forces which fought with each other. Would yoga and increasing enlightenment drive away the muse of poetic creativity? What if the muse was really a product of confusion and when the confusion was gone I would no longer feel inspiration? I had the terrifying thought, *If I'm not a poet, what am I?*

The drive for inspiration led me to wander the city streets and embrace experience wherever it led, to encounter the dark aspects of life I had been sheltered from as a child in suburbia. In the affluent suburbs I had never seen a broken-hearted drunk on the sidewalk drowning his sorrow in a bottle, nor the addict seeking his own form of liberation from suffering at the point of a needle. Who were these people? I yearned to connect with them, to feel their pain and find the common thread of life.

After roaming the city all night, one morning I awoke on a sidewalk in Brooklyn. It was becoming light, and straight ahead was the Brooklyn Bridge, struck by the first rays of sun. Pulled like a magnet, I coaxed my stiff legs toward the majestic arch that seemed to span two worlds.

Some of them are *karma yoga*, enlightened action without attachment to the results; *bhakti yoga*, devotion to a form of God one sees as the beloved Self; *raja yoga*, the Eight-limbed path of meditation described by Patanjali in his *Yoga Sutras; jnana yoga*, the path of knowledge; *tantric yoga*, where all aspects of life are taken as the path; and *ati yoga*, a Buddhist concept pertaining to spontaneous realization in the moment, outside formal meditation.

Gazing at the great web of cables overhead, I wondered what invisible threads connected us to each other, and through what eternity those lines of force guided our lives without our knowing. In the sunrise I gazed into the East River swirling below and out into the ebbing tide of the Atlantic, and wondered toward what destiny my life was flowing. The sun felt good on my face and I watched it rise above the river. Its rays filled me with life and I wanted to merge with it—to become one with the sun. Brooklyn was still in the shadows, so I turned away from the darkness of that shore and crossed the bridge toward the city lit by the rising sun and toward my unrevealed, yet rapidly approaching destiny.

I seemed to have left something behind in Brooklyn, perhaps that part of myself that wanted to hang back in the shadows, and now my path began to unfold rapidly. On completing my yoga the next morning I was catapulted out of my body into cosmic consciousness. Lying on my back with limbs spread in surrender, I lost individual awareness and merged with a universe of unending waves of light undulating throughout eternity— permeated by the sound of *Om*.[50] Here was the awareness of pure being known in the Vedas as *Sat-chit-ananda:* absolute truth, consciousness, and bliss. The goal of yoga had been bestowed as a gift from the Source; how long this transcendental consciousness lasted, I don't know. Suddenly I crashed back into individual awareness, the world of the ego, as I heard the telephone ringing.[51] I lunged for the phone, only to find someone had dialed a wrong number. My anger at the sudden loss of Paradise reminded

---

50 *Om:* an approximation of the *pranava*, the primordial sound, emanating from *Brahman*, from which the Sanskrit alphabet is a further emanation. Brahman is the pre-existing, self-effulgent consciousness whose nature is *Satchidananda*, not to be confused with the Divine personalized emanation, *Brahma*, who is part of the *Trimurti* (Trinity) along with *Shiva* and *Vishnu*. They are personifications of the forces that bring into manifestation, sustain, and dissolve the material universes.

51 The ego is motivated by the Eight Worldly Dharmas, which permeate the human condition, and which exist in pairs: pleasure/pain, gain/ loss, fame/disgrace, and praise/blame. People strive for one polarity and seek to avoid its opposite, and thus preoccupied, rarely find the meaning of life.

me that I was still a human being who sought love, pleasure, and security and tried to avoid pain. I was an individual being with many needs, even a body that sought self-preservation.

I knew this experience was a gift, as my own efforts in meditation had never produced this loss of ego, but from whom had this gift originated? Had Swami Satchidananda, Ramakrishna Paramahansa, Swami Vivekananda, or some other Guru in India decided it was time for me to awaken? Toward whomever had sent this blissful experience, I felt immense gratitude, and I hoped that it would soon be repeated. Unfortunately, that did not happen. However, from that moment, as though I had tasted some rare nectar, the goal of life became the attainment of that sweetness—oneness with the Source.

Life now seemed humorous. What people considered important, I saw had no more reality than a shadow cast by a cloud passing before the sun. It took days to return to relative normalcy. Perhaps I never did, for immersion in the infinite is life-altering. Once experienced, the true Self can never be forgotten. Like a jack-in-the-box that has finally seen beyond its box, it can never be returned the same. What has been seen cannot be unseen.[52]

As I walked down the street, I now seemed to be inside a ball of light that repelled the knife-wielding junkies who had robbed me months before. Bewildered, they bounced away as though hitting a shield, and I walked on my way fearlessly.

For days I wandered the streets without fear, enveloped in an aura of love. Although by the end of the week the glow faded, I was a different person. The desire to hang out in bars was gone, as was the desire to write poetry—and I was strangely unconcerned.

I rose early every morning and practiced yoga. Meditation followed, but I could not attain transcendental awareness no matter how hard I

---

52 Many who have experienced moments of enlightenment think they have reached final "enlightenment"; however growth goes on, and for the attainment of self mastery, that higher awareness must be stabilized and integrated into life as an ordinary human being. In fact, a true Master can pass among humanity unobserved, even being unknown to one's partners, family members, friends, and associates.

tried. I sat for hours slowing the mind, seeking once more to approach the door to eternity, but I was not able to escape the world of relativity.

Leading up to the full moon, Tompkins Square became filled with would-be hipsters beating bongos and conga drums 'til dawn, making escape to higher realms even more difficult. Enlightenment would be easier to attain if I were in the quiet of the Himalayas, I felt. I wished to sit at the feet of a Guru like Ramakrishna or Ramana Maharshi, who could transmit consciousness with a gaze, or even a thought.[53]

---

53 *Shaktipat:* transmission of consciousness by a realized being.

CHAPTER 13

Emissary of the Lord of Death

A friend of the family, Lambert, was at Columbia Presbyterian Hospital dying of cancer. The last time I had seen him was at one of my mother's cocktail parties. He had gone into the kitchen in search of milk to sooth his stomach ulcer, but all he had found was the synthetic powdered cream substitute his own company produced and sold globally. Trying in vain to dissolve it in a glass of water, he was finally condemned to drink the tasteless stuff with lumps floating on the surface.

I found him lying in the basement ward for terminal patients, alone and confused. No one had visited him, as he hated sympathy.

"What's happening to me?" he asked.

"You're dying."

"What, no one told me!"

I was stunned. He was dying without knowing, or perhaps the morphine dripping through his veins had dimmed his memory. I had just read the *Katha Upanishad* and wondered if I should quote him the words of Yama, the Lord of Death:

The knowing Self is not born. It does not die. It has not sprung from anything; nothing has sprung from It. Birthless, eternal, everlasting, and ancient, It does not die when the body dies.

"What's going to happen?" Lambert asked again with a look of bewilderment.

"Your body is worn out," I said, trying to paraphrase Yama's words, "You're going to leave your old body so you can get a new one. There is no death. You're simply going from one room to another. You are leaving the room of pain and going into a new room full of light where there is no pain. Go toward the light. Someone you know whom you love will meet you there. They will take you to your new home and there you will meet your old friends and family you haven't seen in a long time. They will be so glad to see you and you will be happy when you see them."

A peaceful expression came over his face and as he took my hand, with tears in his eyes, he said, "Thank you, thank you so much. I'm grateful you came to see me."

I looked down at him in the hospital bed, the needle of the intravenous drip in his arm, and realized that with all his fine and costly possessions, the trips he had taken to exotic places, he had probably never had more than a passing thought about death—and now it was staring him in the face. With all his millions and the best medical care in the country, was he able to delay death for even a second? Now each precious moment of life was slipping away. When he looked back on his life after death, would he feel he had wasted an opportunity? I heard a few days later that he had died there, alone in the basement. I must have been his last visitor.

CHAPTER 14

The Psychic and the Woman in the Spanish Hat

In the spring of 1971 I heard of a psychic uptown who could tell you what was going on in your life just by looking at you. Since I felt like a cork tossed on the ocean of *samsara* I decided to go see him and learn my future.[54] He had a small church and during the service would go around the room telling people what he saw happening in their lives.

Instead of finding an illumined being, I found someone who seemed tormented. His eyes wandered around the room, staring into space, as though he were communicating with spirits. I knew that we live in a sea of life inhabited by entities existing at different frequencies. As with television, we see only the channel of the frequency to which we are tuned. Perhaps he was seeing several of these channels, but were they the psychic strata of human thoughts and feelings, or could he see into the causal realm of what was destined to occur?[55]

In the second-story room that served as his church, a couple dozen people sat on folding metal chairs. Two candles were on a table before a picture of Jesus. After a brief prayer he led a guided meditation in which

---

54 *Samsara:* the cycle of birth, life, death, and rebirth, which continues until we are purified of negative emotions, and achieve an ego-less state beyond identification with transitory phenomena.

55 The astral plane is the world beyond that of gross physical appearance, but not necessarily of higher consciousness. It is composed of many sub-planes vibrating at different frequencies. The lowest astral plane accessed by most psychics, is filled with human thought-forms that may be perceived as either past or future events. Or, the psychic may merely be projecting their imagination. The lower astral realm is inhabited by disembodied spirits (ghosts) who have not evolved to higher planes, and who may pretend to be great beings, even Masters. In the higher astral planes, which still appear as physical, evolution may continue after death. "Astral" and "etheric" have come to be used interchangeably. As time is an illusion, people occasionally do see "future" events. Destiny, however, is always subject to modification.

we visualized light going out to the world. Then he began going around the room, talking to each person, one after the other. He told a man that he saw a dark energy on one of his lungs and that he needed to give up cigarettes. The woman beside him had a sister about whom she was worried, and he told her she should visit her as planned. The next woman was concerned about her grown son with whom she had lost touch, not knowing if he was still alive, and the Reverend assured her that he might call soon, but not to worry if he didn't. When he came to me he looked into the space above my head and said, "I see that bridges are very important to you. I don't know why I am telling you this, but I see you in the middle of a bridge as though preparing to jump."

"Is this the past or future?" I asked, shocked.

"I can not say, only that I see you on a bridge and it is something very important for you."

He continued around the room telling people what he saw and when we left I heard people commenting on how accurate he had been.

His remark about the bridge made me think of my experience on the Brooklyn Bridge, but should I return? That day on the bridge I had thought for a moment of what it would be like to jump into the cold East River, but instead had made a jump of consciousness. Now I wondered if I should return, that perhaps I had made the wrong choice and would eventually take the plunge.

For the next few days I could not get the bridge out of my mind and the idea of jumping seemed more and more attractive. It would be liberating to jump into space knowing there were no more decisions, responsibilities, or anguish—to throw myself into the arms of the Infinite. Free of this dense body, I could explore the cosmos without limitation. But what if there was a God and I was greeted with displeasure and told that as punishment for suicide I would have to return and start all over again?

Perplexed, I went to see Frank, a psychic friend who lived downtown on Mulberry Street. Perhaps he could shed light on the future. Many said he was the best psychic in New York. Supposedly even the Aga Khan had flown in from Europe to consult with him.

Like the other psychic, he seemed to know what was happening in my life, but he said nothing about a bridge or jumping into the East River. Instead, he saw a woman in a Spanish hat, a woman who would be an important catalyst.

Being a young man alone in the city, this prophecy concerning a beautiful woman impelled me to action. Jumping from a bridge was forgotten and I left Frank's apartment in quest of the woman in the Spanish hat. As I walked uptown I scanned the people I passed. Without realizing how fast I had been walking, I soon reached Central Park. I sat down on a bench to rest, disappointed that the woman had not yet appeared.

Then there she was, a flamenco dancer in black toreador pants, wearing a jacket embroidered in silver, a braid of black hair hanging down her back. On her head was the Spanish hat. I was on my feet in a flash, eager to meet the woman who held the key to my destiny. As I walked behind her, I noticed what I had blocked out at first glance, that she was walking arm in arm with an elderly woman, probably her mother.

How should I approach her? Should I say, "Excuse me, but a psychic said we were going to meet and that we are meant to be together?"

No matter how hard I tried, I couldn't find words that didn't sound ridiculous. I could invite the two of them for tea at the Plaza Hotel across the street, but that also seemed presumptuous. The pursuit slowed until they gradually escaped down the sidewalk.

I ambled along, heavy-hearted, feeling I had missed the opportunity of a lifetime. Then I thought, "What is meant to be, will be. If we are meant to be together, I will meet her again and I will have the courage to speak." However, I decided to call Frank and ask, "Did I just miss the opportunity of a lifetime?"

"No," Frank assured, "The Spanish hat is simply a symbol, an archetypal image of the kind of woman you will be attracted to over the next few years. It is not necessarily one specific woman, and she may not even own a Spanish hat."

Disappointed, I was at the same time relieved. Instead of falling into a complicated romance with the passionate heroine from Carmen, I could remain a yogi and pursue the spiritual path.

Amazingly, years later I met a woman by the name of Stephanie, and when I told her about Frank's prophesy she went to the closet and pulled out a Spanish hat. She had studied flamenco years before and now the hat gathered dust on the top shelf.

Were we meant to be together? Because a psychic had "seen it," did that mean it was meant to be—or did we have free will? Had I carried that hat in my psyche all these years, and was I now going to create a relationship to fulfill the prophecy?

Despite developing a deep friendship with Stephanie, after a few months we found our paths going in different directions. She was attracted to an American teacher of non-duality in Santa Cruz who called himself Master Nome (No Me), while I was drawn to live a meditative life in the desert beyond Mount Shasta.

Of what use had all this psychic insight been? One had reinforced the idea of jumping off the Brooklyn Bridge and the other had implanted an obsession with finding a particular woman. I finally met her naturally, without knowing of her Spanish hat. Years later, Frank told Yoko Ono that he had seen a vision of John Lennon lying on the sidewalk, dying in a pool of blood. Perhaps that insight later helped her reconcile his shooting as karmic, but that night of December 8, 1980, outside The Dakota, John didn't seem to be helped much by that prophecy.

CHAPTER 15

Romance

Not long after the experience of timeless awareness while doing yoga, I quit hanging out in bars. Spiritual consciousness seemed stifled by that atmosphere, needing a purer environment in which to unfold. Also, a romantic interest had entered my life, which balanced the discipline of yoga. Colette was French and, instead of a Spanish hat, she wore a cap she had knit with a crocheted pink flower on the side. I loved her the moment I saw her in the distance.

I had felt the urge to go out that night, but didn't know where. During dinner I had glanced at the *Village Voice* and seen there was a free concert at a small park west of Washington Square. I felt an inner pull I would later learn to recognize as guidance, pushing me toward the door.[56] I got there just as the band was coming on stage. The bleachers were packed but I saw that near the top row of the central bleacher was a solitary vacant seat next to a girl, and inexplicably my heart leapt. As I walked toward her we both seemed to sense there was something special between us. My heart beat fast when I asked, feeling like a moron, "Is this seat free?"

"Of course," she said in a French accent.

I couldn't think of anything to say during the concert, but gazed at her when she turned occasionally and I could see the side of her face. By the end of the concert we both seemed to know we were leaving together. As we walked down the bleachers I asked, "Would you join me for a coffee?

We walked up Hudson Street and I marveled that I had gotten up

---

56 Direct guidance in the moment is felt in what some call the heart, but is actually near the thymus gland, slightly to the right of the sternum. This is where the soul is anchored in the body, and is the seat of the activity of the Three-Fold Flame. When the mind and emotions are still, this flame or energy can be felt. What people call "gut" guidance is felt in the abdomen and usually concerns issues of survival. We are receiving guidance from the Higher Self at every moment, whether we choose to feel and follow it or not.

the courage to speak. Walking beside her seemed natural, as if we had always known each other, and words flowed effortlessly. Finally reaching the White Horse Tavern, we sat down at a small table. As I listened to her voice and observed the softness of her cheek in the candlelight, I felt something miraculous happening.

She said she was a dancer with Merce Cunningham, who had an avant-garde performance group, but she supported herself taking care of people's apartments while they were away. She loved Manhattan and liked the uniqueness of the different neighborhoods. We wandered all over the Village that night and ended up under the arch in Washington Square with a kiss—sealing the beginning of our relationship.

We didn't live together, for she needed space in which to dance and I, solitude in which to write. She would come down to the Village to visit a couple of times a week or I would go uptown and meet her for lunch. We would see a movie, visit a museum, or simply walk in Central Park eating ice cream. For the first time in life I felt it was good to be a human being.

We never argued, and after a year we were as romantic as the night we met. She was my first real girlfriend. The idea of ending our relationship would never have occurred to me, but a destiny began to assert itself that would lead us in different directions. A gap was forming which began to drive a subtle wedge between us. Those who oversee destiny, the Lords of Karma, must have saved that seat beside her at the concert, and those same Masters, knowing now that we had completed our work together, were now separating us.[57] It came so subtly we did not suspect what was happening when she was offered a house in the country for a couple of months with other members of the dance company. They would work on a new routine while I stayed in the City, immersed in the practice of yoga and the study of the *Vedas* and *Upanishads*.

Talking on the phone, I sensed an inexplicable space between us I could not cross. The separation that was going to last a few months dragged

---

57 The Lords of Karma: a group of Masters who keep the records of each person's evolution. They guide one throughout many lives, directing the soul to the parents, relationships, and circumstances required to learn the lessons for which one has come into embodiment.

on—and eventually became permanent. It was the beginning of a period of celibacy which lasted seven years, and during which I would ignore the desire for intimacy to focus on the eternal presence within.[58]

---

58   There is no rule governing the expression of love and sexuality that is appropriate for everyone throughout life, as different paths are appropriate at different stages of development. Ultimately, the Marriage Made in Heaven referred to in the Bible, occurs when the male and female energies are united within the individual, ending the desire to experience outer phenomena.

Chapter 16

The Guru Beckons

"When the student is ready, the teacher will appear," many esoteric books said. The voice of that teacher came through the radio as I was eating lunch. While listening to the National Public Radio station WBAI, I heard someone who was calling himself Baba Ram Dass being interviewed, and was inspired by his words. This was the famous interview that many thousands of hippies later said turned them to look beyond drugs to seek the more enduring joy of spiritual attainment. For many that meant embracing Hinduism or even traveling to India.

Ram Dass, the former Harvard professor, Richard Alpert, was being asked about the experiments he and another Harvard professor, Timothy Leary, had done with LSD.[59] They had found that when

---

59   Richard Alpert was born to a Jewish family in Boston, Massachusetts on April 6, 1931. His father was President of the New York, New Haven and Hartford Railroad and a founder of Brandeis University and Albert Einstein College of Medicine. He graduated from Tufts University in 1952, received a Masters Degree from Wesleyan University and Ph.D. in psychology from Stanford University. He became a professor of Psychology at Harvard, as well as a therapist for the Health Service. His first experience with psychoactive drugs was in 1961 with fellow professor Timothy Leary, when the two of them took psilocybin. He later said, "I didn't have one whiff of God until I took psychedelics" (Sara Davidson, "The Ultimate Trip"; *Tufts University Magazine*: Fall, 2006). He and Leary conducted a double-blind experiment on twenty students of Andover Newton Theological Seminary during a Good Friday church service. Half the students received psilocybin, half a placebo. He said it was clear by the end of the service who had received the psychedelic, one of them shouting, "I see God." He and Leary were both asked to leave Harvard in 1963 but continued their experiments in Millbrook, New York in a house owned by an heir of the Mellon banking fortune. Eventually tiring of these experiments, in 1967 Alpert left for India.

administered under supervision it helped some patients overcome their neuroses. Harvard, however, did not approve of their unconventional experiments and fired them. Freed of academia, Alpert had eventually journeyed to India to gain insight into the changes in consciousness he had experienced with drugs, and to find if that same awakening could be attained naturally.[60]

Little did he dream when he left for India that everything he had studied, the whole rational foundation of his world, would be shaken to the core by a nearly naked old man wrapped in a blanket, and that this man known as Neem Karoli Baba would become his Guru.[61] Even more

---

60   For this whole story read *Be Here Now* (Lama Foundation, 1971), the book Ram Dass wrote, which became a sort of hippie Bible. For additional background read Bhagavan Das' autobiographical account of his adventures, *It's Here Now, Are You?* (Harmony, 1998), also *The Sacred Wanderer* (Sacred Wanderer Productions, 2010) by Ravi Das, the one who helped Bhagavan Das get to India.

61   *Maharajji: Maharaj* (great king) plus *ji* (term of respect), how many address their guru. Neem Karoli Baba (birth date unknown) was named Lakshmi Harayan Sharma, born to a wealthy family in Akbarpur, Uttar Pradesh. His marriage was arranged at age 11, which was not unusual at the time. His wife, Rambeti Ram, with whom he had two sons and a daughter, was the daughter of a wealthy Brahmin family. While still a teenager he ran away and become a sadhu, but his father retrieved him, telling him that he could not leave until his householder duties were completed. He finally left home in 1958 when his youngest child was 11. Because of his inherited wealth, two mansions (*havelis*) he owned in Akbarpur and one in Agra, his family was well provided for. During his time as a wandering sadhu he appeared in many places under different names. His final name came about after a British conductor kicked him off a train for not having a ticket. The train was unable to continue, despite all the efforts of the engineer, until the conductor apologized and invited the sadhu back on board. The town at which this happened was Neeb Karori (translated as Neem Karoli). Although he spent much time in meditation he came to be known as a *bhakti* yogi, inspiring his devotees to love and serve God in the form of humanity. He expressed great love for not only the Hindu Gods Ram and Hanuman, but Jesus as well. One of his favorite expressions was, "Love everyone, serve

mind-boggling was his own transformation into a Guru, one who would return to America to inspire the new Woodstock generation emerging from the soul-wrenching travails of the Vietnam War.

Wandering in India he had run into Bhagavan Das (Servant of God), a tall ex-surfer who took him into the foothills of the Himalayas to meet his own Guru, Neem Karoli Baba. On arrival, Maharajji had beckoned the suspicious professor forward and described how Alpert had been looking at the stars the previous night, thinking about his dead mother, who had recently passed away. He went on to reveal more details of his life, with which he seemed intimately familiar.

"She died of spleen," Maharajji said, pointing to his side.

At that point, realizing that this old man in a blanket knew his innermost thought, his logical mind hit a wall and he burst into tears. He had a sort of meltdown and began sobbing uncontrollably at Maharajji's feet.

When he recovered somewhat he asked, "How can I achieve enlightenment?"

Thinking that he would be told to be ascetic and follow a strict meditation practice, he was shocked when instead Maharajji said, "Ram Dass, just love people and tell the truth."

Later on he added, "Just be in your beingness. That knowingness "I Am" has created the entire universe. Hold on to that. Nothing has to be done."

As the radio interview concluded, for the first time I thought about going to India. I wondered, maybe I also have a Guru, perhaps even Maharajji? I saw myself walking the same path Ram Dass had to the temple in the Himalayas and prostrating at the feet of Maharajji. Would he greet me the same way? Perhaps he would say simply, "My son, at last you have arrived." Then he would touch my third eye and put me into cosmic consciousness.

---

everyone." Many miracles have been attributed to him, including healing the sick and bringing the dead back to life. Well known Westerners who have been drawn to him include: Steven Jobs, founder of Apple Computer; Julia Roberts, the actress; and Larry Brilliant, former director of philanthropic projects for Google.org. American devotees have set up a temple dedicated to him in Taos, New Mexico.

Ram Dass at the feet of Neem Karoli Baba

CHAPTER 17

The Guru Under the Tree

I went back to my farmhouse in the country for the summer. A trip to India still seemed only a remote possibility; nonetheless, I began to live like a yogi. Every morning I spread my mat on the front lawn overlooking the Hudson River with the Catskill Mountains in the distance, practiced yoga, and meditated. In the afternoon I worked in the vegetable garden, walked through the forests, or drove across the river to Woodstock for tea. One day at a café in Woodstock I ran into a woman in white who introduced herself as Sherry, a yoga instructor. Later I discovered she was a renegade descendant of the Rockefeller clan, trying like the rest of us to survive on her own, free of family pressure. Over tea she told me about her Guru, Ramamurti Mishra, who was not only a yogi but also a medical doctor and Sanskrit scholar, a fascinating combination of talents.[62] When she said that he lived in nearby Monroe, New York, at Ananda Ashram, which he shared with Swami Satchidananda, my former yoga teacher, I decided to make the short drive to visit him.

After leaving my car in the ashram parking lot, I walked around the beautifully kept grounds of what had once been a private residence, and went in search of Dr. Mishra. I had never seen an ashram before and felt self-conscious. Wearing old blue jeans while everyone else was wearing pure white, I wondered if I was holy enough. In the distance I heard the uplifting sound of Sanskrit chanting, which felt eerily familiar.

---

62 Ramamurti S. Mishra, M.D. (1923–1993), later known as Shri Brahmananda Sarasvati, was a western medical doctor, neurosurgeon, psychiatrist, professor of medicine, Ayurvedic physician and authority on Sanskrit. His mother was a Guru in India and his father a high court judge and practicing astrologer. At the age of 6 he appeared to die for 36 hours; however, as his father prepared to light the funeral pyre he returned to his body. He founded the Yoga Society of New York and Yoga Society of San Francisco and authored the highly acclaimed *Textbook of Yoga Psychology* (Baba Bhagavandas Publication Trust, 1997).

Its vibration drew me magnetically down a path past the large house to a well-kept emerald lawn. Under the spreading branches of a huge evergreen tree a group sat at the feet of a dark-skinned man in an orange robe, and I recognized the image I had dreamed of since childhood. Many times I had seen this man chanting in a strange language before a group of white-clothed students under this tree. Drifting toward me in the still air of the summer morning, the chanting filled my soul with peace. Not wanting to interrupt the melodic rhythms, I stood still on the group's perimeter. Then the man in the orange robe, whom I now realized must be Ramamurti Mishra, looked up and gazed at me. Beams of white light shot from his eyes into mine, seeming to penetrate my soul. I realized then that he knew me completely. I did not have to go to India; my Guru stood before me. He smiled and beckoned that I should sit at his feet. I felt disoriented, my mind floating in space, memories of past lives in India and visions of future events seeming to collapse into the present moment.

Turning his attention back to the group, the Guru continued chanting and my consciousness soared in bliss to higher realms. Here was the being I had known I would one day meet, a meeting that would start a new life.

After class I followed the group back to the house and Dr. Mishra came up beside me. He didn't waste a moment. His words indicated that I was correct in assuming he knew me.

"So, you were born in the West this lifetime!" he said, seeming amused.

"Yes," I replied, my mouth dry with excitement. I wanted to ask him what else he knew, how we had known each other in past lives, and what was supposed to happen now, but my mind was too overwhelmed to speak.

He opened the door to the house and as we entered I was shocked when he asked, "Have you been initiated yet?"[63]

"What?" I stammered.

"Would you like me to initiate you?"

I was not sure what initiation entailed, but said that I hadn't. He motioned to sit on the floor of the living room, and then sat behind me on the sofa. Without further discussion he placed his hands over my eyes,

---

63 Initiation: (Latin, *initiationem*) to be led inward, pertaining to secret ritual; however, in the esoteric traditions a transmission of consciousness is sometimes imparted by the Master.

pulled my head toward him and began chanting a mantra above my head. Energy coursed through my body and my chakras spun like sparklers, an indescribable bliss surging through my being.[64] Then he removed his hands and rose to his feet.

"Meditate on *That*," he said. "*That* you experience in the center of your being near your heart will take you to *Brahman,* the supreme Source. *That* is all you need. Hatha yoga is good for the body, but only Raja Yoga will take you to Brahman. What you meditate on you become. Meditate on God and you will become God."

Everything had happened so unexpectedly I did not realize the gift I had been given. I remained on the living room floor, unable to rise, still immersed in bliss as the wheels of colored light within continued to spin. As instructed, I meditated on *That*. Focusing on the inner feeling, I kept my eyes closed, ignoring the people passing through the room. Finally I was able to rise and join the others in the dining room, but did not feel like eating. I sat at the table near Dr. Mishra, hoping that he would impart some further instruction, but he seemed to ignore me and soon I left for home to be alone.

I returned to Ananda every weekend to see Dr. Mishra, but these visits were different. My new Guru said I needed to purify my subtle nervous system so the spiritual energy could flow unobstructed. Since he was an Ayurvedic as well as western medical doctor I had great respect for the breadth of his knowledge and trusted him implicitly. His mastery of both eastern and western methods highlighted the strengths of each and I saw how both could complement each other.

Over the summer he imparted ancient purifying and energizing methods that had been transmitted by the ancient *rishis,* which would make the body a better conduit for the energy he had awakened.[65] As the

---

64 *Chakras:* (wheels) spinning vortexes of energy that largely determine how we perceive and relate to phenomena. These major centers, located along the central channel of the body, must be purified of negative energies and harmonized to make the body a pure vehicle of higher consciousness. There are minor energy centers in other parts of the body.

65 *Rishis:* sages (*Rishikas*: feminine)with direct perception of the Infinite, authors of the *Vedas,* written down 2,000–1,000 BCE from a

subtle channels of the body opened, for the first time in my life I felt as though it was functioning as intended. With every breath I felt prana circulate through my sinus cavities, filling my brain with illumination. This regimen of cleansing took at least an hour, beginning before sunrise every morning, followed by meditation. Soon I felt totally alive, vibrant and sustained in heightened awareness.

At the end of that transformative summer of 1970 Dr. Mishra announced that he was going to San Francisco to teach Sanskrit at the California Institute of Asian Studies for the winter.[66] Sadly, I realized that my time with him was coming to a close. How could my Guru abandon me? I had made a commitment and assumed that he had also. The news was as upsetting as a marriage partner suddenly announcing plans to file for divorce.

He said that I had been initiated into the practice that would take me to God Consciousness, but I knew I was not there yet and my mind overflowed with unanswered questions. The great Gurus like Ramakrishna, Vivekananda, Yogananda, and Neem Karoli Baba had guided their disciples every step of the way, hadn't they? Perhaps Dr. Mishra was only an *upaguru* (temporary teacher) until I found the *sadguru,* the ultimate teacher who reflected my own soul. Perhaps there was a Guru for me in India after all?

To my great joy, before he departed, Dr. Mishra addressed this unanswered question. I was sitting with him in the living room when he looked directly into my eyes and said, "So, you're going to India?"

"Well, I'm feeling the pull."

---

more ancient oral tradition. In the *Rigveda*, thirty women sages are mentioned. The *Saptarishis* (Seven Great *Rishis*) are the emanations of Divine Intelligence who bring consciousness into the material world. In the Western tradition they are called Elohim or *Chohans* (Masters) of the Seven Rays.

66 California Institute of Integral Studies (CIIS) was founded as the result of a recommendation by the philosopher Sri Aurobindo (Bengal, 1872–1950) to Dr. Haridas Chaudur. He and his wife Bina came to San Francisco to found an institution whose aim was to bridge the East and West through education.

"You could look up Swami Chidananda at Sivananda Ashram."

Then he uttered what I had unconsciously desired to hear from my departing Guru, "You have my blessings."

"At last I have the name of my true Guru, the one awaiting me in India," I concluded. If I had listened more closely I would have heard that he had not said that Swami Chidananda was my Guru, or even that I should go to India. He had simply reflected my own projection of what I wanted.

Ramamurti Mishra, later known as Swami Brahmananda Sarasvati

With every day the pull to India grew stronger. I attended a free dance performance at Cooper Union by the renowned classical Indian dancer, Vija Vetra. She appeared as a jeweled Goddess forming *mudras* with her hands as she whirled through space.[67] Suddenly a beam of light flew from her hand and struck the center of my forehead and in that instant I knew I was going to the East. That beam of light from her hand had opened my inner eye, in which I saw India. With that image was a knowing that a great adventure was about to begin, one that would change my life forever. I felt the Guru beckoning—an invitation to journey east.

To have a Guru was absolutely essential to attain enlightenment, the ancient texts said. Even the great Swami Vivekananda, who had brought the knowledge of yoga to the West at the World Congress of Religions in Chicago in 1898, had sat at the feet of the God-Man, Ramakrishna. In India more devotion is frequently given to the Guru than to God because the Guru is God in human form, embodied for your benefit. Even if the Guru is not enlightened, it is said that if you totally commit to that form he will, none-the-less, serve as a vehicle for your own enlightenment.

There is the legend of a Tibetan lama who after many years of guiding younger lamas to enlightenment shocked them one day by saying, "I wish to step down now as your Guru. I have been so busy guiding you over the past thirty years that I have not had time to do the spiritual practices I have been teaching. Now I will have the time, so you can be my Guru and guide me to enlightenment."

I later heard that Neem Karoli Baba said,

Whoever may be your Guru—he may be a lunatic or a common person—once you have accepted him, he is the Lord of Lords.

When I returned to Manhattan in the fall, I told Colette that I would be in India for only a month or possibly two, and we said goodbye. She was busy rehearsing for her dance performance and neither of us dreamed that this separation would be permanent. When I returned she would have free time again, and we would have many beautiful experiences to share. It wasn't until I finally returned that I realized the meaning of Thomas Wolfe's poignant words, "You can't go home again." When I finally did return, neither Colette nor I were the same people and the home we had created in our lives was gone.

---

67   *Mudra:* hand gesture that can transmit energy as well as meaning.

CHAPTER 18

Journey to the East

At Kennedy Airport I stood in line for the flight to London with a group of young Americans dressed in white with *malas* around their necks—obviously on a spiritual path.[68]

"We're going to see Guru Maharajji," one of them said.

"The Guru of Ram Dass?"

"No, the thirteen-year old *Sadguru*."[69]

I had never heard of him, and said that I was going to India to see a Guru in Rishikesh.

"Why go all the way to India to see a Guru when you can meet the Sadguru from India who is in London? He is a perfect Master and above all other Gurus. You can stay at the ashram with us in London."

Since I needed a place to stay on arrival, I accepted their offer. What could I lose? Maybe hearing Ram Dass on the radio had only been to get me searching.

In London I found myself sitting at the feet of a chubby, thirteen-year old kid they called Guru Maharajji, who claimed to be the only one on Earth in possession of what he called *Knowledge,* unique spiritual methods he was willing to transmit to the faithful.

"I am here to give you the knowledge which only I can give," he boasted.

"Wow, what *chutzpah*," I thought, "but you never know; he must have something to be able to attract all these followers."[70]

---

68 *Mala:* string of usually 108 beads plus a Guru bead, used to count the recitation of mantras, a process called *japa.* Each bead represents one of the 108 channels of the subtle nervous system, also the four aspects of each of the 27 lunar mansions, as well as the possible number of character flaws needing to be purified.

69 *Sadguru:* perfect Master. Although *Maharajji* is a term of respect, this boy used it as his actual name.

70 *Chutzpah:* (Yiddish) arrogant audacity.

"If he's so enlightened," I wondered, "how can he be so boring?" He droned on and on, day after day, about the evils of materialism, and how only he could teach the techniques that would free us of that materialism.[71] Finally, I couldn't take his arrogance any more and asked, "What's wrong with the way I meditate now?"

"How could *you* possibly know how to meditate," he replied, puffing up his chest.

"Why you spoiled brat," I wanted to say, but held my tongue.

After days of listening to him market knowledge like a dishwashing detergent, I succumbed. "What the heck, I'm already here; I might just as well try it and see what happens."

Either we were found worthy or the boy had exhausted himself, but the *Mahatmas* finally told us that the great moment of our initiation had arrived.[72] After assuring us that Knowledge was from God so was totally free, and that we would not be required to take any vows, we were ushered into a small room by the Mahatma.

The door closed and the excitement mounted as we waited breathlessly for the secret of the ages. Then the Mahatma said, "Now that the great moment has arrived you need to surrender your mind, body, and all your material possessions to Guru Maharajji, for from now on he will take care of all your needs."

"What a liar," I thought. "I guess when he said 'free' he meant 'no fixed price,' but he expected you to donate everything you owned!"

Since I had come this far, I was not going to miss these secret teachings now. From studying law I knew that fraud cancels every contract from the inception. I crossed my fingers behind my back, signifying before God that I did not consider myself bound by terms imposed so deviously.[73]

---

71 A couple of years later he was arrested for trying to smuggle a suitcase full of watches through Indian customs. They had been given to him by devotees as a symbol of their renunciation of materialism. He has since renounced his Divinity, resumed his birth name, and travels extensively promoting world peace.

72 *Mahatma:* great soul, Master. He applied this term to the Indian men who served him and performed the "knowledge" transmission process.

73 Fraud: "An intentional perversion of truth for the purpose of inducing

After waiting this long no one left the room, and in a hushed voice the Mahatma began explaining the secret techniques. I was shocked to hear that after waiting all these days the practices turned out to be ones I was already doing!

I had wasted enough time in London. Now I knew how so many kids were brainwashed into joining cults. Deprived of sleep and surrounded day and night by other enthusiastic followers telling you that you're doing the right thing, your discriminating intelligence is worn down. From this experience I began to trust my innate feelings about spiritual teachers more than what people said about them, and to look to see if they also transmitted compassion, wisdom, and *dharma*.[74] Even more important, I looked to see if they put their teachings into practice.

This experience with a pretender only increased my desire to be connected with an authentic Guru, the one I believed that was awaiting my arrival in Rishikesh. Instead of hitchhiking through Europe I decided to expedite my arrival and boarded the Orient Express, the notorious train on which James Bond had traveled in the film *From Russia with Love*. As the train was long rumored to be used by secret agents, I kept an eye out for unusual characters as we crossed the English Channel into France.

By the time the train had reached Zagreb, Yugoslavia (now Croatia) nothing exciting had happened and, wearying of the monotony, I got off. In any case, it didn't seem appropriate to go on a vision quest using such comfortable means of travel. Greater personal sacrifice was needed, so I began to hitchhike. Rides came easily through Yugoslavia until nightfall, when I found myself stranded. After a long wait by the side of a desolate road, a crowded bus stopped and picked me up. I traveled through the night down through Bosnia, Kosovo, and into Macedonia. Leaning against

---

another in reliance upon it to part with some valuable thing belonging to him…." (*Black's Law Dictionary*, 6th ed. 1990)

74   *Dharma:* the practice of that which upholds righteousness, natural harmony, and one's life purpose in conscious adherence to spiritual law. In addition to *dharma* and *vidya* (spiritual knowledge), the highest teachings must also convey *shanti* (peace), *prema* (divine love), and *sathya* (truth).

the window I had a fitful sleep, dreaming of a terrible war between ethnic groups that would ravage the region in the near future.[75]

In the morning we crossed the border into Greece and I awoke bruised and stiff. The driver was shouting, gesturing me to get off, but I replied that I wanted to continue on to Istanbul. He said he would not drive any further, drawing an imaginary knife across his throat. After centuries of enmity between the Greeks and Turks the buses would not cross the border. I exited to find myself on a flat, barren plain—literally the end of the road. I asked the way to Istanbul and the driver pointed to the bridge over the Evros River. As I was neither Greek nor Turkish, I felt I would be safe.

As soon as I made the choice to walk across the barren wasteland an intense wind began blowing in my face. I felt the spirits of the dead, of armies long gone—that they were the force in the wind lashing at my clothes, trying to draw me into the conflict they were still waging on invisible planes. Crossing the bridge over the river, I felt the wind shouting, "There is no Guru waiting; only suffering lies ahead on your journey to the East."

Yet, a force pulled me onward across the bridge—the excitement of the unknown. I was certain that ahead I would find the door to a new world. If I had the courage to continue, the door to higher realms would open, and I wondered, "Have I come this far to turn around?"

Thinking of my mother's friend I had seen dying in the hospital in New York, I thought, "It's better to die on a quest than go alone, drugged, and with tubes sticking in you."

Summoning my inner force, I leaned into the blasts and pulled myself along the railing to keep from being blown into the rippling marshes below. When I finally arrived on the far shore, the wind strangely ceased and there was calm. Seeing they had lost their battle, perhaps the spirits had retreated. I looked for someone to check my passport, but there was no checkpoint at this border, no one who cared if I entered this country or not. Maybe they left the border control up to the spirits in the wind? Those who tried to sneak across at night were found shot in the marshes in the morning. Perhaps they believed that anyone entering during the day had earned the right.

---

75   The Bosnian War did break out in 1992, about 22 years later.

On the horizon were the minarets of what seemed to be the Emerald City of Oz, matching the illustrations in the book from which my mother had read to me at bedtime as a child.[76] I had not known that such a place existed. I was glad that I had proceeded, for already a new world was opening. I watched as the orb of the setting sun sank into the purple mists rising from the dark earth of the freshly plowed fields.

A truck full of workers returning home from the fields suddenly stopped nearby. A man flashed a white-toothed smile, leaned over with his muscular, sun-tanned arm, and lifted me up among the other men. The truck lurched forward toward the minarets of the mosque in the town ahead, and I basked in the camaraderie of the men joking with each other. It felt good to be alive. That feeling of rightness confirmed I was going the right way.

The truck stopped in town and we jumped from the tailgate. The men pulled me into a café, and I had no choice but to accept their hospitality. The town seemed to welcome me like an old friend returning home. The aisle of the café was so narrow there was room for only a row of small tables on each side, so they took turns at my table. One after another of the swarthy workers ordered tea, raised the glass in a toast, and tossed it down. Sitting there in that café I felt at home—that strangely, I belonged.

---

76 *The Wonderful Wizard of Oz*, L. Frank Baum (George M. Hill Co., 1900).

CHAPTER 19

Mysterious Talisman

The coup by the military in March of 1971 had not established a stable government able to bring peace or economic improvement to the people, and I awoke in the morning to find that shots had been fired. The Turkish People's Liberation Army was kidnapping foreigners and holding them for ransom. I was told it would be safe in Istanbul so I got on a bus crowded with people headed in that direction, hoping to avoid running into roving groups of rebels. Winding through the passes where the risk instead was of being robbed by bandits, it was a long, tense journey. Finally I fell asleep against the window and only woke in the morning as the bus pulled up at the gates of Istanbul. I staggered stiffly down the steps to see the sun rising over the minarets of the mosques—still giving me the impression that I was in the land of Oz. Inhaling the exotic smells lingering in the morning haze, I shouldered my backpack and stumbled toward the marble columns that were part of the city wall. It was an arch known as the Gateway to the East—beyond which, it was said, was the beginning of the Orient.

I was awestruck, realizing that I was standing in the footsteps of Emperor Constantine. In the third century after Christ he had built a wall around the city, and this gate was now all that remained. How many conquerors had lost their lives attacking this city, whose ashes now mingled with the dust of their ancestors? I didn't see any sign of the current revolution, no armed men in the street; however, I stood out as an easy target in the crowd and was on my guard. I thought of retreating to the bus and heading back the way I had come, but the crowd pushed me forward. I felt lost, not knowing which way to go.

Then, a couple of urchins grabbed my hands and led me toward the kiosk where I could get a bus downtown. I had been warned about letting anyone get close, especially kids like these. They could slit your pocket with a razor in a flash and take your passport. I held tightly to my possessions, sure that I was about to be robbed. Certainly they wanted *baksheesh* (a tip) and would plead for as much as they thought they could get. Once I took out my wallet they would probably grab it and run.

However, to my surprise they began circling as though in a welcoming dance. As their mouths opened in carefree laughter I marveled at the perfection of their teeth, which seemed dazzlingly white in the morning light. I had never seen teeth of such perfection.

The happiness that flashed from their eyes dissolved any effort to be rid of them. As I succumbed to their charm, one of them put a warm arm around my waist and ran his small fingers through my hair. While distracted, the other boy pressed close. Suddenly I saw a glint of metal and a weight fell solidly on my chest. I looked down to see a substantial silver coin hanging around my neck from a silver chain.

"Swami, swami, this will protect you," they chanted gleefully.

Tears welled up in my eyes as they pushed me onto the bus that had just stopped at the kiosk.

"Goodbye, Swami, goodbye!" the angelic boys shouted before disappearing.

Wanting to wave back, I searched for them in vain. As the bus lurched ahead I looked down at the brilliant coin hanging from the chain. It was an English Half-Crown, held to the chain by a silver bracket in the shape of a five-petaled lotus—a familiar symbol which I vaguely recalled having seen somewhere.

Instead of robbing me or asking for money, these beggars had bestowed a medallion of obvious value; and why had they called me Swami? I was not yet wearing the white clothes of India. I did not solve this enigma until a year later when I saw this same five-petaled lotus above the gate at the *ashram* of Sathya Sai Baba.

CHAPTER 20

Mother India

From Istanbul I journeyed east into Afghanistan. From Kabul I had hoped to go through the Khyber Pass, but on December 3, 1971, Pakistan initiated a pre-emptive airstrike against India and I barely escaped on the last plane before all airports were shut down. Others who waited to go through the pass were trapped by artillery barrages.[77]

The plane landed in Delhi, and I took the bus into the heart of the city, aptly named Connaught Circus, a circular park surrounded by a road. Here all types of humanity, buses, rickshaws, and water buffaloes mingled in a cloud of asphyxiating exhaust. The shock of India hit full force. I was on the other side of the world, far from the comfort of home. With no escape, I felt panic. This was not the tranquil India of Kipling's *The Jungle Book,* which my mother had read to me as a child, nor did it resemble the pastoral films of Satiyajit Ray, a tambura droning melodically in the background. The scorching heat, noise, and exhaust fumes of rickshaws were overwhelming. I thought of getting back on the shuttle and returning to the airport, where I was sure I could get on the next flight back to New York.

The bus pulled away, however, and I was stranded. Seeing a green area in the center of the vast Circus, I walked across the street, sat under a tree, and shut my eyes to meditate. Instead of the spirituality I had expected, I sensed an overwhelming desire for material things—that I was in a sea of

---

77   Pakistan killed almost 2 million Bengali Hindus in East Pakistan. After the Pakistani Air Force bombed 11 Indian airfields, on December 3rd Prime Minister Indira Gandhi initiated a counter attack. The United States supported Pakistan against India under the direction of Nixon and Kissinger, while the Soviet Union supported India. Military operations ended on December 16th, with the overwhelming victory of India and the establishment of a free Bangladesh. Despite America's military and political support of Pakistan, I was, nonetheless, warmly received by the Indian people wherever I went.

desire. As if in confirmation, two young men, ignoring that I was sitting cross-legged in *padmasana* with eyes closed, sat down and began asking questions.

"What is your native place, Sir?" one asked.

"The US."

"How many cars do you have?"

"One."

"What, only one?"

"And what is your purpose in coming to India?"

"To find a Guru."

"What!" they shouted, incredulous, "Why would you want to do that? Don't you know the Gurus are all fakes, just looking for money? You have everything in America. You're just wasting your time coming here." Disgusted, they got up and prepared to leave.

"So, what do you do?" I replied.

"We are students of engineering. After we get our degrees we are going to America to work in high tech."

"I was in engineering," I said, "but I quit to seek the spirit."

They looked at me in disgust, glancing back over their shoulders as though leaving a pariah.

I had to get out of Delhi. Remembering the Srivastavas, an Indian couple I had met on the Orient Express, I decided to accept their offer to stay with them. I flagged down a rickshaw and, despite the chaotic traffic that seemed to go in all directions simultaneously, arrived safely at the train station. There was just time to phone the Srivastavas that I was coming before boarding the train toward Haridwar.[78] Dr. Srivastava was a professor of engineering at the university near Haridwar.

Before the last stop I disembarked and found Professor and Mrs. Srivastava and a dozen of their friends and relatives at the station, waiting to offer a warm greeting. In India the guest is seen as God, a

---

78   *Haridwar:* (*Hari,* Vishnu; *Har,* Shiva; *dwar,* gateway). Haridwar is regarded as a gateway to God, one of the seven most sacred places in India and an ideal place to begin a pilgrimage. Here the Ganges descends into the plains of India, and is one of the four locations where millions of Hindus gather for the spiritual festival known as a Kumbh Mela.

beautiful tradition; however, I soon discovered that there were certain expectations of that Divine guest. I was expected to stay at least three days and eat three helpings of each chili-spiced dish at every meal. Fulfilling this obligation led to chronic indigestion. In later travel this was further stressed by the continuing consumption of spicy food, which was all that was available in most places.

On the third day before I left, I was taken to a clothing shop and outfitted in white cotton *Khadi* cloth befitting my spiritual quest. As a further parting gift, the Srivastavas draped a mala of huge *Rudraksha* beads around my neck.[79] I was deeply touched. Arriving in one of the poorest countries in the world, I had been invited into a stranger's home and treated like royalty. One of their relatives drove me to an ashram on the banks of the Ganges. They assured me that here I would be well treated, for the Guru had many western followers. I decided to spend the night there, and next morning head into the foothills of the Himalayas to Rishikesh, where I was sure *my* Guru waited.

---

79 *Khadi:* cloth that is hand-spun and woven as part of the movement started by Mahatma Gandhi to break India's dependency on Britain. It is comfortable, but wrinkles easily. A new form of Khadi cloth is now being produced, which has become a fashion as well as a political statement of India's independence. *Rudraksha:* Eye of Shiva. The bead is a large, multi-faceted seed from a species of evergreen tree, and is reported to have protective as well as healing properties.

CHAPTER 21

At the Mercy of the Child Guru

As the car pulled away from the gate I looked up at the sign over the ashram gate that said Premnagar (City of Bliss). It sounded familiar and I had a sinking feeling. My worst suspicion was confirmed as I walked down the path to the ashram's front door. Fate had brought me once again to the feet of the child Guru I had last seen in London. He had just arrived on a jumbo jet with three hundred westerners he called "Premies."[80] I would just have dinner and get an early start in the morning.

The ashram, used to hosting only small groups of Indians, had no idea how to deal with that many people, especially westerners. The only running water was a single spigot and the toilets had stopped working. The field behind the ashram had become the latrine. In rural India, where toilets and privacy are unheard of, people are used to relieving themselves in public; but for westerners this was a shock that took a while to assimilate. Cooking was also done outside and flies swarmed happily back and forth from field to the food. Within twenty-four hours nearly everyone had dysentery. However, we were still expected to help prepare meals and sweep the temple grounds, which they called Karma Yoga.

In the morning I awoke with a burning fever. Having slept on the cement floor of the temple, I was powerless to avoid the *darshan* of Guru Maharajji.[81] This time he sat in the midst of an ornately decorated altar on a throne several feet above the audience. It was just before Christmas and the Hindu shrine was decorated with twinkling, colored lights, which appealed to the westerners missing the holiday festivities at home.[82] I was

---

80 "Premie," derived from *prema:* Divine love. Not to be confused with "preemie," born prematurely.

81 *Darshan:* sight of Divinity, audience with a Guru or saintly person, a regular occurrence in ashrams.

82 *Hindu:* (Persian) refers to the people beyond the Indus (Sindu) River, also the origin of the name India. The ancient name of the country was Bharat. *Bha:* Light/Knowledge/God; *rata:* devoted. Hence Bharat

shocked to hear Maharajji boast, "Why are you thinking about Jesus? Forget about Him, because I am that same being here now."

Instead of leaving in the morning as planned, I lay on the cement floor for days, burning with fever, and moving in and out of delirium. The Hindu Gods in their various peaceful and wrathful forms looked down on me from the shrine, gradually merging into a blur of flashing colored lights. Twice a day the child Guru gave darshan, ranting on and on about his greatness, and I began to wonder if, in the midst of this increasing sense of unreality, I had been carried off to one of the astral hells by the *asuras* (demons) depicted in pictures on the shrine.[83]

"The reason you are sick," a devotee said one day, looking down on me with obvious displeasure, "is because you still haven't accepted Guru Maharajji as God."

When I could no longer stand the boasting of this teenage, petty tyrant I dragged my mat outside onto the porch.[84] There I could at least look out into the fields shimmering in the heat. As I was lying there one afternoon, trying to ignore the incessant droning of the flies, I thought I heard one of my favorite songs from the 60s. Or, was it my imagination? As I listened, I heard it more distinctly, coming through the stillness of the afternoon. It was now unmistakable—Bob Dylan's "Mr. Tambourine Man," which I'd last heard in Greenwich Village at the fountain in Washington Square.

Was I delirious? Or was someone really playing that song? I hadn't seen any electrical outlets out back, so I struggled to my feet and shakily walked around the side of the temple to follow the song to the source. There,

---

(India) is the land of the people devoted to God. The religion was not called Hinduism but *Sanatana Dharma*, the path of righteousness leading to liberation.

83   *Asuras:* demons who were at one time *devas* (Gods), but who gradually degenerated due to increasing pride, vanity, disobedience, ignorance, and aggression. Both classes of beings war with each other, even today. *Deva:* (from Proto-Indo-European *deiwos:* celestial, shining), also the root of *deus:* (Latin) God, and the English word Divine.

84   Encountering a petty tyrant can help one confront one's own inner tyrants. "My benefactor used to say that a warrior who stumbles on a petty tyrant is a lucky one." *The Fire From Within*, Carlos Castaneda (Washington Square Press, 1991).

sitting on the steps, was a forlorn girl with a mini turntable on her lap. She had brought it and the vinyl album all the way from London—saving the batteries for a special occasion—which for her, as well as me, was now.

Listening to Dylan's voice rasping out over the field, I had a sort of satori—that I was the tambourine man—searching for my own song, which no one else could give. I needed to pursue my own truth. I kept walking and started to feel better. The further I got away from the ashram the better I felt. With no idea where I was going, I felt drawn toward a green line of trees in the distance. I stumbled toward them, and when I arrived, I pushed through the greenery, through the branches and vines— and there it was, the river that was the soul of India, the Ganges—which seemed to have been beckoning for eternity.

I had read *Siddhartha* before I left on this quest, and remembered how Siddhartha had achieved enlightenment—not by following the Buddha, but by living a normal life—finally sitting on the bank of the Ganges, listening to the sound of the sacred syllable, *Om,* which he heard murmuring.[85]

Without thinking, I stripped off my clothes and plunged into the holy river descending out of the Himalayas. Every cell was suddenly charged with light. I pulled myself up onto the riverbank refreshed, and realized that all signs of illness were gone.

I dressed and walked along the river barefoot. I had never felt so free, free of obligations and possessions. My passport and wallet, indicators of my identity that I had never been without, were back at the ashram. I had no money, no identity, yet was filled with inexplicable joy. Wherever I wandered I would be taken care of by Mother India.[86] I had finally run away from home, as I had tried to do as a child, but now there was no obligation to return. The warmth of the sand beneath my feet and the whispering of the river were constants reminders of the presence of the Mother.

---

85   *Siddhartha*, Hermann Hesse (1877–1962). The protagonist discovers that truth is found only through polarities, that every extreme includes its opposite, and that no words can contain the ultimate meaning of existence. We can only discover the ultimate truth within ourselves.

86   Temples are maintained in India that provide wandering spiritual seekers with meals and temporary lodging. It is believed that one accumulates good karma by assisting those on the spiritual path.

CHAPTER 22

Wristwatch Baba

Walking along the Ganges I felt an exquisite sense of oneness, my mind merged with the sky, body with the earth, and soul with the river. Yet, I was still a separate ego yearning for total immersion in the absolute—an ego-less oneness with God that I had experienced, but wanted now as permanent reality. I yearned for the Guru who would transmit this awareness as Ramakrishna had transmitted it to Vivekananda, and as Babaji had transmitted to Yukteshwar, thence to Yogananda.[87] Ramamurti Mishra's touch had brought me to the door, but now I needed the final touch to push me through that door of consciousness into the infinite, supreme reality. At Rishikesh I hoped to receive that boon from Swami Chidananda. If not from him, could there be someone else? I remembered the ancient saying,

When the student is ready, the teacher will appear.

I felt a sense of excitement, knowing that a moment of complete *samadhi* could occur at any moment, awaiting only the Guru's blessing.[88] Hardly had that thought arisen when I saw a *sadhu* in an orange robe coming along the riverbank.[89] He walked slowly, appearing to be lost in inner contemplation, and so I stopped to await his arrival. Perhaps he was the one? Was this the Guru for whom I was waiting?

A few feet away he stopped and raised his eyes. Surely he would beckon me to sit, and reveal that he knew my innermost thoughts as Ram Dass

---

87   Babaji was the Guru and initiator of a series of yogis, each of whom served in the same capacity for their follower: Lahiri Mahasaya, Sri Yukteswar, and Paramahansa Yogananda. This fascinating account is given in Yogananda's classic, *Autobiography of a Yogi.*

88   *Samadhi:* absorption in higher states of consciousness. In the highest state, *nirvikalpa samadhi*, the self is immersed in absolute oneness, and individual self-consciousness disappears.

89   *Sadhu:* wandering renunciate.

had experienced with Neem Karoli Baba. Then he would whisper a mantra or touch my third eye.

Just as I expected, the sadhu motioned me to sit in the shade of a tree. We sat together on the riverbank and I waited for the event that would mark the end of my earthly search, the attainment of liberation. Seemingly in answer to my thoughts, he beckoned me closer and began to speak. In flawless English he said, "Would you like something?"

"Yes, yes," I said, wondering if perhaps he wanted me to ask outwardly for what was in my heart.

"Would you like something for your mother?"

"I beg your pardon?" I asked, thinking I hadn't heard correctly.

"Would you like something for your mother?" he repeated. "Or maybe something for your sister, or a sweetheart?"

With that, he pulled up the sleeves of his loose fitting robe and revealed both arms lined with wristwatches. From hand to shoulder, his arms were covered with watches of all imaginable styles; he was a veritable walking jewelry store. As I looked in shock, hardly believing my eyes, he continued, "Very good quality, and best price."

I stumbled to my feet, realizing that I had been taken in by someone as slick as the con artists who sold stolen jewelry on Second Avenue in New York City.

"Hey, where are you going? Are you American? For you I have a special price!"

Backing away, humiliated, I felt a lump in my throat as my dream of instant samadhi dissolved. Hadn't Ramamurti Mishra said that I should go to see Swami Chidananda in Rishikesh? I had been too hasty. I vowed, "Tomorrow I will go to Rishikesh and prostrate at the feet of the true Guru!"

CHAPTER 23

Spinach Baba

At last I arrived in Rishikesh. A boatman ferried me across the river and I remembered how Siddhartha, in Hesse's story, had become enlightened ferrying people across the river rather than by following the Buddha. Just as I was about to ask the boatman if he needed an assistant, we reached the shore, and seeing a naked sadhu wading into the Ganges, I went to join him. Imitating his example, I stripped off my clothes and chanted *Om Namah Shivaya* three times. I poured the glacial water over my head and then completely immersed myself in the water cascading from the Himalayas—the brow of Shiva, according to Hindu belief.

I emerged feeling rejuvenated and spiritually cleansed for the imminent purpose—finding my Guru. Setting off upstream toward Sivananda Ashram, I was ready finally to implore Swami Chidananda for liberation.

Swami Sivananda (center) in Rishikesh
with Swami Chidananda (first on his left)

It had been almost two months since I had begun this journey, and I was satisfied that I had not taken the easy route, unlike those westerners who had boarded a jumbo jet and flown direct. After lengthy travel and a long illness I was finally arriving at my Guru's ashram with the eagerness of one lost in the desert nearing an oasis. Swami undoubtedly knew that I was coming, as Neem Karoli Baba had anticipated Ram Dass, and most likely had a room waiting. If Swami did not greet me personally I would leave my pack in the room, and then go to the canteen for the refreshing juice of a green coconut. I could then go back to the room and lie down to rest until the Guru called.

After a tiring walk in the scorching sun, I stood before the ashram gate, which was opened by a stoop-shouldered man in spectacles whose rotten teeth jutted from his mouth.

"Yes?" he questioned, seeming annoyed at the intrusion.

"I have come to see Swami Chidananda," I stammered, relieved to have finally arrived at the destination assigned to me months before.

"Impossible," the old man said, beginning to shut the gate.

"But I've come a long way to see him, I was sent by Ramamurti Mishra!"

"Who?"

"Ramamurti Mishra!"

"Never heard of him."

"Well, may I come in and go to my room? I'll wait until Swami returns. I've come a long way."

"I'm afraid that's impossible."

"Why is that?"

"The ashram is full."

I was sure there was a mistake, that once Swami knew I was there he would straighten things out.

"Well, may I come in and wait until Swami comes back?"

"No, not possible."

"Not possible, why?"

"Swami Chidananda is currently in New York giving lectures," the old man said with annoyance. "He will not be back for a month!"

The door shut in my face and again I felt the flush of humiliation. The energy of anticipation that had sustained my travels for the past few months now dissipated. I had pursued a delusion. I should have known that finding a Guru would not be that easy. I was tired and exhausted and felt that I would soon collapse from the heat. I stumbled back down the dusty path to the river and sat in the shade of a Shiva temple. As I took a drink from my canteen, I tried to figure out what to do.

"Dear God," I thought—if there even is a God who knows and cares about me—please show me what to do next."

Perhaps in answer to my prayer, a young German couple happened by. Seeing that I was dejected, they sat down and struck up a conversation. When I told them why I was so forlorn, the girl said, "Perhaps our Guru is yours also, and he sent us to find you? He lives just upstream. Come with us and we'll take you to him."

I had nothing else to do, except for the fact that I hadn't had food since early morning and wanted to get something to eat. Tired of the rice and dhal I'd been eating since arrival in India, I was craving vegetables as fresh as the ones I used to pick from my garden—in particular, spinach. For days I had been fantasizing about eating a bowl of steamed spinach drenched in butter. There were plenty of restaurants in town, but I knew it was futile to seek plain spinach; in India the vegetables are cooked to a pulp and filled with chilies.

"Come see our Guru first and you can eat later," they begged.

I remembered the words of Jesus:

Seek ye first the kingdom of God and his Righteousness, and all else will be added unto you.

Having gone without food this long, I reasoned that I might as well seek the Guru first, so I stumbled along behind them as we wended our way upstream. In twenty minutes we came to a peninsula of sand and rock jutting into the river. As I rounded a boulder I came upon a nearly-naked man with a large belly, sitting cross-legged on a tiger skin. There was no tent, blanket, fire pit, or other sign that he lived here; he just seemed to hang out here. His devotees prostrated at his feet, but since I didn't believe in bowing, I simply brought my hands together in *namaskar* and sat at a respectful distance.[90]

---

90 *Pranam:* sign of respect, which acknowledges the Divinity in both

He soon turned his gaze on me, but since he was a *muni* baba, said nothing.[91] If he was my Guru, I wondered how that would be communicated. I assumed he would give some kind of sign, but nothing was happening. The longer I sat there the more hungry I became, and I began thinking about where I would find a restaurant in town.

Without fanfare the yogi reached behind his back and brought forward a shiny, stainless steel container, which he offered. I crawled forward hesitantly and took the hot container in my hands. I was shocked to see a mass of steamed spinach smothered in *ghee* (clarified butter). On top were a couple of toasted chapattis, also dripping ghee. The spinach was lightly steamed, exactly the way I used to prepare it from my garden back on the farm.

I looked at him in surprise, "For me?"

He nodded. I wanted to be sure it wasn't his dinner, but now didn't wait for a second invitation. The spinach was so delicious I didn't even think about the miracle of its appearance out of thin air. When finished I thanked the yogi and put the empty container on the sand near him. Suddenly I was overpowered by the desire to sleep and could not resist lying down in the sand.

How much time elapsed I did not know. When I awakened the sun had set behind the hills, and a purple haze had descended on the river. The German couple had left but their Guru still sat there gazing at me. I felt totally nourished, and waited now for some sign or indication from the yogi, but he said nothing. Because he had created the spinach I had been craving out of thin air, did that mean he was my Guru? Although I didn't feel particularly enlightened, I wondered if he had transmitted a special blessing while I was asleep. Despite his powers of mind reading and

---

the one expressing it and the one to whom respect is being shown. This respect can be shown through six different forms, one of which is *namaskar*, where the hands are folded with the tips touching the forehead. In *ashtangana pranam* one prostrates face down, flat on the ground, with arms stretched over the head.

91 *Muni:* silent. The latest Buddha was called *Sakyamuni Gautama:* member of the Sakya clan, Gautama family, who has vowed silence. He probably maintained silence only during his six years of asceticism.

precipitation I didn't see how our relationship was going to progress if he was not going to talk.

"What am I supposed to do now?" I wondered, unsure of the etiquette. Surmising that the main event was over and that there were no acts to follow, I rose to depart.

"Is he going to utter some parting word of wisdom?" I wondered, but he remained silent. The yogi continued to gaze blankly into space, not giving any indication that he cared what I did. Realizing that our meeting was at an end, I bowed and left. It was getting dark, and as I walked down the path toward town I was glad I didn't need to look for dinner—for the delicious spinach and chapattis had been most satisfying.[92]

As I left town I came to a statue of Saraswati, the Goddess of Wisdom, and stopped before her to pray for a Guru who, in addition to bestowing dinner, would also guide me on the path of wisdom and liberation.[93] At the riverbank the boatman was no longer there, so I used the bridge to cross the river.

---

92   Only forty years later did I realized the great blessing this nameless yogi bestowed, a blessing still felt.

93   *Saraswati:* the Goddess of knowledge, wisdom, art, science. She is worshipped by yogis for her chastity and dedication to spiritual attainment. The name of Abraham's wife may have originally been Saraswati, as the Bible says she was first called Sarai, a shorter form of Saraswati, or possibly Sari: (Hebrew) princess.

CHAPTER 24

Ram Dass

On the sweltering bus back to Delhi it reached one hundred twenty degrees, and I wrapped a shawl around my face to keep out the blowing dust. To make the journey worse, several Indian engineering students heckled me with the same three questions, which they repeated over and over: "How much money do you make? How many cars do you have? What is your purpose?"

The first time the questions were asked I replied, "I'm living on savings. I have one old car. I am seeking enlightenment."

"Ha! Ha!" they shouted to each other, "He's seeking enlightenment! What a joke!" Then the questions were repeated with only slight variation for hours on end. It was how they amused themselves to pass the time. Was this how Saraswati was answering my prayer for wisdom?

Arriving finally in Delhi at the end of the eight-hour ride, we disembarked from the bus and I addressed the lead heckler, a huge man wearing a bright orange kurta and black, western pants,

"You have made this the worst trip in my life, but I still know that God is in your heart."

The haughty mask of his face suddenly cracked, his upper lip quivered and he burst into tears. Kneeling on the ground, he touched his forehead to my dusty feet and sobbed, "Forgive me, swami, please forgive me."

Craving a cold shower, I checked in at the Palace Heights off Connaught Place, a cheap hotel that I had heard was friendly to westerners. Once in the room I discovered that there were no showers and that I would have to bathe Indian style, using a cup to pour the tepid water as I squatted over the drain in the floor. Afterward I went out on the terrace overlooking the city and sank into a comfortable chair. Finding a Guru was proving to be a lot harder than I imagined. I wished that I could connect with Maharajji, the Guru that had initiated Ram Dass into the path of the heart and had been my original inspiration to go to India; however, I didn't have his address. It had never occurred to me to get that before leaving home. I had assumed that Swami Chidananda was my Guru.

In a few minutes, seemingly in answer to my thoughts, a couple of Americans came out on the porch and we struck up a conversation. They said that Maharajji was not far away, in Vrindavan, the town where Krishna had spent his youth. He was in the Hanuman temple and gave darshan twice a day. This exciting news inspired me to leave the next morning in search of Neem Karoli Baba.

It was only a few hours by train to Mathura, and then ten kilometers further to Vrindavan. I expected that Krishna's birthplace would be as beautiful as in the ubiquitous hippie posters, with blissful cows and peacocks gazing at the *gopis,* who were eternally in love with their lord; however, it turned out to be just another crowded town where the gutter was an open sewer.[94]

Not seeing any gopis or feeling the presence of Krishna, I boarded a rickshaw for the remaining ride to Vrindavan. There I found the cheap hotel where Maharajji devotees stayed and got a room. But, where was the Hanuman temple and how would I get there? I sat on the bed, perplexed. Finally, hoping I would run into someone who knew how to reach the Hanuman temple, I opened the door and went outside into the corridor. Suddenly, the next door opened and a tall, balding man with a gray, scraggly beard emerged. Our gazes met and an endearing smile appeared on his face. I realized with a shock—it's Ram Dass!

"So, what brings you here?" he asked.

"Actually, you did," I confessed. "I heard your interview on public radio in New York."

"Ahhh," he sighed, knowingly.

I didn't discover until later that he often wistfully regretted that interview that had attracted so many to seek out his Guru. Now he no longer had Maharajji to himself, but had to share him with a throng of spiritually starved American hippies.

Since the moment seemed appropriate, I got up the courage to ask the question that had been on my mind since I had first heard that interview, "Do you think Maharajji could be my Guru too?"

"Well, it's certainly obvious that you've been called here. You'll just have to go and check him out, won't you? It might take a while but in time you'll know."

---

94 *Gopis:* cow-herd girls, particularly those devoted to Lord Krishna.

"You really think I've been called here?" I said in amazement, wondering if this was the confirmation I sought.

"Well, you're here aren't you? You couldn't be here if you weren't meant to be here, right?"

"Yes, I guess so," I agreed, forced to accept his irrefutable logic.

Ram Dass gave directions on how to reach the temple, then excused himself to return to his room,

"I'm going back into samadhi now. I was meditating and Maharajji told me to come outside. I guess it was to give you directions, so he must be expecting you."

I thanked him and returned to my own room to meditate, but I was so excited at the thought that Maharajji was expecting me and had sent Ram Dass to give directions that I paced the floor, hardly able to wait to see him.

As I was burning with impatience, I left the hotel. Since I had plenty of time before darshan, I decided to search for the forest where Krishna had played his flute and danced with the gopis, but after walking down a dirty, crowded street in the direction people pointed, I found only a few stunted trees in a sandy lot.

As I began walking back to the center of town I encountered another westerner, who introduced himself as Ravi Das. He was also there to see Maharajji. Walking together he said, "I think I just met my Guru."

"Really? You mean Maharajji is not your Guru?"

"Well, I thought he was when he gave me my name, but he has never said anything to me since then. Anyway, I was just walking along and this sadhu comes up to me, looks me in the eye, and says, 'My son, I am your Guru and I want you to take me to America.' I don't know what to think; he seemed so sure. He told me to come back tomorrow and he would initiate me."

As we walked back to the hotel I thought of Wristwatch Baba, and wondered how many sadhus there were who were total fakes, and how many of them ended up in America where a lot of gullible kids believed everything they said.

Finally, the time had arrived to visit the temple. Following the directions Ram Dass had given, I hoped to attend the evening darshan. He had said it would take about forty-five minutes on foot but after a while

I began to feel lost. The barren road just meandered through the fields toward the horizon. Since India was teeming with noisy life everywhere, to be suddenly alone created the feeling that something was wrong. It felt surreal, as if I was between worlds, the past gone, but the future had not yet arrived. I floated in a void of no reference points to anything with which I was familiar. A part of me wanted to turn around and go back, yet another part continued to draw me forward. I wondered where I was being led—and for what purpose?

Finally I came to a crossroads that seemed to resemble the one Ram Dass had described, and I turned onto a dirt road. Sure enough, there was the small temple surrounded by a wall. After I took a few paces a gate opened and Ram Dass emerged with half a dozen westerners in white.

"You're too late!" Ram Dass shouted, upset.

"Too late for darshan?"

"No, too late, period. Maharajji said *jao*—split—go away. When we get too attached to his form, he sends us away. Come on, we're all going back to town."

Rejected again by the Guru! I felt that my trip to India had been for nothing. Do I even have a Guru?

As we walked back toward Vrindavan I looked at the people walking beside me and wondered what had brought them all here. What force had touched their hearts in the streets of the cities, in the rural villages, in the communes of America, to inspire them to come all the way to India—to walk the dusty, sweltering roads and sit at the feet of an old man in a blanket?

I looked at the girl beside me who could have been the "girl next door," wearing a sari, with a scarf over her head that restrained her golden hair. After introducing myself I asked her name.

"Karuna. It was Susan Wolfe but Maharajji calls me Karuna."

"So, what brought you here?"

"One day right after high school graduation in Des Moines my boyfriend, John, and I were looking through *Be Here Now*, and the moment I saw Maharajji's picture I knew I had to see him. I couldn't explain it. My boyfriend had a job waiting for him, but he was very sweet and said, 'Do what you need to do and I'll wait for you.' We wanted to get married, but

I'm waiting for Maharajji's blessing. I have surrendered to the Guru, so I can only do what he says."

"How long have you been here?"

"A year."

"Doesn't your boyfriend miss you?"

"Oh, yes, he's so sweet, but I can't go home until Maharajji gives me his blessing."

Then I turned to the guy on my other side, Ted, who I discovered was the only other person in the group apart from me who had not asked Maharajji for a Hindu name.

"So, Ted, what brings you here?"

"Well, I work for a company in the San Francisco area that puts on rock concerts. We put up tents. But, since it was holiday time and there were no concerts, I had a month off and wanted to go somewhere, some place new I'd never been before. The idea 'India!' popped into my head and I thought, 'Why not?' I had just enough money saved, so I bought a ticket."

"But how did you decide to come see Maharajji? Were you on some spiritual path?"

"No, I don't do yoga, meditate, or do anything spiritual. I just wanted to go someplace new, someplace warm."

"So, what brought you to Maharajji?"

"Well, after I got off the plane in Delhi I took the shuttle into town, then got into a rickshaw and asked to go to the train station. There was a train just leaving so I got on board. I had no idea where it was going. I just wanted to get out of the city and see some of India. After a while I became bored with the train and got off. I didn't know where I was, but at the station there was a guy in a bicycle rickshaw beckoning. He told me to get in, so I did. He rode way out into the country, then stopped and told me to get out. That was right here. Just as I was wondering where I was and what to do, that door in the wall opened and Ram Dass, whom I recognized from a magazine, came out and said, 'Come in or you'll be late for darshan.' So, here I am."

As we walked we began discussing what to do next. One of the devotees said, "Hey, I've got an idea, let's go to Varanasi. It's supposed to be the holiest city in India. Hindus go there when close to death, because they believe that if you die in Varanasi your soul goes straight to *Vaikuntha* (Heaven)."

"Yeah, and a lot of Gurus have their ashrams there too," someone agreed. "We could share a houseboat on the Ganges for almost nothing."

Before I realized what had happened I found myself included in the Maharajji satsang, and on my way to Varanasi.[95]

---

95   *Satsang:* literally, the company of truth. A group that follows a common Guru or spiritual teaching.

CHAPTER 25

Houseboat on the Ganges

Travel is a microcosm of life. You cannot be attached to how the journey unfolds or if you will even reach the destination you had in mind. Traveling in India is a constant lesson in surrender, which lead me to the realization that the destination and the path are one.[96]

I stood in line at the train station for an hour trying to buy a ticket. When I finally reached the front, the clerk said I was in the wrong line. I discovered there was one line to find out what trains were available, another line to see if that train had any vacancies and to make a reservation and a third line to actually buy the ticket. Of course, by then a couple of hours may have elapsed and your chosen train might be full, and you would have to go back to the first line. Having finally reached the head of the reservation line, the clerk wobbled his head back and forth in a confusing gesture that might mean yes or no, and that I eventually learned meant, "I acknowledge your presence but am not going to say anything for which I might be held accountable."

After checking my chosen train he said, "So, sorry, Sir, all booked. You must choose another date."

Three hours later, after being jostled around in the sweltering heat and still not having a ticket, I was so desperate I escaped outside. All I wanted was to drink the juice of a green coconut, go back to the hotel, and collapse. Walking down the steps a young man approached and, apparently reading the despair on my face, said, "Where do you want to go please, Sir? Just give me your money and I will get the ticket for you."

"What? Give you my money?"

I was incredulous that a stranger would ask for money and expect me to trust that he would return with a ticket.

"On which date do you wish to go, Sir?" he continued.

I told him the date and he plucked the money from my hand plus an extra ten rupees for his service.

---

96   For more on this, read *The Path is the Goal: A Basic Handbook of Buddhist Meditation*, Chögyam Trungpa (Shambhala, 2011).

"You just wait here, Sir," he said, reassuringly.

Then he was gone up the steps into the station—and I was sure out the back door.

The thieves here are a lot more polite and clever than New York, I thought, but fifteen minutes later the man returned with the ticket in hand.

"My cousin is a clerk with the Railway," he explained, beaming from ear to ear. "Next time, Sir, come to me first."

It hadn't occurred to me that Indian railways overbook like US airlines, selling more tickets than they have seats. I soon found myself on a third-class train with no air-conditioning and standing in the aisle, hanging onto a railing. Hours later someone exited and I was able to sit down, squashed between others on a hardwood bench. Around midnight I was exhausted. Not finding anywhere to lie down, no one paid any heed as I climbed into the overhead luggage rack and soon fell asleep.

In the wee hours of morning I woke with sore ribs where I had slept against a metal bracket. Looking around for a better place to recline, I spied a place on the floor in the corridor outside the latrine. Lying there on the floor, I pulled my thin cotton shawl over my ears to deaden the sound. I woke when people stepped over me to use the toilet and the lavatory door slammed inches from my face. Passing in and out of sleep, I had the thought, *Surely I have reached the lowest depths of human existence.*

Feeling more dead than alive, I arrived the next morning in Varanasi. I left the station and walked down to the Ganges, hoping that the sight of the sacred river would help revive me. I heard the chanting of the Maha Mantra (Hare Krishna), which had been continuously chanted on this spot for the past several thousand years—its words eventually reaching even my old neighborhood on the Lower East Side.[97]

---

97 The repetition of a mantra, even the word God, creates a vibration which changes a location forever. The greater the consciousness, the more powerful the vibration. Thus mantras and I AM Affirmations, when said with full consciousness of the Source, can be focused to affect our reality.

Varanasi, view of the cremation ghats from the Ganges

Clouds of incense billowed skyward, commingling with the smoke of the bodies burning on the *ghats*.[98] While absorbing the transcendent energy of the chanting, I watched people throw garlands into the river, bidding their recently cremated loved ones goodbye.

Some of the satsang had arrived earlier and I ran into a group trying to strike a bargain to rent a houseboat. Their haggling was interrupted by a westerner, who introduced himself as Fantuzzi. He carried a conga drum under one arm and a one-stringed instrument called an *ektar* under the other, and seemed a blend of sadhu and rock star.

"Hey, guys, I've already got a houseboat, so why don't you all stay with me?"

Soon a dozen of us were being rowed by a boatman out to his houseboat, which was anchored offshore from the burning ghats. From the boat we could watch the funeral pyres send their smoke skyward and hear the chanting of mantras from dawn to dusk. Mixed with our *bhajans*

---

98   *Ghats:* steps leading down to a body of water, frequently used for religious rituals. In Varanasi they are used as a place to cremate bodies.

(devotional songs), life onboard was like a *mela*.[99] There were times when almost everyone went ashore, leaving things relatively quiet except for the perpetual chanting of the mantra that drifted out from the shore. At these times I would drop into a meditative state where the sense of the independent self ceased.

Having heard the reputation of the Ganges as the physical form of the Goddess Ganga, who descended to Earth to cleanse humans of their sins, I decided to immerse myself in her sacred waters. As I watched the bloated body of a water buffalo float downstream I prayed that the legends of the river's ability to purify were true. A partially incinerated skull floated past. Then I chanted *Om*, and dove into the murky water.

Surprisingly, the water did not feel dirty. Rather it seemed effervescent as Champagne, and produced an exhilarating effect. I emerged feeling rejuvenated, hoping that the Goddess had dissolved any negative karma.

---

99   *Mela:* a fair; however, the Kumbh Mela is a gathering at which millions of Hindus come together to enact religious rituals. It is held in remembrance of a meeting at which the Gods and demons fought over *Amrit,* the nectar of immortality, which was contained in an urn called a Kumbh. The ritual dates back thousands of years and is described in the *Bhagavata Purana,* the *Mahabharata,* the *Ramayana,* and other texts.

CHAPTER 26

The Bliss-Permeated Mother

On Christmas eve Fantuzzi announced that Anandamayi Ma, the woman saint Yogananda had written about, was at her ashram on the hill overlooking the Ganges.[100] Since it seemed an auspicious occasion we decided to visit her, hoping that since we were westerners she might grant us an audience on this special night that celebrated the Christ.

She was born in East Bengal, now Bangladesh, on April 30, 1896. Her parents were very poor, spending most of their time singing devotional songs. She spent the early part of her life in spontaneous absorption of the Divine, often staring into space for hours at a time. Teachers interpreted her constant happiness and disregard for what was happening around her as stupidity, and neighbors thought she was insane. At age 13 her family arranged a marriage, as was the custom. However, whenever her husband touched her she would become unconscious, and when he tried to consummate their marriage he received an electric-like shock. He apologized profusely and became her devotee. She renamed him Bolonath and they continued to have a celibate marriage.

She offended some, including her father, as she refused to bow or touch the feet of elders as was the custom, saying, "Why bow when you yourself are everything?" She gave no formal teachings and refused to be called a Guru. She had no agenda except to travel wherever invited by her devotees. She taught that to serve yourself, serve others; and by serving others you serve yourself. She told Paramahansa Yogananda, "My consciousness has never been associated with this temporal body."

We were excited to meet her and hired a boatman to row us ashore.

---

100 Mahatma Gandhi was her devotee, and when he went through hardship she consoled him. Kamala Nehru, wife of the Indian Prime Minister, was also her devotee. At Anandamayi Ma's death in Dehradun, August 27, 1982, over 25 ashrams had been dedicated to her. Many regarded her as an embodiment of the Divine Mother, much the same as the current Mata Amritanandamayi, called The Hugging Saint.

Anandamayi Ma, the Bliss-Permeated Mother

Since it was the custom to make an offering to a Guru, we bought a box of sweets to present. Then we climbed the hill to her ashram and found ourselves seated before a lady in a white sari emanating a tranquil beauty. With hardly any wait we were told to go forward and kneel before her. She looked bored and smiled wanly as we presented the sweets. She held her hand over the box and then returned it, nodding that we were dismissed. As we went back to our place in the crowd I felt disappointed that she had not kept them. Even though Yogananda credited her with

132

many astounding feats, including returning the dead to life, she seemed barely present, and I felt she could hardly wait until everyone left so she could again be alone. Inwardly I made the wish that I could meet her alone some day, away from the ashram filled with followers—alone on a country road. Of course, I knew that the chance of that happening was nil, as she rarely left the ashram, and then only with a dozen attendants. She seemed to belong to her devotees, who jealously guarded her as their private property. Even if I were to meet her outside the ashram, we would not be able to talk, for she was also *muni*, having many years ago taken a vow of silence.

We left feeling disappointed that our contact had been so brief. At least we felt fortunate to have met a saint Yogananda had mentioned in *Autobiography of a Yogi*, the last of those he had written about who were still alive. To see a great saint was considered a blessing with possibly far reaching effects, some of which might not be noticeable for years.

Stupa at Sarnath, where Buddha gave his first teaching

CHAPTER 27

Finding the Buddha

B uddhism intruded itself into my consciousness with the thud of a book landing before my face on the deck of the houseboat. I had been lying face down and now looked up to see the yellow book with red title, *Meditation in Action,* by Chögyam Trungpa Rinpoche, lying inches from my nose. A light went off in my head as I stared at the title and received its message—meditate in every act—which had arrived at precisely the right moment. The West emphasized action, the East meditation; but it was the union of opposites that was needed.

I was shocked at how unconventional this Lama was, that he ate meat, drank alcohol, and even had sex with female students. Then I thought, "Who am I to judge the actions of an enlightened being—or anyone, for that matter?[101]

After months wandering in India I was ready for the simplicity taught by the Buddha. Keeping track of the thousands of Hindu Gods had become tiresome. Their pictures were in every shop and rickshaw and their statues in every public place. Each deity had multiple forms, and I had despaired of ever learning all their names and relationships.[102] They appeared to be one big incestuous family that argued and even fought wars amongst themselves, each having to be worshiped in a different way. Was mastering this phantasmagoria of deities really necessary for

---

101 A person's level of enlightenment cannot be determined by one of a lower level of realization. Hence, it is meaningless to claim that someone's Guru is enlightened, or that one Guru is more enlightened than another.

102 God manifests in personal form as Vishnu, who has 1000 names. He descends to Earth 10 times as an Avatar, among them Rama and Krishna. Vishnu's consort is Lakshmi, also known as Maya. Krishna alone is called by at least 108 names, among them Gopala, Govinda, Mukunda, and Jaganatha, pertaining to different times, functions, and conditions. The Gods are also frequently not monogamous, some having a profuse number of children.

enlightenment? Of course, a *pandit* (pundit) might say they were symbolic aspects of the Divine within, that God is formless but can also appear in the form the devotee wishes. All forms are simply manifestations of the great, unchanging reality of God Consciousness, which is participating in the play of the Divine *Lila*.[103] However, most Indians seemed to treat the Gods as totally real and requiring a great deal of daily attention.

After a week on the houseboat and tiring of the constant chanting, to clear our heads some of us decided to visit Sarnath, where Buddha gave his first teaching. There I found myself among monks with saffron robes who emanated a pristine clarity of mind. As they were not worshipping anyone outside themselves, they had a simple openness and presence in the now that was refreshing.

I had been among *bhaktas* for so many months (devotees who cultivate love of external forms of Divinity) that I had almost forgotten that the goal was not attachment to form—no matter how beautiful that might be—but liberation.[104] The clarity of these monks was so noticeable that we decided to pursue Buddhism and visit Bodh Gaya, the place where Siddhartha Gautama supposedly achieved enlightenment to become the Buddha.

We discovered that the famed meditation Master S. N. Goenka was about to offer a Vipassana retreat, and soon we were on the train to learn this ancient method that the Buddha had used to awaken. Arriving late at night, we were shocked to find that this hill town was much colder than we expected, and our thin clothes offered little warmth. By the time the train arrived at the station in Gaya, it was so late that there were no taxis or rickshaws. We finally found an old man with a bullock cart whom we finally persuaded to take us the remaining five miles to the center of the Buddhist world. Trying to generate some warmth, we huddled together as we bounced over the bone-jarring road. I kept reminding myself that everything is impermanent and that all suffering is due to identification with the illusory self.[105]

---

103 *Lila* (or *Leela*): the Divine play. Sometimes called *Rasa Lila*, the dance of the Gods. *Pandit*: pundit, Brahmin scholar learned in Sanskrit and the Vedas.
104 *Bhakti Yoga:* spiritual path of devotion.
105 Buddha elucidated the Three Marks of Conditional Existence.

Around four in the morning we finally arrived at the massive wooden gate of the ashram, only to find it locked. We knocked, but no one stirred within the high walls of the compound. I thought of scaling a wall and opening the gate so we could find a warm place to rest inside, but the walls were studded with broken glass. Resigned to our fate, we huddled against the gate and took turns reading the *Dhammapada* by flashlight, waiting for signs of life from within.[106]

When the gate finally opened around six, I learned that breakfast would not be served for a couple of hours. I decided to get warm by walking into town and visiting the famous Bodhi tree under which the Buddha had sat, and on the way having a cup of hot chai. Perhaps I too would have the same sudden realization under the tree, and then not need to take the course.[107]

It was a beautiful tree with heart-shaped leaves—and I prayed to Buddha for permission to sit under it and meditate in the very spot where he had attained realization. As I didn't hear the inner voice of disapproval and since no one was around, I climbed over the low railings of the fence and sat with my back against the tree's massive trunk. I prayed to experience the Buddha, to feel his presence and light, which I had read was dazzling. I yearned to experience the light of such a being, which I felt would be life-changing. However, I could not still my mind, for I kept thinking, "I'm sitting where Buddha sat!" The very act of dwelling on an external Buddha kept me from experiencing my own Buddha nature. Perhaps that is why Judaism and Taoism do not focus on any particular form, but try to realize Divinity everywhere.

Anicca: Everything is impermanent and in constant flux; *Dukkha:* The desire for what is impermanent leads to suffering; *Anatta:* Suffering is maintained by identification with the non-existent ego. Understanding these truths leads to *prajna:* wisdom, which is the antidote to suffering, and to *Nirvana:* ultimate liberation from the samsaric cycle of birth and death.

106 The *Dhammapada:* a compilation of the early teachings of the Buddha in verse.

107 I discovered later that this tree was an offshoot of the tree under which Buddha had meditated.

The Bodhi Tree, where the Buddha achieved enlightenment

I was also feeling nervous about having climbed the fence and soon opened my eyes to see myself surrounded by a dozen people taking photos. Fearful of being arrested by temple guards, I quickly climbed back over the fence and headed back to the ashram for breakfast. I arrived just as the gates were being closed for the beginning of the retreat. They would be kept closed throughout the ten days to minimize distractions. No one would be allowed in or out.

Relieved to find a huge cauldron of oatmeal with jars of yoghurt, raisins, and cashews awaiting our return, the question then arose, "Is the desire for food an obstacle to liberation?"

Buddha had said that all attachments were obstacles to be surrendered, but as I enjoyed the sweet taste and warm, comforting feel of the oatmeal in my mouth, I could not feel that it was wrong. I gave myself permission to enjoy breakfast without suffering, reminding myself that the oatmeal as well as the body consuming it were impermanent.

Dwelling on impermanence, I realized the call of nature to the restroom, a call I decided to heed prior to the start of instruction. Asking for directions, I was sent into the administration building where I walked down the central hall with rooms on either side—at the end of which I was told I would find the lavatory. As I walked down the dimly lit corridor, I glanced into what appeared to be empty classrooms. A light emanated from one of the rooms, and as I passed I glanced through the door and saw that the source of the light was a monk in a saffron robe. The room was illumined by the golden light that emanated from his head. Two monks stood before him with hands clasped, heads bent in rapt attention to his words. I paused in shock, wanting to enter the room and bow before this being. If anyone was a Guru, this was he. However, the restroom was calling, so I decided to heed nature first. I would only be gone a minute and would then return to bow before the luminous monk and ask his blessing.

When I returned, however, the room was dark and empty. Where had he gone? As the gates were locked, I knew he had to be somewhere in the ashram. I looked everywhere, but could not find him. Perhaps he had come to participate in the teachings? Eagerly I looked in the large room where the instruction was about to begin. It was packed with would-be meditators, but he was not among them. The only non-westerner was the Burmese instructor, S. N. Goenka, who had just begun talking about how to observe the in-breath and out-breath, the instruction for which I had come all this way, yet all I could think about was finding the being I had seen in the now-empty room.

Despite the urge to continue the search, I forced myself to sit and learn this method, which is what the Buddha himself had finally used to cut through maya. As I observed the sensation of the breath flowing in and out I began to feel more present in my body in the here and now, and the desire to leave slipped away. In addition to being aware of the flies buzzing in the room, I was nonetheless able to also watch other thoughts as they came and went. This was very different from the meditation I had practiced since childhood, where the sense of self disappeared. Now I was observing thoughts and emotions emerging and dissolving on the screen of the self, yet a self I was beyond. I began to experience the emptiness of all phenomena and understand the meaning of the mantra, *Gate, Gate, Paragate, Parasamgate, Bodhi Svaha*[108]

---

108 *Prajnaparamita* mantra: One of the best known Buddhist mantras

Gone, gone, gone beyond, gone completely beyond, Awake! So be it!

When the session ended, I left the room and continued the search for the luminous being, but I couldn't find him or the other monks. Only westerners had enrolled in the course, so I went to the office and asked, "Where did the monks go?"

"What monks?" the director asked, with a blank look on his face. "There are no monks here. This is a lay retreat."

"I saw three monks in saffron robes down that hall before the instruction began," I insisted, but he shook his head.

"Maybe they went into town?" I persisted.

"The gates have been closed since breakfast," he said with annoyance, "so no one could have left the ashram."

I left the office disappointed and asked others if they had seen the monks and knew where they were staying, but no knew had seen them. The luminous being and his disciples had simply disappeared.

---

from the Heart Sutra (traceable to 7th century CE), the core Buddhist teaching given by the Bodhisattva Avalokitesvara to Sariputra. It states that the essence of enlightenment is in the realization of the inherent emptiness of the five *skandas* (aggregates): body, thought, feeling, impulse, and consciousness.

CHAPTER 28

The Blissful Mother Grants My Wish

New Year's Day, 1972, dawned in Varanasi without any new miracles or news of any noteworthy Gurus in town. Maharajji had not reappeared. No one even knew where he had gone after telling us *jao* (go away). We were tired of the floating ashram and hearing "Hare Krishna, Hare Rama" chanted day and night, so one day we decided to find a place that might prove more peaceful. Some wanted to go north to Nainital, where they knew Maharajji would eventually re-emerge, but many of us who had recently read *The Aquarian Gospel of Jesus the Christ*, decided to go to Jagannath Puri. It was here, according to the author Levi Dowling's vision of the *akashic record*, that Jesus had spent two years studying with the pandits in the temple.[109]

For six thousand years there had been a temple on that site, which was regarded as one of the four most sacred places in India. These places were considered to be the homes of the Gods.[110] Many great saints had visited Jagannath Puri, among them Sri Chaitanya, who was worshipped by his devotees as a reincarnation of Lord Krishna. It was he who chiefly promoted the Maha Mantra (Hare Krishna, Hare Rama) and prophesied that it would eventually spread throughout the world, a prophecy fulfilled five hundred years later with the global popularity of George Harrison's song, *My Sweet Lord*.

---

109 *Akasha:* space, aether. The akashic record is the imprint that all experience leaves on the subtle environment of space. A location can be physically or etherically revisited and the record of what transpired there clearly seen. Our every thought, emotion, word, and action is recorded in the akasha as surely as though filmed by a video camera.

110 Adi Shankaracharya, the great eighth century philosopher and founder of the school of Advaita, taught the unity of the *Atman* (soul) with *Brahman* (the absolute). He said that it was the duty of all Hindus to make a pilgrimage to these four sites. It is called the *Char Dham Yatra:* (*Char:* four; *Dham:* abode; *Yatra:* journey).

Jagannath Temple in Puri, Orissa

According to Dowling, Jesus taught the local fishermen, who were of the untouchable caste, how to connect directly to the inner God Presence, thus incurring the wrath of the temple priests who depended on their devotion for support. For this transgression of their authority he barely escaped with his life. Even to this day non-Hindus are forbidden to enter the Jagannath temple on threat of death.[111]

---

111 *The Aquarian Gospel of Jesus the Christ* (Levi H. Dowling, 1920) has been criticized as historically inaccurate, for the present Jagannath Temple was built in the 11th century CE; however, it is built on the site of previous temples, the records of which go back to Vedic times thousand of years BCE. The problem western historians encounter is that they consider only written records historically acceptable, while

After a sweltering, third class train ride lasting two days and nights, we arrived at the coastal town of Puri. As I stepped from the train I rejoiced in the refreshing sea breeze blowing off the Bay of Bengal. The towering temple spire in the distance drew me like a magnet, and the closer I approached the more I could feel its spiritual energy. I could easily believe that this was the place, rather than Bodh Gaya, where Sakyamuni Buddha achieved enlightenment.[112] Ram Tirtha, an American whom Maharajji implied was the reincarnation of a great Indian yogi by that name, knew of a place to rent. Soon we were living in a white bungalow on the beach that we came to think of as our ashram. From its flat roof where we climbed to do yoga and inhale the ocean breeze we could see the temple on the horizon and feel the transmission of its spiritual energy.

Here we practiced yoga, meditation, and read the Indian classics, the *Bhagavad Gita, Yoga Sutras of Patanjali, Srimad Bhagavatam*, and the *Upanishads*, and discussed their meaning. It was easy to see why Jesus had come to India, for it was obviously the ancient center of spirituality. India will again be that center of ancient wisdom once she has grounded her spirituality in the earthly know-how of the West.

Ram Dass and a few other Maharajji devotees were living in a house up the beach and would sometimes drop by for dinner. We ate like yogis, with our only meal in the late afternoon, usually a salad of fresh mango,

---

many records were passed down in the oral tradition, which they never examine. The story of a western saint Issa (which means Divine Being)— Jesus—and his travels in India and Tibet, is well known throughout the Far East. *The Unknown Life of Jesus the Christ* (Nikolas Notovitch, 1890) also describes these travels. Max Muller later tried to disprove this book because later monks denied its existence. However, they may have been under pressure to discourage further inquiry along these lines, or simply wanted to discourage further tourism in order to preserve their privacy and seclusion.

112 There is almost as much controversy about the life of the historical Buddha as the life of Jesus. There is a debate about which teachings are actually Buddha's, for if we accept all 84,000 as authentic he would have had to have taught eighteen hours a day, seven days a week, for the entire forty years that he was active as a teacher.

cherimoya, coconut, custard apple, banana, and cashews, drizzled with coconut milk, honey, and lime juice. Later we would stroll on the beach, ankle deep in the warm water, breathing the cooling sea breeze and watching the sunset. After dark, the waves threw green, phosphorescent pearls at our feet, a fascinating phenomenon of the tropics that I had never seen.

One day after I had gone up the beach to invite Ram Dass for dinner, we walked back along the Bay of Bengal. As the warm waves washed over our feet and we watched the gold and purple fingers of the sunset, I expressed my gratitude to him for having inspired my trip to India. It was something I had wanted to express for a long time. He had not only inspired me, but an entire generation. I felt a camaraderie at that moment that men feel only rarely, as perhaps when facing death in war or the other kind of death—the dissolution of the ego. Here we were, two affluent Americans, having renounced all the material advantages of the West, walking nearly naked on a beach in a far off land in quest of something intangible. Was what we sought even real and, if so, would we find it? He had given up his family's wealth and a prestigious professorship at Harvard, and I had given up a possible career as an aerospace engineer and all the benefits of growing up an affluent American with connections to the highest levels of business and government. In the silence there was the bond of something transcendent.

Finally Ram Dass said, "You know, there are many times when I regret ever opening my mouth about Maharajji. My life was so much simpler before that. Now I have to deal with all these people wanting to hang out. A lot of the time I don't even really like them that much. I don't understand; why is it that they want to be around me?"

"They feel your love," I said, touched by his revelation.

"But I don't love them. In fact, I wish they would go away and leave me alone."

"Well, people feel love, the love that's in your heart."

"That's the love I feel for Maharajji."

"It's still love, no matter what you call it."

As we continued in silence I realized that whether love is for a Guru, person, animal, or even a flower, when we feel that love it radiates to the whole world. Soon we arrived at the bungalow, where everyone was waiting to begin dinner.

Although I had not thought much about Jesus since being forced to attend Sunday school, now I found myself thinking about him often. It was not just because the *Aquarian Gospel* said he had been here; I could feel his presence. One day as I walked the dirt road to the Jagannath temple, my inner sight was opened. Like Levi Dowling, I too saw the akashic record and saw the Master walking beside me—and saw that I had known him in those times when we had walked together on this very road. It was an eerie feeling, as when you first see yourself in a video and can hardly believe it's you. I saw that Jesus had brought our group of Essenes from the West to study with the Vedic pandits, but because he had shared their teachings we had needed to flee.

Walking up the dirt road into town to buy rice, I entered a thatched roof hut filled with burlap sacks of grain. As the shop was crowded, I stood in line, silently chanting a mantra to keep from being impatient. My eyes were focused on the back of the woman in front of me, her white sari indicating that she was either a widow or a renunciate—not surprising, as Puri attracted spiritual seekers from all over the world. Little did I dream that this woman was no ordinary seeker. After purchasing her rice and dhal and dropping the packages in her sack, she turned around and I saw that it was none other than Anandamayi Ma. Out of the five hundred million people in India, here was the great saint before whom I had prostrated only weeks before, praying that I would meet her alone some day. Now here she was before me. I was in shock.

Quickly I ran next door to a sweet shop and purchased a bag of delicious Mysore *pak burfi* (Indian milk sweet) and rushed back just as she was leaving. I planted myself in front of her and speechlessly held out the sweets. I wondered if she would only bless and return them as she had before, but she took the package, opened it, and smiled with obvious pleasure before tucking them gingerly into her bag. Holding my hands together in pranam, I bowed and then stood aside for her to pass. She smiled again, bowed, and started up the road.

Was I going to let this opportunity pass? Here was chance to make a personal connection with the woman about whom Yogananda had said, "I had found many men of God realization in India, but never before had I met such an exalted woman saint." Of all the realized beings he had written about she was the last still alive. This was the chance of a lifetime.

I wanted to be polite, however, and not offend her or bring her out of her exalted consciousness.

I thrust the money for the rice into the shopkeeper's hand and headed out of the shop and back up the road toward home. By coincidence Anandamayi Ma and I were walking in the same direction and my long legs soon brought us together again. Knowing it would be considered impolite for me to address a woman on the street, let alone a world-renowned saint, I hesitated to speak. However, since we were both walking the same way and I noticed her basket was heavily laden, I finally got up the courage and offered to carry it for her. She smiled but politely refused the offer.

I was surprised then to hear this saint who had reportedly not spoken to anyone in many years begin speaking. She addressed me directly in her native Bengali and, miraculously, I seemed to understand every word. As we walked barefoot up the muddy road we talked like old friends. Her face was radiant, and as we walked I felt she much preferred this simple life to that of the ashram, where she was the constant focus of her devotees.

"What brings you to India?" she asked.

"I heard Ram Dass on the radio, so I came here to find my Guru," I replied excitedly.

"Ram Dass?" she asked, with noticeable interest.

"The American Ram Dass," I clarified, as there was a popular Indian saint, Papa Ram Das.

"Ah, I see," she said, seeming to be appreciative of my quest. "And have you had success?"

I shook my head, realizing that I was conversing with one who was, herself, a revered Guru, and about whom Yogananda had said, "She was oblivious to her outward garb as a woman—she knew herself as the changeless soul…."

"Is she my Guru?" I wondered, "She has obviously answered my prayer. If she is my Guru, will she tell me, or should I ask?" I wondered, as before, about the correct etiquette to inquire if someone is your Guru. Waiting for her to announce that I was indeed her *chela* (disciple), she smiled sweetly and, without saying anything, kept walking.

After a few minutes we came to a crossroad and she nodded her intention to turn left. I did not discover until later, when others of the sangha I told about this meeting tried to find her, that she had an ashram down that road. As we parted I regretfully said goodbye.

Continuing along the road I marveled at how she had gone shopping alone instead of allowing her devotees to get what she wanted. It seemed that perhaps she found being a Guru wearying, and enjoyed occasionally just being a normal woman. A current manifestation of the Divine Mother known as Mata Amritanandamayi (the Hugging Saint) also sweeps the floor when she likes and does not hesitate to sit in the kitchen peeling potatoes.[113]

When I returned to the bungalow still in shock over the meeting everyone asked, "What happened to you?"

"What do you mean?"

"Why, you're glowing!"

I told of the encounter with Anandamayi Ma and how she had answered the prayer I had made in Varanasi on Christmas Eve. These people had also been there that evening when she dismissed our group with a nod. I never dreamed she would answer that prayer. This encounter was the first of several meetings with the bliss-permeated mother that would change my life forever.

The energy of the Jagannath Temple was like a magnet. Every morning I followed its pull as I went down the same road Jesus had walked two thousand years previously. The road was lined with beggars and lepers seated on straw mats and they held out their arms, imploring me for help as I passed. I always wanted to give them something to assuage their suffering, but knew that I couldn't feed them all. I thought of what Jesus had said, "The poor you will always have with you," so walked on my way saying prayers for them. The closer I would come to the temple the more raised I would feel by its tremendous spiritual energy.

One morning at sunrise, while meditating on the roof, I suddenly realized the immanence of God in everything, and that the same light of the sun was not only in me, but also in everyone. Filled with compassion,

---

113 Ammachi has established schools, medical facilities, orphanages, and offered disaster relief for thousands. For more on her life and mission, see: www.amritapuri.org

I ran out and bought as much rice as I could carry, a few kilos in each arm, and walked toward the temple, giving rice to the beggars. In each person's eye I saw myself, that I was the one inhabiting that body, who had taken on that form to have a multitude of experiences.

When I ran out of rice I continued on my way, but word spread ahead that an American giving away rice was headed toward town, and by the time I arrived at the temple a mob of beggars and street urchins was waiting. Before I knew it they had surrounded me and started clawing me, ripping my clothes to obtain the rice they assumed I still carried.

Consciousness of oneness suddenly evaporated as the adrenaline of danger surged through every cell. I threw the empty rice sacks up in the air and, as they fought over them, dodged away. Finding the sacks empty, they ran after me in pursuit.

Like a shot, I tore down the street along the side of the temple, with the mob getting larger at every turn. My long legs kept me ahead of them, and as I rounded the far side of the temple I saw a man standing on the platform of a vegetable shop at the end of the street, gesticulating wildly and offering protection.

With the mob closing in, I ran full speed. He held out a hand, while with the other hand he brandished a club over the heads of the mob. He pulled me onto the platform several feet above the street and when they saw his whirling club they soon dispersed. After a while he flagged down a bicycle rickshaw so I could leave without attracting attention, but I left feeling devastated.

Where had I gone wrong? I had been in God consciousness, seeing everyone as part of myself, then a few minutes later was running for my life. Perhaps these people were where they needed to be to learn the lessons they had chosen and it was not up to me to change that? Perhaps Jesus had come to the same conclusion when he had said, "The poor you will always have with you."

Riding back from the temple, still dazed, I was not prepared for the electric shock of spiritual energy I suddenly felt. I turned to see its origin and there, once again, was Anandamayi Ma, standing at the side of the road with her hands clasped in pranam. She was in a state of God consciousness so profound that it pierced the veil of maya in which I dwelled. Suddenly, I was the God presence she saw. Rising to my feet, I bowed, nearly falling from the rickshaw that was lurching up the dirt road. As I passed, she remained with head lowered, her hands clasped in adoration. My heart beat wildly, and I was forced to sit to keep from falling out of the rickshaw. Looking back, I saw the bliss-permeated mother still standing motionless by the roadside. The rickshaw lurched ahead and I lost sight of her in the crowd, but her blessing still reverberated within.

On returning to the bungalow, I quietly climbed onto the flat roof without being noticed, and turned my attention inward. I longed to see within the Divinity she had seen—and to which she had bowed. I felt that she had placed a rosebud within my heart whose petals were unfolding, filling me with bliss. The more I put my attention on that rose, the more powerful the joy became. I realized then that the greatest gift you can give another is to see their perfection—for what you see, you bring into being.

Anandamayi Ma

Neem Karoli Baba

CHAPTER 29

At the Feet of the Guru at Last

I was to see Anandamayi Ma once more, this time at the Tota Gopinatha temple. I was sitting with a group from the satsang, in the courtyard before the statue of Lord Chaitanya, reportedly one of Krishna's later incarnations. Accompanied by several of her devotees, she came in and sat in the dirt on the women's side. After she sat she singled me out of the crowd, but this time she only nodded. The friends I was with, some of whom may have been skeptical that she was in Puri after having been told at her ashram that she was not there, now whispered, "Look, Anandamayi Ma!"

However, this time there was to be no personal contact, for after the puja her devotees whisked her away. I realized with sadness that I would never see her again. Our meeting had been the answer to my prayer, and the blessing she had given needed no repeating. If I were to visit her at her ashram in Varanasi I would once again be just another face in the crowd. Would I ever find a Guru who was always accessible the way Ram Dass had? I envied him and Krishna Das and my other friends who had a personal relationship with Maharajji. I didn't realize it at the time, but even Ram Dass was no longer receiving as much personal attention as he had at the beginning, and he was being forced to rely more on the Inner Guru.

Soon it was rumored that Maharajji had emerged from seclusion and was back in Kainchi at the Hanuman temple.[114] Everyone was headed back to see him as soon as possible, and I joined the pilgrimage—hoping that in Maharajji I would at last find the personal Guru I was seeking.

Once in the foothills of the Himalayas we stayed at the Evelyn Hotel in Nainital, a half hour bus ride from the Hanuman temple. It was owned by a loving devotee, K. K. Sah, who treated us like family.

---

114 We discovered later that Neem Karoli Baba was in Puri the same time we were; only he was living in the Jagannath temple. He and Anandamayi Ma were old friends.

Maharajji was well known for taking good care of his devotees, and especially seeing to it they were well fed. He said that Westerners were so deprived of love as children that feeding us was equivalent to giving us the love we had missed.

When I first saw Maharajji I was not impressed. He lounged on a cot, nearly naked, with beautiful American girls caressing his feet. As he seemed oblivious of my presence, I sat in back against the wall to observe. Occasionally he joked with Ram Dass or other devotees who had front row seats. However, Ram Dass blushed occasionally, as he was sometimes the butt of Maharajji's jokes. Being close to the Guru was not always blissful. It was like being close to the fire—sometimes you got burned. I felt as though I had been invited to the meeting of an exclusive club from which I was now excluded. I had found a Guru who welcomed personal relationships with westerners, all except me. I decided not to force the issue. I would wait and see what unfolded.[115]

Though I had been so moved on hearing Ram Dass' story of his first meeting with this Guru, I began to wonder what Maharajji's power was over him. Here was a brilliant Harvard professor, now sitting adoringly at the feet of a fat old man in a blanket. Had Maharajji hypnotized him or had Ram Dass simply taken too many drugs and finally lost his mind? Maharajji didn't say much, mostly making small talk; what he did say was usually not profound, much like what I heard in church on Sunday:

Tell the truth—Don't judge—Love people and feed them.[116]

Nor did Maharajji give *shaktipat*, the transmission of consciousness that Ramamurti Mishra had bestowed on me and for which Baba Muktananda was well known.[117] What had won Ram Dass' over—that Maharajji had read his

---

115 Many had photos taken of themselves with Maharajji, which at the time I thought was vain, so when photos were being taken I usually disappeared. Hence, in writing this book I could only find one for inclusion.

116 Sathya Sai Baba was known for a similar teaching: *Love all, Serve all.* Isaac Tigrett, a Baba devotee and creator of the Hard Rock Cafes, had this written on the walls of the cafes.

117 Baba Muktananda (May 16, 1908 – October 2, 1982), born into a wealthy family in Mangalore, India. He became a disciple of Bhagavan Nityananda, who awakened him spiritually with a transmission of light from his eyes. He was a Guru of Americans Hilda Charlton

mind? Psychics in New York had read my mind, but I had not surrendered or given my power to them. Later I heard him say that what wrought the change was the fact that "He knew everything about me, everything bad I had ever done, and still he loved me; I felt forgiven."

Whatever Maharajji had done, it had opened Ram Dass' heart, and I longed for that same love; yet Maharajji continued to ignore me and I watched with curiosity and impatience.

Days went by and nothing seemed to happen.[118] Wasn't the Guru supposed to occasionally talk to you? We would show up mid-morning for darshan and then Krishna Das and Jai Uttal would lead heart-opening bhajans. Finally, that love began to awaken devotion—a blissful form of bonding with Divinity I had never experienced.[119]

Maharajji would make us stand and chant for hours, reminiscent of the Hare Krishna followers I'd seen on the street in New York. One time we were chanting *Sri Ram, Jai Ram, Jai Jai, Ram Om,* and just as I was about to leave in despair, I was filled with ecstasy. Those bhajans were always uplifting but that ecstasy never came again. More often I would stand obediently, singing with the others, wondering when Maharajji would relent and allow the session to end. I began to realize that I must not be a bhakta, but if not that, what? What *is* my path?[120]

---

and Rudi Rudananda and founded Siddha Yoga in the US. His main ashram was in Ganeshpuri, India, where Ram Dass visited him briefly. *Shaktipat:* transmission of spiritual energy, which can be given by a gaze, touch, or thought.

118 The illusion that nothing is happening is frequently what the mind perceives about situations where it is not in control. The parting words of the 16th Karmapa to Dr. Mitchell Levy just prior to death were, "Nothing happens."

119 Both Krishna Das (www.krishnadas.com) and Jai Uttal (www.jaiuttal. com) later became world famous for their devotional music and were nominated for Grammy Awards.

120 Even bliss is not the end of the path, but a passing state that comes and goes at various stages of awakening. Those who seek only bliss go to astral realms at death, which the Buddhists call "God Realms." These are places of temporary bliss, of which one eventually tires, and then one seeks re-embodiment in order to gain self-knowledge, wisdom, and ultimate liberation.

*Left to right: Peter Mt. Shasta (at top), Ram Dass (kneeling),
Jai Uttal, Ganga Dhar, and Maharajji (in blanket)*

In the afternoons Maharajji had everyone fed—meals which were mostly white rice, peeled potatoes, *dhal* (a spicy lentil soup), and sweet, milky chai. I mostly drank chai, as my stomach still could not handle solid food. A few of the more health conscious ones complained one day to the Indian women who were cooking, "Instead of white rice, white potatoes, and white sugar, can't we have steamed vegetables, brown rice, unpeeled potatoes, whole-wheat flour chapattis, and *jaggery* (unrefined brown sugar)?

The next day as people began to eat everyone looked at one another. The food had indeed been changed: lunch was white potatoes and white rice, seasoned with white sugar. Even the chai had extra sugar. After that, everyone ate what Maharajji offered—lovingly cooked by his Indian devotees and given without charge.[121] We got the message that our thoughts about what we ate were more important than the actual substance. One day he quoted Jesus:

> *It is not what goes into your mouth that defiles you, but what come out of your mouth.*

One day an Indian man who had just been released from the hospital was brought to the temple by his family. He was sickly and could hardly eat anything. He did pranam to Maharajji, who then handed him a brown paper bag of *puris* (deep fried chapattis) from which oil was dripping. Maharajji told him to eat them and come back the next day for more. As greasy food was the last thing to feed someone with stomach problems, we were sure the food would kill him. However, he returned the next day looking stronger and soon made a complete recovery.[122] It was said that despite their appearance, the puris must have been charged with healing *shakti* (primordial energy).

After several more weeks of being ignored I became increasingly

---

121 At no time was anyone asked to pay for anything other than their hotel bills and personal expenses. Maharajji and the temples where he resided seemed to be supported by voluntary donations (*dakshina*) from devotees.

122 Amazing stories about Neem Karoli Baba, collected from devotees and compiled by Ram Dass, can be read in *Miracle of Love* (Hanuman Foundation, 3rd ed. 1965).

impatient. I had accepted Maharajji as my Guru, but he had not reciprocated. In fact, he acted as though I wasn't there. Still sitting in the back against the wall, I decided that since Maharajji was most likely not my Guru I would leave the next day—and at that moment a large banana dropped into my lap.

I looked around to see if someone had thrown it, but it had simply dropped out of the air. Since many people reported miracles happening around Maharajji, I took it as a sign that at least he knew I was there, and that I should postpone departure. But, when was he going to talk to me? And would he raise me into *Nirvikalpa Samadhi* so I would merge forever in limitless consciousness?

In the afternoon I ran into Karuna, the blond girl in love with her high school sweetheart back in Des Moines, whom I had met in Vrindavan on my first attempt to see Maharajji.

"Any word from Maharajji yet?"

"No, he still hasn't told me to go home."

"Oh, that's too bad."

"I'm sure he's just testing me," she said, wistfully.

"Testing you on what?" I replied. It seemed she was already purity incarnate.

"To see if I have any selfishness, or if I'm totally ready to serve God."

"You seem selfless already," I said.

"But I want to be totally free of ego, to be the perfect devotee, like Hanuman kneeling before Lord Rama."

A group walked by who were going to sing bhajans and invited Karuna to join them. She said goodbye and went with them.

The next day I again sat at the back of the room while most everyone else sat as close to Maharajji as possible, hoping to get even a look from the eye of the Guru. Karuna and some of the other girls sat against his cot, caressing his feet.

"Why am I here?" I asked again, for nothing seemed to be happening.

Then I noticed that Ted, the guy who set up tents for rock festivals, was sitting with his back to the front wall, slightly behind Maharajji and to his right side. His face also bore an expression of skepticism. Eyes staring at a spot on the cement floor, he occasionally raised them to cast a questioning look at Maharajji.

Suddenly the Guru whirled around and, with the palm of his large hand, whacked Ted on the head. His eyes flew open in shock as he looked, open-mouthed, at the being that had dealt the blow, obviously waiting for some explanation. Maharajji turned to the Indian devotee standing on his left who was serving as translator, and said, "I had to do that to show this guy I know he's here. He's been sitting here for a month and thinks I didn't notice him."

The two of them burst out as though they would die laughing—as though someone who seemed omniscient, who was seen in multiple locations simultaneously, would not be aware who had been sitting next to him for the past month!

Maharajji, Neem Karoli Baba

Later, when I talked to Ted, I asked him what he had experienced.

"I'm so embarrassed; I had just been thinking, 'I've been here for a month and I bet this guy doesn't even know I'm here.' Then, whack! I don't mind him hitting me; in fact, I'm glad. But, what gets me is that he must also have heard all my judgments and bad thoughts about him."

I walked away, amused, for I was sure this message was intended for me also; however, that did not make all the time hanging out and waiting for something to happen easier. I began wondering, "Is there something *I* can do to speed the process of awakening?"

I had never taken LSD and wondered if now might be the time. After all, I was hanging out with Ram Dass, who had been notorious, along with Tim Leary, as one of the drug Gurus. Drugs had been a prominent feature of the 60s, and Ram Dass and Leary had been two of the first modern researchers into its potential. Now Ram Dass' message was that drugs were not necessary, that you could achieve clearer, more sustained consciousness in meditation. This message was a cultural turning point.[123] Although I spent a lot of time with Ram Dass I never brought up the subject of drugs, as I felt that, to him, it must be a thing of the past, and that on the yogic path the ingestion of an external substance was superfluous.

During the 60s, when mind-expanding drugs were supposed to have been so prevalent, I seemed to have been protected from connecting with them. Whenever I found the person who was supposed to have the drugs, or went to where the drugs were supposed to be, I was invariably told, "Oh man, I just gave away the last hit. You should have been here five minutes ago."

However, as I was feeling bored with Maharajji's seeming rejection, one day I confessed to Ram Dass how desperate I was feeling. "Nothing is happening," I complained. "I'm not even seeing Maharajji in dreams!"

"So, how do you feel about that?"

---

123 Timothy Leary (Ram Dass' partner at Harvard) and ethnobiologist Terrence McKenna became completely dependent on the frequent ingestion of various psychotropic drugs to maintain their altered states. Maharajji said that LSD was "yogi medicine"; however, one takes medicine only when indicated, not as a daily diet.

Sensing my need for guidance, he had morphed back into the skilled clinical psychologist he had been at Harvard.

I told him I felt like a failure. I had not achieved success in the material world and now felt I was a failure in the spiritual one as well. I had not even been successful as a hippie, where all you had to do was let your hair grow and swallow a pill. Now, standing before me was the world renowned psychedelic Guru of the 60s. I had smoked some marijuana one summer in Ibiza, but that was it. I felt like a sinner confessing to a priest.

"Yes, Peter, what is it?"

"Well, I'm kind of embarrassed to say this, but I've never taken acid."

"Yes, I know," he smiled with compassion.

"Really, how could you tell?"

"Well, you still have a few edges."

I wondered if he was totally edge-free? I remembered when he'd gotten angry at two guys playing chess where we were staying, at the home of one of Maharajji's devotees. "Chess is not spiritual," he'd shouted.

Hoping that he would supply me now with the long desired LSD, I hinted in vain. He smiled benevolently and said, "When the time and place are right, it will manifest."

What better time and place better than now? If I was going to take LSD, what could be better than to take it here in the Himalayas from the hand of Baba Ram Dass? But, it seemed Ram Dass didn't see it that way.

Satsang, Nainital, 1972

CHAPTER 30

With Gangotri Baba

I heard of a powerful yogi, Gangotri Baba, who lived in the hills below Nainital.[124] Since I still seemed on hold with Neem Karoli Baba, I decided to visit this sadhu and broaden my horizons. He was the son of a wealthy Brahmin family, who had become a medical doctor. For sport he had taken up amateur boxing and become quite good—too good, apparently—for one day he killed a man in the ring. In repentance he had not only given up boxing, but his medical practice as well. Renouncing all worldly endeavors, he had taken up the life of a sadhu. He had wandered as a beggar throughout India before returning to live on a hillside down the mountain from town.

He told a fascinating story, that while traveling down a back street in Delhi one afternoon, a stranger had come up to him whom he realized was the Guru who had for years been guiding him in his dreams. He told him that his time of wandering was over, then put his arm around his shoulders and physically transported him to the Himalayas. After a period of instruction he was told to return to the hillside beneath the village where he had grown up. Here he was to continue his spiritual practice and heal those who came to him. His Guru was the great Babaji, whom some called Hariakhan Baba, and Gangotri Baba now invited me to stay with him in his small lean-to on the side of the hill.[125]

---

124 It wasn't until later I learned that British psychologist, R. D. Laing, had stayed with this same yogi for several weeks, and had left just before I arrived. The yogi, whom he gave LSD, said he could achieve the same state of consciousness with a mantra, although it took longer.

125 There is much debate about the Babaji who Yogananda wrote about. Since the word "Baba" means father, and "ji" is often added as a term of respect, there are thousands of Babajis, some better known than others. Ram Dass' Guru was also called Babaji. Even the Babaji Yogananda wrote about gave contradictory statements about his age, telling some that he was born in the third century CE, while telling others that he was 500 years old. Another Babaji, Hariakhan Baba, who bears

161

After a few days with him I withdrew from my backpack a couple of books I'd brought along. One that was published by the Theosophical Society contained a foldout chart of the multi-dimensional nature of reality, showing different spheres of consciousness all connected by various lines. Curious about what Baba would say, I showed him the chart. He cast a brief glance at the complex drawing and then dismissed it by saying, "You will never find God in a book."

Speechless that he had discarded all occult studies with one sentence, I put the book away. Hiding in the bottom of my pack I then saw the paperback of Walt Whitman's ecstatic poem, *Leaves of Grass*. Wondering what he would say, I showed it to him and he read,

What do you think has become of the young and old men? And what do you think has become of the women and children...? They are alive and well somewhere.... The smallest sprout shows there is really no death....All goes onward and outward, nothing collapses, and to die is different from what any one supposed, and luckier.

"A great siddha!" he said, obviously impressed. "Who is he?"
"Walt Whitman."
"An American?"
"Yes," I said, proud that we had produced at least one poet who earned the respect of a Himalayan yogi. He sat thoughtfully for a moment, as if comprehending that a westerner had actually written something transcending a delusional view of reality. With a shrug he surmised, "Well, he must have been a sadhu in a past life!"

---

little resemblance to the drawing in Yogananda's book, appeared in the Kumaon Hills from 1890 through 1924. Several followers said they saw him enter a river and in mid-stream dissolve into a ball of light, never to be seen again. Mahendra Brahmachari traveled around India for thirty-five years interviewing people about their experiences with "Babaji," and published the stories as *Punya Smriti*, under the name Guru Charnasrit; however, were all those people talking about the same Babaji? This issue was further confused in 1970 by a new claimant, who called himself Haidakhan Baba, and who drew many western followers.

One day Baba put a circular mirror in my hand and sprinkled ashes from the fire on it. As he wiped it clean and whispered a mantra, it suddenly became a living screen on whose surface a succession of past lifetimes began appearing. I saw a movie of past incarnations and was appalled at the hundreds of lifetimes, many of which were simply about trying to survive. There were lifetimes as a farmer where I toiled all day in the fields to eke out a living for my family. I was a soldier on countless battlefields, killing or being killed, often as a youth. I was a merchant with little thought other than to accumulate wealth.

"What a waste," I thought, as I watched all those lifetimes devoid of awareness. I had been like the man I had visited in the hospital in New York, who had hardly thought about God until one day the moment of death arrived unexpectedly—as it often does.

Looking further into the past, I saw that I had been a spiritual teacher, but lacking the requisite patience. When the students could not apply what seemed simple lessons, their faces filled with bewilderment and I abandoned them. All the people in my life were those with whom I had been in relationship lifetime after lifetime. Time and again we came back into contact with each other so we could learn our lessons and advance one more step on the path of evolution. Finally I saw that talking often did not accomplish as much as silence, that simply being was often the best teaching. Eventually, I learned that the greatest teachers were often those who said little. The truth is already written in the heart and needs only to be awakened—often accomplished by a touch, a word, or merely the presence of one who knows.[126]

As the phantasmagoria of the past lives in the mirror ended, I was filled with gratitude for my present life and the opportunity it offered. I was firmly established on the spiritual path, free of dependencies, and could go all the way this lifetime. Like an eagle freed from its cage, I could soar above the Himalayas into the sky of pure consciousness, then fulfill my destiny by bringing that perception back to Earth.

Time ceased as we meditated, and I felt one with the ancient rishis

---

126 Some great teachers, such as Ramana Maharshi, were completely silent. Years later, I realized the greatness of "Spinach Baba," whose silence still reverberates through my being.

transmitting the ancient, changeless wisdom. At night other yogis from the surrounding hills came to visit, and we often spent the night around the fire, sometimes until dawn. Every few days we cooked some rice, but living in that altered state of the yogi, even that little food did not seem necessary.

Gangotri Baba in the Himalayas, 1996
(Permission by Exclimber)

CHAPTER 31

The Sadhu Goes to Court

We would rise before dawn, meditate, and do silent mantra practice. Then we fetched water from an icy stream and did a ritual purification, pouring it over our heads and letting it cascade over our bodies while chanting *Om Namah Shivaya.*[127] Back at the fire, we drank hot tea and watched the sun rise over the hills.

However, one morning something changed. Baba dug in to a trunk hidden under a blanket in the back of the lean-to that I had not seen before, and pulled out a new *lunghi,* a cloth he wrapped around his waist. He put the ceremonial ashes of a Shiva sadhu on his forehead, draped his Rudraksha mala around his neck, and pulled the *trishula* out of the ground.[128] As he walked away, grasping the trident like a spear, he shouted over his shoulder, "Keep an eye on things."

"Hey, where are you going?" I shouted after him.

"Court," he mumbled, heading down the path.

"Court?" Had I heard correctly? I could not have been more surprised

---

127 *Om Namah Shivaya:* a mantra which existed prior to the evolution of the concept of Shiva as an actual being. Shiva was originally an adjective, meaning the auspicious and primordially pure essence of the Self, which exists independent of external phenomena. *Om:* the sound of creation, itself composed of three sounds: A-U-M. Then come the five syllables, each of which is a *bija* (seed) sound for an element: *na* (earth), *ma* (water), *shi* (fire), *va* (air), *ya* (akasha/ether). When chanted consciously as a mantra these elements are purified, as well as purifying the chakras and one's entire being. Over time this consciousness was personified as a being associated with the nature God *Rudra,* and later partially merged with *Agni,* God of fire, and *Indra,* king of heaven, as the modern Lord Shiva. Although modern usage translates the mantra as "I bow to Lord Shiva," the true meaning pertains to the non-dual consciousness that is the heart of the Vedas.

128 *Trishula:* metal trident carried by many Shiva sadhus, representing the spiritual trinity.

if he had said he was going to see his stockbroker. Why would a sadhu, one who has renounced all worldly possessions and attachments, go to court? I followed him at a distance to see where he went. From the hill it seemed that the path led nowhere. Then, like an apparition, a black Mercedes four-door sedan came around the bend and inched to a stop. To my amazement, the half naked sadhu opened the back door and climbed in. The door slammed and the car accelerated down a dirt road I had not seen, leaving a cloud of yellow dust hanging in the still air.

I went back to the lean-to and sat before the empty fire pit to meditate and wait for Baba's return. As Agni, the God of fire, was sacred to him, I was surprised that he had allowed the flames to go out. Since I had been there, he had always kept the fire burning to maintain a spiritual focus, which I knew was intended as a reflection of the inner fire.

Baba returned around dark, accompanied by another Shiva sadhu, and by their demeanor I could tell things had not gone well. They took me into their confidence and explained why they had gone to court.

A year before, in 1970, a young man had appeared in the village of Haidakhan, claiming to be the reincarnation of Hariakhan Baba— Gangotri Baba's Guru—demanding the return of not only his ashrams from his past life, but his former bank account as well. Since it was well known that Gangotri Baba had been a *chela* of Hariakhan Baba and was still in contact with him on inner planes, he was asked to testify as to the truth of this claim, the veracity of which no one would know better. However, it seemed there were powerful political and economic connections involving local landowners, and the judge gave everything to the young man claiming to be the reincarnation of Hariakhan Baba. He also claimed to be the reincarnation of the original, deathless "Babaji," the eternal Guru about whom Yogananda had written, and the Guru of my patron, Gangotri Baba.[129]

---

129 A number of westerners, including the founders of the Rebirthing Movement, Leonard Orr and Sondra Ray, had fascinating experiences at "Hariakhan Baba's" ashram and accepted him as their Guru. Mr. Orr claims to teach the attainment of physical immortality, which he says he learned from this "Babaji" who, however, died of a heart attack at the approximate age of 34 in 1984. Years later on the slopes of

The two sadhus stayed up late into the night around the rekindled fire, talking about the political and financial machinations that had taken place in court that day, but I grew weary and finally lay down. Awakening as usual before sunrise, I saw that the other baba had gone. Gangotri Baba never said another word about the case and our daily ritual continued anew.

Thursdays are Guru Day in India and people from the nearby village made a pilgrimage to our camp to ask Baba for healings, blessings, and other boons. He would take *vibhuti* out of the fire and command the fire spirits to go into it, and then wrap the ash in paper and tell the person to take it home.[130] He instructed them to use the ash at a specific time when he would go into meditation and command the spirits to come forth to do his bidding and dispel negative forces.

This would be good to know how to do, I thought, as well as how to activate a mirror to show past lifetimes, and I wondered if Baba would teach this. Since I had at last found a being who appeared enlightened, and who would not only converse with me but let me live with him—I got up my courage one day to ask for what I had been seeking.

"Will you be my Guru?"

He paused thoughtfully and said, "I can't give you an answer right now. Taking on a chela is a great responsibility."

"How come?"

"Well, suppose I give you a mantra and you don't do it properly or for the right number of repetitions. Then I'm responsible and would have to do them for you."

"Oh, I hadn't thought of that."

"I will go into seclusion and ask Babaji."

Mount Shasta, while I was praying to make contact with Babaji and an ascended being appeared in a white robe and said, "I was 'Babaji,' but I no longer maintain a body on the physical plane. I can appear wherever I wish, and in whatever form, as the occasion requires."

130 *Vibhuti:* sacred wood ash from a consecrated fire, which destroys even the memory of evil and causes the remembrance of Divinity. Sai Baba says that, as our bodies will soon be ash, it is also a reminder of the preciousness of life.

Days passed with no answer, however. I didn't want to ask him again, as he could hardly have forgotten so serious a request. Yet, time dragged on with no answer, and it seemed that once again I was going to be deprived of a Guru.

Once again, nothing seemed to be happening and I began to miss Maharajji. It was the love and devotion, the feeling of the spiritual family that I missed—Krishna Das, Jai Uttal, and the rest of the sangha singing bhajans, and the love that Maharajji beamed back to us.

Then something happened that precipitated my unexpected departure. Baba had a scar on his back that looked like the zigzag of a lightning bolt, which he said was caused by the kundalini going up the wrong side of his spine. Some vertebrae must have shifted out of alignment, causing him pain. Familiar with the hippie method of adjusting the spine by "walking" on the back, I offered to treat him. I did not realize, however, that by touching him with my feet I was violating an ancient cultural taboo. Not only were you never supposed to touch anyone with your feet, due to the negative energy flowing out, it was considered impolite to even point a foot in someone's direction—and I had stood on his back!

He rose from the ground with a scowl on his face,

"Tomorrow you will leave!"

"What?"

"You need to leave!"

Suddenly I realized that he felt defiled, and I was appalled at what I had done. I had violated the trust of my would-be Guru. Then I wondered, if he can be so easily upset by a well-intentioned desire to help, is he really as enlightened as I thought? If not enlightened, then I don't want him as a Guru. Though Babaji was his Guru, and he could work certain miracles, I realized that I had never felt his love. It seemed that he, too, still identified with ego, and possessed vanity—even anger. I thought that overnight he might relent, but the next morning Baba sat staring into the fire and did not look up when I said I was leaving.

"I am grateful for everything," I said, bowing in pranam, yet the sadhu continued to stare into the fire. Throwing my pack over my shoulder, I left Gangotri Baba's campsite and walked slowly up the dirt trail toward Nainital and the Maharajji satsang.

CHAPTER 32

Meeting of the Gods

The next night at the Evelyn Hotel in Nainital I was awakened by a familiar presence in the room. When I opened my eyes, there was Gangotri Baba standing near the bed, looking at me. I was relieved to feel that I had been forgiven now, for he invited me on a journey.

"Come with me to meet the Gods."

"What?" I could hardly believe my ears.

"It is *Purnima,* the night of the full moon, and the Gods are gathering. Leave your physical body, come with me, and I will introduce you to them."

That the Gods were meeting together in one place and that I was invited exceeded my wildest dreams. The bewilderment I had felt toward them would now be ended with a personal meeting; yet, for some inexplicable reason, I hesitated. No energy impelled me to leave my body; in fact, I felt the contrary, to stay put. Effortlessly, without thought, I heard the words leave my mouth, "No, go without me."

"What?" he shouted, "This is the chance of a lifetime! How can you not want to see the Gods?"

"Because I AM GOD!"

I felt the irresistible power of my Higher Self surge forth with such conviction that I was shaken to the core of my being. For the first time I expressed my own God dominion, and Gangotri Baba stepped back in shock. With a scowl he disappeared, leaving me sitting up in bed, alone in the dark room. Had I missed an opportunity I would later regret?

The longer I thought about meeting the Gods of ancient myth, the more curious I became. Finally, curiosity got the better of me and I lay down, giving myself the suggestion to fall sleep and leave the physical body. Soon the outer self was asleep, and in obedience to that act of will, found that I had stepped forth in the etheric body.[131] As soon as I repeated

---

131 Leaving the body consciously is often called astral travel, which also implies the danger of going into the lower astral realm, which is inhabited by malevolent entities and destructive thought-forms.

his name I felt his vibration and followed his path through the ethers like a dog following a scent. Soon I had caught sight of him and held back to watch from a distance.

There was a semi-circle of about two dozen Gods, pictures of whose exploits, loves, and conflicts adorn calendars all over India. Even banks and taxis display pictures or statues of chosen deities. A number of Sadhus were going around the semi-circle in a sort of reception line, personally conferring with each God and receiving a blessing. There was Gangotri Baba being greeted by the other sadhus, then entering the line himself. I knew that I could go forward now and join him, but again I was held back by the Atman, the inner Divine Presence. I continued to watch from a distance, marveling at how these Deities resembled so closely the ubiquitous pictures and statues synonymous with Hinduism. What puzzled me, though, was their lack of light. No uplifting radiance emanating from them, as I would have expected from Divine beings.

Suddenly, I realized that these were astral Gods, and that I was in the psychic world of humanly created thought forms. These beings were created by human devotion, and their existence was sustained by human consciousness. Man created these Gods in his own image, aspects of his own consciousness. These Gods could not grant liberation, only mirror the consciousness of those who created them. Without the energy supplied by human devotion, they would fade away. This is why the Source within had prevented me from offering myself to them, and why it is written in the Old Testament, Book of Exodus, "Thou shalt have no other gods before me."[132]

Leaving the body should only be attempted with permission from the Masters and the Higher Self and for a specific, benevolent purpose. It is achieved by 1) Focusing attention on the etheric body (Soul), to which you are connected at all times, 2) Intending what you wish, and 3) Merging awareness with that Higher Self.

132 I meditated with Shivabal Yogi, whose disciple, Shivarudra Balyogi, said that at one time the Gods had appeared to him and offered him anything he wanted, including superhuman powers. Realizing it was a test, he politely refused. Shortly afterward, he achieved full self-realization.

Shocked by what my inner vision had revealed, I quickly retreated and soared back through the night sky to Nainital. Soon I re-entered the sleeping, physical form lying in bed, that during the day served as a protective vehicle. In the morning, the image of those astral gods assembled in the foothills under the light of the full moon was still clear and vivid.[133]

A few days later I ran into one of the girls from the satsang by the name of Shanti and we had chai together. When she said that she hadn't seen me around for a long time and wondered where I had been, I told her of my stay with Gangotri Baba.

"Oh, him!" she exclaimed, screwing up her face in apparent disgust. "He doesn't like women."

"Well, he is celibate."

"No, I mean he doesn't *like* women."

"What do you mean?"

"Gayatri and I went down to visit him," Shanti explained, "and he made a lot of lewd remarks about us to another sadhu who was there."

"What!" I said, shocked. "Maybe you misunderstood?"

"No, he kept asking us, 'Where are your boyfriends?' Then he said to the other sadhu, 'They sleep with a different man every night.' They were so rude, I couldn't believe it; they treated us like prostitutes."

I realized now that, like many monks in different parts of the world, although they had chosen to live away from women, the unresolved desire was still there. Despite their closeness to the Source, on some very basic levels they had not integrated aspects of their own humanity.

---

133 Sai Baba also says that the Gods are aspects of our own consciousness, that we bring them into existence by our desire to experience those aspects of ourselves. A western example of deity creation is Santa Claus, the all-knowing being who rewards children for being good and punishes them for being bad. He was created less than a hundred years ago by artists, writers, and advertising agencies, which drew on the legends of several cultures to create a composite Deity. This myth is still vigorously propagated by parents throughout the West. Even though the book of *Genesis* (1:27) says, "God created mankind in his own image," the converse is also true; mankind created the Gods according to its own images. Evolution is a co-creative experiment in which humanity and God reflect each other.

CHAPTER 33

Cosmic Consciousness and LSD

I continued to think about the remark Ram Dass made that I still had edges, and the thought of this character defect ate away at my self-esteem. Did I really have edges that were so apparent, and if so, what were they? Ashrams were full of people who neglected looking at their psychological problems to pursue enlightenment exclusively, and I didn't want to be one of them. I knew that there was no escape from these issues and that in the end everyone has to come back and confront these unlearned lessons. After seeing my past lives in the magic mirror, where in many, little spiritual progress had been made, I wanted to see what wounds needed healing, even if that meant using LSD. Though Ram Dass had helped pioneer its medical use at Harvard, he hadn't yet volunteered to supply any. I remembered Ram Dass' words, that if God wanted me to take LSD, it would manifest by itself. As if in response to that thought, the next day a Maharajji devotee who was also staying at the Evelyn Hotel, approached on the patio and said, "Hey, man, close your eyes and hold out your hand."

I did as requested and felt something drop into my palm. When I opened my eyes, there was a small, white pill.

"Clinical Window Pane LSD-25—the best you can get."

"Really?" I said, my jaw dropping open. He wouldn't tell me where the LSD had come from, but I suspected Ram Dass.

"Don't take it now. Wait until late at night when the hotel quiets down. It will put you in a state of cosmic consciousness."

As he had suggested, I waited until night had fallen and the hotel was quiet. I lit a candle and stuck it on a chair, which I pulled up close to the bed. Beside it I placed the tablet of acid. Waiting until there were no sounds, I sat with eyes closed, attention focused inward as I observed the rise and fall of my breath. I awaited the opening of the doors of perception that would reveal the cosmos.[134] Sure enough, soon I was above the Earth—conscious

---

134 "If the doors of perception were cleansed, every thing would appear

of the entire cosmos, aware of galaxies beyond our universe. I was universal intelligence without limits; yet there were also "others" with whom I was in telepathic communication, whom I realized were also parts of the great One. The Window Pane acid had truly thrown opened the window of the self to reveal the vastness beyond.

The candle had burned down and begun to flicker. Gradually I opened my eyes and looked at the clock. It was around midnight. Perhaps I should lie down and get some sleep? Leaning forward to blow out the candle I was shocked to see that beside the candle, still untouched, was the small, white tablet! I had not taken the LSD, simply anticipated its effects. That focus alone had launched me into cosmic consciousness. Could it be that simple? *What your attention is upon, you become!*

The initial question still remained, however. Had I gotten rid of the edges of my personality? Was the experience I just had the same as actually taking the physical substance? Here before me was the LSD I had been trying to obtain for years, that had now been dropped in my hand. It seemed that I was meant to take it, so I popped the tablet in my mouth with a prayer and washed it down with a glass of water.[135]

---

to man as it is, infinite. For man has closed himself up, till he sees all things through narrow chinks of his cavern" (William Blake, "Marriage of Heaven and Hell"). This line inspired Jim Morrison to call his rock group "The Doors." It was also the inspiration for two famous books by Aldous Huxley that have been combined in *The Doors of Perception and Heaven and Hell* (Harper Perennial Modern Classic, 2009). It also inspired the title of Huston Smith's *Cleansing the Doors of Perception: Religious Significance of Entheogenic Plants and Chemicals* (Sentient Publications, 2003). Both Huxley and Smith connected with Timothy Leary and Ram Dass at Harvard. They conducted some of the initial research on the clinical application of psychoactive substances when administered in appropriate doses in supportive clinical settings. According to research, when properly administered, peyote and psilocybin have been found to be less dangerous than most other pharmacologic substances. Prof. Huston Smith was largely responsible for the legalization of Peyote by the U.S. Congress for use in the Native American Church.

135 LSD stimulates the pineal gland to produce DMT, which it produces

Nothing happened at first, and I thought that since I had already experienced cosmic consciousness the pill would have no effect, but in twenty minutes I began to feel a tingling as though my nerves were dissolving. I regretted taking it and thought, why did I do this?

Suddenly, I was sucked back out through the window of mundane consciousness once again into the cosmos. A powerful force was pushing me beyond the gates of linear thought, beyond the illusion that I was a separate being in control of my life. Once again I realized that I was not separate from God—that I AM GOD—as I had experienced without the LSD, only now it had a driving power that burned through every cell.

Hours later it began to recede, and as I started to come down, I tried to hold on to that awareness. I prayed, "How can I keep this consciousness?" A majestic man in a white robe appeared in my mind's eye. Though he was the image of mastery he smiled warmly, seeming to know me, and spoke with firm, yet gentle, power, "To stay in God Consciousness say I AM THAT I AM."

I repeated this affirmation that was as old as time, and the awareness of my own Divinity returned. I heard within, "Keep saying I AM, because I AM is God. You have already discovered that what your attention is on, you become. Every time you say those words you will remember *who* and *what* you are—that you are God."

As he promised, when I said "I AM," the consciousness returned. After imparting those magic words, the mysterious being departed without telling me his name. I would not know who he was for another year, when he would appear in physical form in Muir Woods in Northern California.[136]

---

naturally in smaller quantities during meditation and other peak moments. Rick Strassman, M.D., did U.S. Government funded research from 1990–1995 at the University of New Mexico on DMT, which he describes in his book: *DMT: The Spirit Molecule, A Doctor's Revolutionary Research into the Biology of Near-Death and Mystical Experiences* (Park Street Press, Later Ed. 2000). Maharajji said that LSD was like window shopping; it enabled you to see what you wanted but could not give it to you.

136 For a description of this encounter read the first chapter, "Rendezvous in Muir Woods," in *Adventures of a Western Mystic: Apprentice to the Masters,* by Peter Mt. Shasta (Church of the Seven Rays, 2010). Or,

For the rest of the night, whenever identification with the three-dimensional world started to return, I would say, "I AM THAT I AM," and I would be drawn back into the awareness of the multidimensional, Cosmic Self.

As the rosy-fingered dawn spread over the eastern hills, I went outside, and as I saw the sky, the bliss of being one with the Creator washed over me. As others emerged from their rooms and I looked into their eyes, I saw that same Creator in them. How long would this experience continue? Forever, I prayed.

After breakfast we went over to Kainchi to see Maharajji and receive his darshan. Feeling that I was not one of Maharajji's favorites, I usually let everyone file in before me to the small room where he gave darshan. Then I would enter and sit against the back wall. Seeing my reluctance to enter, someone took me by the sleeve and pulled me inside. Although Maharajji had not looked at me the entire month I'd been there, this time as I walked past his cot he turned sideways, looked directly into my eyes, and asked, "Who are you?"

"Who am I?" I repeated, freezing in my tracks. The intensity of his gaze burned into me. Again, he repeated the same question, this time with even greater insistence, "Who are you?"

Standing there in front of the seated sangha, I felt embarrassed by the attention. What did he want? Finally I blurted out, "Maharajji, I've been sitting here for the past month."

"But, who are you?" he repeated, shouting.

I had read enough *Advaita* to know that he did not want my name, where I was from, or what I did, but the absolute *who*. But what should I say? As I looked into his eyes I realized that he too knew that he was God, and at that moment I was God looking at God. During all those weeks I had been sitting against the back wall feeling neglected, he had known all along that I was there. It had only been my ego that had been neglected, clamoring for attention.

I was filled with the desire to honor that Divinity. Without thinking, I reached into my bag and pulled out a package of incense and lit the entire bundle. Without embarrassment, I stood in front of Maharajji and

read it online at: www.AscendedAdventures.com/excerpts.html.

did a puja, circling his head with the smoking wand. Amazed that no one stopped me and that Maharajji sat there, eyes closed, I concluded the ritual. Having filled the room with smoke, I put the incense outside and returned to my place against the back wall—once more anonymous.

Now that Maharajji had acknowledged me I thought our relationship would change, that perhaps he would invite me to sit in front, but that didn't happen. It seemed that once again I had become invisible. Nothing more was going to happen, and I was going to sit there all day being ignored. Perhaps during those long hours I should practice self-inquiry? Maharajji had asked the same question Ramana Maharshi asked everyone:

Who are you?

When I got beyond the obvious answers, knowing that I was not the body, the mind, or emotions, I ended up in the head, experiencing an electrical short circuit. Yet, I knew that it was only by getting out of the head that the question could be answered and the true self realized. The real question I should be asking was not, "Who am I?" but,

Who is the "I" that wants to know?

As I dwelt on that, again I transcended the self and returned to the self-realization of universal consciousness,

I AM.

By afternoon, when the chemical effects of the LSD had worn off, I was shocked at my behavior in front of Maharajji, that I had circled his head with fifty sticks of burning incense. Even more surprising was that no one had stopped the ritual. I had violated the etiquette for being in the Guru's presence, which was usually enforced by the Indian devotees, but no one had done anything to interrupt the spontaneity. The entire episode seemed to have been orchestrated by Maharajji.

Free now of the chemical's effects, I could see that LSD was, as Maharajji had said on one occasion, "yogi medicine." It had provided an insight, but I also saw that a substance could not replace sustained self-awareness. That would require further years of meditation, experience, and practice.

CHAPTER 34

Who Is My Guru?

Even though Neem Karoli Baba had finally shown some interest in me, I began to feel that he was not my Guru. Although everyone showed slavish devotion to him and I continued to hear of miracles he had performed, I did not feel much benefit from hanging out hour after hour. While Ram Dass and the others sat adoringly at his feet, singing songs of devotion, I was becoming more and more frustrated.

Finally, I saw Maharajji sitting alone on his cot one afternoon. This was the first time I had seen him without anyone else around. I knew, "It's now or never." Gathering my courage, I dashed up to him. Knowing that I had to be brief, I dispensed with formalities and blurted out the question that had been on my mind. Ever since I had first heard Ram Dass' radio interview in New York, I had wondered if Neem Karoli Baba might also be my Guru. Realizing now that he was probably not, I shouted, "*Who is my Guru?*"

He cocked his head to one side and, squinting at me, shouted, "Jesus Christ!"

"What? Is he swearing at me?" I couldn't believe what I was hearing.

"Jesus Christ," he said again, his eyes now flashing intensely.

"Jesus Christ?" I replied. Had I come all the way to India to receive the same proselytizing I received from the Jehovah's Witnesses who knocked on my front door so many Sundays? I wanted the name of an earthly Guru, one at whose feet I could sit and receive instruction.

Seeing the blank look on my face, Maharajji began shaking his fist, shouting even more animatedly, "Jesus Christ, Jesus Christ, Jesus Christ!"

Hearing Maharajji shouting, two Indian men came running to protect their Guru, and I retreated. Although I had just finished reading about Jesus' adventures in India in *The Aquarian Gospel*, how could he be my Guru? How could I receive instruction from someone so far away and infinitely busy? I could not imagine he even knew of my existence. I left the temple and caught a bus back to Nainital.

179

Not only was I confused by Maharajji's pronouncement, but I was also suffering from dysentery. I had not been able to eat anything more than coconut milk for forty days, and had reached a state of surrender regarding staying on the physical plane. I felt surrounded by an ever-increasing light into which I was dissolving. Sometimes I would hear the cosmic *Om,* and when I closed my eyes I would feel everything dissolving into self-effulgent light. I was looking forward to leaving earthly existence behind. I knew that death was only an illusion, a move from one room into another more beautiful and spacious one. I wondered if the edges Ram Dass had seen were now gone. I did not actually want to die, but accepted that rapidly approaching possibility.

Dwelling on Maharajji's shocking statement that Jesus was my Guru, I decided to test if that could really be true. I did not want to commit suicide, an act I had contemplated once before and which I knew would only cause rebirth in the same condition, but I wanted to see if Jesus would save me if I were about to die. I knew that with my digestion in its precarious state I had to be very careful what I ate, so I decide to throw myself on God's mercy by eating a huge Indian meal and seeing if I was saved. The last meal I had tried to eat had caused such stomach pain and diarrhea that I had thought death welcome. If Jesus were truly my Guru, this would be an opportunity for him to make himself known. If he did not, I was ready to move on to a higher world where physical survival would not be such a problem.

The main street of Nainital ran along the shore of the lake, and soon I came to one of the best restaurants in town. After entering I hesitated, as most of the Indian guests were well dressed in western attire, and I resembled a ragged sadhu. However, the waiter motioned me to a table and I ordered a number of mouthwatering dishes from the vegetarian side of the menu. It would have been reasonable food to order prior to my journey to India, but I realized now that it would probably be my last meal. While eating, I reviewed the scene of that morning, with Maharajji shaking his fist and shouting over and over, "Jesus Christ." If I had not been able to contact Jesus from a church in America, how was I going to contact him now from a restaurant in India?

The place had been quiet when I entered, but now a disk jockey hidden in a cubicle in the corner began playing Bollywood music. I found

180

the singsong whining about wished-for romance annoying, and looked forward to leaving. Since my stomach was not yet showing any sign of distress, however, I ordered *gulab jamun,* dense, round dumplings soaked in sweetened rosewater. I was sure that this sugary dessert, eaten on top of the spicy meal, would be the coup de grace.

After finishing, I paid the bill in a hurry, not wanting the distress that was certainly on its way to arrive while I was still in the restaurant. I thought it advisable to get back to the hotel and the security of the bathroom as soon as possible. Walking toward the door, suddenly the music scratched to a stop and a western song began, a song from the late 60s that had been popular during a painful time in my life. Hearing it now brought a lump to my throat. As I walked out the door I heard, "Jesus loves you more than you could know."

I felt as though stabbed in the heart, and tears came to my eyes. I realized that whenever I had heard those words in the past I had always felt loved—that even though my logical mind said that Jesus couldn't possibly know who I was, those words always touched my heart. I felt now that, despite appearances, everything was going to work out all right.

I stumbled down the step into the street. It was dark, except for a few lights along the shore of the lake. As I walked back toward the hotel, a man in white came up from behind. He walked beside me so closely that our shoulders almost touched. I wondered if he was going to ask the usual questions—where I was from, how many cars I had, and what my purpose was—but instead he gazed into my eyes and asked with true concern, "Why are you here?"

"What do you mean?"

"You are an American, aren't you? So, what are you doing in India?"

"I'm on the spiritual path, looking for my Guru," I replied, hoping this would satisfy him.

"But, you don't need India for that."

"Why not?"

"Because, you have Jesus," he smiled, a light flashing from his eyes. With those words he abruptly stopped, and without saying another word, turned around and walked back the way he had come. That was strange, I thought, and I stood there wondering why he had said that. It was the third time that day I had heard the name Jesus.

181

Jesus

Back at the Evelyn Hotel, I was amazed that my stomach felt fine and, miraculously, I fell asleep. When I woke in the morning I felt better than I had in a long time, and discovered I was able to eat a normal breakfast. Afterward I went out on the porch with a cup of chai. As I looked out at the lake and the sun rising over the mountains, I felt somehow that I had been blessed.

CHAPTER 35

The Kumbh Mela

My tranquility was disturbed when I overheard that Maharajji had again told everyone to *jao*, get lost. He suggested we attend the *Kumbh Mela*, a spiritual gathering fifty times the size of the Woodstock Festival. It would take place in Allahabad at the junction of three rivers, the Ganges, Yamuna, and the legendary Saraswati. The later had dried up long ago, but was still considered to exert its spiritual influence. Vedic texts prescribe that it take place when Jupiter enters the sign of Aries on the New Moon in Capricorn.[137] It was at a previous mela at this location that Lahiri Mahasaya, the Guru of Sri Yukteswar, met the renowned Babaji, who Paramahansa Yogananda wrote about in *Autobiography of a Yogi*. Yukteswar was Yogananda's Guru. I was told that Maharajji had said in parting, "It is very auspicious, at the moment of the conjunction of the planets, to drink the water from the river."

Instead of a spiritual vibration, the mela felt more like a trade show with yogis, Gurus, and all types of spiritual teachers coming from all over India to promote themselves. Far from being free of ego, the mostly naked sadhus seemed to vie to see who was the greatest renunciate, who had the longest dreadlocks, the most outrageous face paint, or who could get into the river first. Some of the younger sadhus simply sat in the sand looking forlorn; perhaps they were simply wondering when they would be fed. Although some women were present, it was definitely an outpouring of male energy reminiscent of a college football homecoming weekend, where the fraternities were trying to recruit new members. No one was meditating—definitely not the spiritual event I had expected.

---

137 *Mela:* gathering, usually for spiritual purposes. The *Maha* (Great) *Kumbh Mela* takes place every twelve years. This was the *Ardh* (half) *Kumbh Mela,* which occurs every six years, and was attended by about ten million yogis, sadhus, and spiritual seekers. The most recent Maha Kumbh Mela in 2013 in Haridwar was attended by over 100 million people during the almost two months it lasted. On the most auspicious day, over 30 million people entered the Ganges near that location.

Clouds of smoke from ritual fires billowed skyward as I scanned the crowd for some sign of Babaji. I tried not to judge the obvious pride of those sadhus who strutted vainly, remembering that Babaji had chastised Lahiri Mahasaya for that same flaw when he had appeared to him here one hundred years before. Despite feeling closer to Jesus after the experience I had with him in Nainital, I still felt I needed a Guru in physical form, one at whose feet I could sit and ask questions, and where would be a more likely place to find that Guru than here at the Kumbh Mela?

Kumbh Mela, Allahabad

With every passing minute, however, that hope waned. It was hard to imagine that any great soul would descend into such a chaotic melee. I yearned to leave the hot, noisy crowd, but realized that first I had to act on Maharajji's suggestion to bathe in the river and drink its sacred water. The auspicious moment was at hand and the planets met in conjunction. Shoulder to shoulder with thousands of devout Hindus, I walked into the confluence of the three rivers and waded waist-deep in the muddy water. This was not the pristine, glacial source at Badrinath, and I felt a moment of doubt as I looked into the muddy waters.

186

"Do I really want to drink from this river that has passed through thousands of villages and in which millions of people bathe, wash their clothes, and dispose of their dead?"

Surely, this was a test of faith. Although Maharajji was not officially my Guru, he was still the one to whom I felt linked by destiny, and at whose suggestion I was here. Would he say to do something harmful? On the one hand there was common sense screaming that every drop of this water was inhabited by a million microbes, any one of which could cause great distress or even death. I remembered the open sores and missing limbs of the lepers on the road to the Jagannath Temple, and wondered if this might be the exact place where they had contracted the disease.

On the other hand, there was the path of surrender; if I ignored appearances and had implicit trust in the Guru, I would be protected, blessed, and granted liberation. Which path was right?

Allowing most of the brown water to seep through my fingers, I said a prayer for protection and licked the last drop that still clung to my palm. After all, Maharajji had not said how much to drink, only to drink water from the river, which I had now done. Perhaps now, Babaji or some other great Guru will appear, I hoped, since I have passed this test of faith. Emerging from the river, I looked eagerly for Babaji's face among the crowd. Many sadhus tried to attract my attention as I walked up the beach, inviting me to join their camps, but as I looked into their eyes I did not see in any of them a light of recognition.

With a sadness mixed with relief, I withdrew from the mela, moving away from the smoke and noisy mob, and headed back toward the home of Maharajji's devotees, where I was a guest. Walking back through the streets, I felt with each step that I was going to be leaving India soon. I hadn't found my Guru, and "What are you doing here?" echoed in my head, the words spoken to me by the man in white on the street in Nainital. I'd had enough of the teeming streets of India, yet the idea of returning to the West's oppressive materialism was not appealing either. I was caught between two worlds and belonged to neither.

I finally arrived, exhausted, at the pink house on Church Lane that was the peaceful home of Dada and Didi Mukerjee, some of Maharajji's closest devotees.[138] Coming out the gate in an immaculate, white outfit, was fellow American, Ram Tirtha. His face shone with inner radiance and I thought, "Here is one who is more enlightened than any sadhu I encountered at the mela.

"Wow, you look like you've had a hard day," he said, taking a quick look at my anguished face.

"Yes, I'm thinking of heading home. I love the Indian people and the spiritual energy, but living here is too difficult."

"Well, I know a place in the States that has the same energy as the Himalayas."

"You do? Where is that?"

I was incredulous, but I was only familiar with the East Coast and knew little of the rest of the country.

"Mount Shasta—the sacred mountain in Northern California. It's one of the meeting places of the Great White Brotherhood."

"Great White Brotherhood—what's that?"

"They are Masters who were once human but who have raised their frequency, like Jesus did when he ascended, and who now live in higher dimensions. From that octave they guide the destiny of humanity.

"When I'm in the States I go to Mount Shasta," he continued, enthusiastically. "I sit on a rock high on the side of the mountain and read the "I Am" books. Through them I can tune in to the Masters and feel their energy. It's no different than being high in the Himalayas."[139]

The idea of an organization of enlightened beings, who not only knew me but also guided the destiny of humanity, stretched my credulity. If they were guiding humanity, why did the world appear to be such a mess? However, here was a wise friend telling me these masters existed, so I tried

---

138 Sri Sudhir Mukerjee (1913–1997), professor of economics at Allahabad University. *Dada* means elder brother, *Didi*, elder sister. Maharajji spent a part of each winter at their home. He wrote two books about Maharajji, *By His Grace: A Devotee's Story*, and *The Near and the Dear: Stories of Neem Karoli Baba and His Devotees* (both published by Hanuman Foundation).

139 *Unveiled Mysteries, The Magic Presence,* and the *"I Am" Discourses,* by Godfre Ray King (Saint Germain Press).

to suspend disbelief and keep an open mind.

Ram Tirtha then suggested that while I was still in India, if I was not going to depart for America immediately, I should visit the Theosophical Society near Madras. This was where the Masters had guided Madame Blavatsky to establish their organization, whose mission was awaken humanity to the truth of God within.[140]

I thanked Ram Tirtha, who was on his way to the mela, and entered the gate of the Mukerjee home. I was tired and wanted to lie down. Soon I fell asleep. I woke in the morning, gripped by severe stomach cramps and diarrhea. It seemed that Maharajji's blessing had not deterred the amoebas of the Ganges. Perhaps I should not have surrendered to the external Guru, but followed my own God-given common sense? Perhaps the consciousness of the paramecium I had slain in high school had returned to teach me compassion, that any suffering caused consciously to any sentient being travels in a circle and returns to its creator.[141]

---

140 The Theosophical Society was founded in New York City in 1875 by Helena Petrovna Blavatsky, Henry Steel Olcott, William Quan Judge, and others, and was moved to India a few years later. Its stated objectives were to "form a nucleus of a universal brotherhood of humanity; study comparative religion, philosophy, and science; and investigate the unexplained laws of nature and the powers latent in man." It was understood that this nucleus was the outer, exoteric manifestation of the Great White Brotherhood of Masters which existed on etheric planes, and which was brought into manifestation outwardly at this time to further the Masters' purpose of aiding human evolution.

141 A secondary blessing was that, in learning to heal myself, I studied homeopathy and various other healing arts, which have enabled me to help others.

CHAPTER 36

Seeking the Masters

Next morning I felt in no shape to wander around India, and I sought medicine from an Ayurvedic physician. I asked Ram Tirtha if he knew of a place in India where I could rest and regain my health. Again he mentioned the Theosophical Society in Adyar on the outskirts of Madras. It was an eight-hour train ride and would provide a quiet, comfortable place by the ocean where I could have food without hot spices.

Despite my exhaustion and bedraggled appearance I was warmly welcomed at the Theosophical Society and given a quiet room in Leadbeater Chambers. The grounds were as beautifully kept as a country club, spreading for over two hundred acres where the Adyar River flows into the Bay of Bengal. There was a spiritual radiation here similar to Rishikesh, indicating the place was used by spiritual beings as a focus of some high activity.[142] I was greeted warmly by John Coats, the president of the Society, who invited me to have dinner at his home the next evening with the other Theosophists in residence at the time.

First thing next morning I visited their library, the largest metaphysical collection in the world, and opened a copy of *Unveiled Mysteries*, the "I Am" book Ram Tirtha had recommended. Despite my anticipation I was disappointed, for in the Foreword there seemed to be the same materialistic outlook I had sought to escape. The author said that in the Ascended Master Octave the book was "bound in a cover of jewels"—as though attempting to impress the reader. I had grown up seeing unhappy women adorn themselves with gems. It seemed that the author had not yet developed *vairagya*, detachment from the senses, which is the *sine qua non* for a beginner on the spiritual path. However, I was still curious about these teachings Ram Tirtha had recommended, so I put aside my prejudice and read further.

---

142 When I visited Adyar many years later, that beautiful spiritual radiation of the Masters was gone, and I hardly recognized the place.

The essence was that each of us is an individualized manifestation of God, which is called the I AM Presence (*Atman* in Sanskrit), that is invoked by the words "I AM." We can invoke the power of those words to create whatever we want, the teachings emphasized. That seemed too simple, however, for if that were true wouldn't everyone be happy? Furthermore, the book seemed focused entirely on the manipulation of human conditions, and not at all on self-realization, the actual attainment of God Consciousness. Obviously, simply saying "I am God" did not produce instant enlightenment, even though that is what the mysterious, etheric Master had told me to say when I took LSD in Nainital, and which had prolonged the state of elevated consciousness. As I said "I am God" now, I saw that if one identified with the lower self, that could also amplify the ego. This clinging to the personality and its selfish objectives is what the Buddhists call self-cherishing, which leads to re-embodying on the samsaric wheel of birth after birth. If these teachings really came from enlightened beings, there had to be a secret to making them work that had been omitted. Attaining God Consciousness was obviously more complex than saying two words. I wondered, "What is the secret of I AM?"[143]

I shut the book in disappointment and went back to my room to practice the hatha yoga, pranayama, and meditation I had learned in New York. These methods had been used by yogis for thousands of years and been proven to lead to enlightenment. The only question was, how long will that take? At least these yogic techniques seemed to improve my health and awareness.

Intent on forcing a spiritual breakthrough, I redoubled the intensity of my yoga practice, but suddenly it backfired. While simultaneously doing

---

143 There are even one-word mantras that yogis claim have led to enlightenment, such as *Ram* (an ancient embodiment of God known as an *Avatar*, who ruled a part of India). Maharishi Mahesh Yogi also dispensed many one-word mantras to still the mind. In *Three Magic Words* U. S. Andersen discusses the use of the three most powerful words in the English language, "I AM GOD" (copyright 1954 by U. S. Andersen; free download: www.scribd.com). He explains that by saying these words not out of ego, but silently from the heart, one can reprogram the unconscious mind. Realization, however, usually requires time and patience.

the "breath of fire" during a headstand, a needle-like pain stabbed my left ear. At the infirmary the doctor said I had ruptured an eardrum. He blew antibiotic powder into my, ear canal and said I should discontinue yoga. In my zeal for sudden enlightenment I had forgotten the cardinal rule, that yoga should only be practiced under the guidance of a yogi. Wasn't finding that Guru why I had come to India in the first place?

Not being able to do my usual practices, my spiritual path seemed blocked. Longing for guidance, I decided to visit the sacred Banyan tree. Many sages had meditated under this tree. After escaping Tibet, it was one of the first places the Dalai Lama had visited, and it was under this tree that Krishnamurti had given his first teachings. From its central trunk its branches spread over two hundred feet in every direction, additional trunks extending down from its branches into the earth. It was a living symbol of the one Truth, which sent down many manifestations into the world.

I sat under the Banyan tree every day. As I couldn't do yoga, I meditated on the inner light—a simple meditation that Saint Germain gave in *Unveiled Mysteries*. I had come to the Theosophical Society hoping to penetrate the great mysteries, and this practice seemed boringly simple. However, in every book through which I searched in the Theosophical Library, I found that meditation on the light was the core of every religion. So, I continued with the instructions Saint Germain gave, imagining and feeling that light expanding from center of my chest to every cell of my body and then radiating into space. He said to end the meditation with I AM affirmations to reprogram the negative tendencies of the mind and make it a transmitter of light. Day by day, the feeling of peace and the awareness of inner light expanded, and I began to feel interconnected with all life—like the spreading branches of the tree under which I sat.

It seemed that in bringing the celestial light down into the human self, I was uniting the apparent disparity between the East and West, the teachings of escape from the world through Nirvana and the teachings of mastery in the world. Reading the *Bhagavad Gita* again, I saw that mastery of the self and the world was exactly the path that Lord Krishna described to Arjuna.[144] In this ancient text the concepts of duality and non-duality

---

144 *Bhagavad Gita:* (Song of God) a part of the great epic, *Mahabharata,*

are united in the teaching of selfless service and spiritual warriorship in daily life.

One day, sitting under the tree, I felt pulled to walk to the beach where the property ended on the Bay of Bengal. It was here in 1909 that C. W. Leadbeater had been walking with Annie Besant, the president of the Society, when she had asked him when the next World Teacher would be discovered. At that moment they came upon the young Krishnamurti sitting in the sand and, supposedly seeing the magnificent aura around the boy, Leadbeater said, "That is him."[145] Thus began the education of the one who later, in denouncing the dogma of Theosophy, would be instrumental in initiating an era of self-inquiry and spiritual freedom that came to be known as the New Age.

While standing there on the dazzling white sand, contemplating the synchronicity of that moment of Krishnamurti's discovery, I beheld a small, bedraggled dog staggering up the beach. He was one of those pathetic strays whose life in the streets of India was a constant fight to stay alive. Here, "dog eat dog" was a literal reality each dog faced daily. I marveled that this one dog had escaped the streets of Madras to arrive at my feet on the very spot where the World Teacher had been discovered—as though guided by some high instinct. He walked a few steps and then looked down at the sand beneath his feet, then walked a few steps further. As the water lapped at his feet, he seemed horrified at the approach of death, and struggled to hold his head up and continue down the beach. He swayed on weakening legs, poised between two worlds, knowing that if he fell he would be swept away by the incoming tide. I admired the bravery with which he faced his death, and chanted Vedic mantras for his liberation. Then I left him to his solitary process, which I felt he wanted to complete without distraction. Next morning when I returned, his body was a hundred yards down the beach, tossing in the surf.

---

generally considered to have been composed by Ved Vyasa between the 2nd and 5th centuries BCE.

145 Krishnamurti later denied he was the World Teacher and, in reacting to this role expectation placed on him from childhood, repudiated all teachers, masters, and gurus. Instead, he encouraged self-observation, but without espousing any methods.

Still not able to eat much, I was in a weakened condition, and the dog's passing had a profound effect. I, too, stood at the separating point of two worlds, and wondered if it was time, like the dog, to leave my body. Behind me a great teacher had been recognized, initiated, and trained for world service; before me the ocean blissfully beckoned toward higher planes of existence.

Spending most of my time in meditation, I became increasingly aware of the special energy that pervaded the grounds of the Society. It had been brought into being by Madame Blavatsky at the request of the Ascended Masters, intended to serve as their vehicle for educating and spiritualizing humanity. I tried to contact those omniscient beings, many of whom had still been in physical bodies in the late eighteen hundreds when Blavatsky was alive. Despite feeling that I was there as their guest, I did not receive any direct reply. Feeling once again ignored by the Gurus I had come to find, I buried myself in metaphysical research in the library, trying to read Blavatsky's great works, *The Secret Doctrine* and *Isis Unveiled*. Although containing interesting information on the evolution of humanity, I found them of no practical assistance in the process of awakening.

Then, one day after meditation, as I sat looking at the floor, I felt an extraordinary energy and realized that I was in the presence of one of these Great Ones. My inner sight opened like a flower at the arrival of the morning sun, and I beheld a being in a white robe and turban whose fine features and aquiline nose were familiar. Before I realized it, I was in my finer body, ascending with him above the buildings and the grounds of the Society. There in the ethers I beheld an immense, white marble library that served as a repository for the sacred texts of the world from the beginning of time. Here the history of humanity was preserved, the sacred writings of Lemuria and Atlantis and the missing scrolls from the Library of Alexandria.[146]

---

146 Although some ancient texts say that the Royal Library was accidentally set afire by Julius Caesar, others say that only a storage house in the port burned. The scrolls that disappeared contained the origins of Christianity, which seem to have come from the teachings of Apollonius of Tyana, a widely respected and well-known seer of the first century.

195

As we approached the dazzling edifice, I felt what remained of normal consciousness ebb away, and my physical body was forced to lie down. Not for several hours did I awaken, and then feeling different—lighter and more etheric. Many nights I dreamed that I went to this library to learn, but in the morning when I awoke I found it hard to remember. For almost a month this process continued. After rising every morning I wandered to the banyan tree to meditate, then strolled along the Bay of Bengal—but on inner planes a great inner transformation was taking place. When it was time to leave, although much of the specific memory of what had been imparted had faded, I retained the clear memory of the tall, turbaned Master.

One day I entered the large main temple, where formal meetings were held for official members. With its high ceiling and marble floor and pillars, it resembled a huge mausoleum. However, standing out in gold letters across the main arch were these words:

There is no religion higher than Truth.

Then the memory of that great Master returned. I remembered that he had appeared in childhood and brought me to this temple in my etheric body. He was called the Lord Mahachohan, and he had pointed out these words and said, "This is your work in this life: Learn the truth that transcends all religion, dogma, and superstition, and share that truth with others."

These scrolls were likely stolen in 391 CE by Theophilus, Bishop of Alexandria, and may now be in the Vatican Library. These scrolls tell of a saint who travelled to India and Tibet, where he was known as Issa (anointed one), and came back to the West to give the teachings of the inner God Presence. Jesus is the name given this saint by the Romans. Christ is a word derived from the Greek, *Kristos*, in turn derived from the Sanskrit, *Krishna*, meaning the consciousness that cannot be destroyed. See: *Apollonius The Nazarene: Mystery Man of the Bible,* by Raymond Bernard (Health Research, 1956).

Lord Mahachohan

CHAPTER 37

Who Am I?

While in Adyar I ran into a friendly American and fellow guest at the Society by the name of Truman Caylor Wadlington. He talked extensively about a yogi he had met, Ramsuratkumar, about whom he was so enthusiastic, he had written his biography. When I asked what he taught, Truman couldn't tell me anything. Like many of the muni (silent) babas, he didn't give any teachings, but it was obvious Truman regarded him as one of those God-intoxicated beings who saw God everywhere—manifesting what Ramakrishna had called Divine madness. I wondered, however, how you could distinguish that from true madness, especially if they rarely spoke? His popularity seemed mainly to arise from the fact that he had sat at the feet of Sri Aurobindo and the Advaita teachers: Papa Ramdas, Ramana Maharshi, and his student Poonjaji (Papaji)—and that he now lived in the street.[147] The core of Advaita is inquiry into the Self, by asking "Who am I?" Hopefully, then one realizes the timeless, eternal, true Self, existing beyond body, mind, and ego.

There are many who have had tastes of this Oneness and, learning to speak in the Advaita phraseology, have become Gurus of non-duality. No matter what the problem or question you ask these people, the answer is the same, "Who is it that wants to know?"

Or they condescendingly say, "If you knew who you were, that wouldn't be a problem, would it?"

This implies that enlightened people have no problems, which is not true, or that they feel zero responsibility for others. This is a philosophy that suits wandering sadhus or Gurus, whose needs are all met by others, but does not apply to most people who live in the world.

---

147 These later three Gurus popularized *Advaita:* non-dualism. Papaji told a number of well-known western teachers who sat at his feet that they had achieved enlightenment, only to retract that endorsement after they had left.

In a warm climate like India, one can live in a cave or under a tree in a state of Oneness, cared for by devotees who leave a pile of banana, mangoes, and nuts for the Guru, but in a cold climate like Tibet or other northern latitudes it takes more than detachment to survive. The realization that life is an impermanent illusion does not solve the problems of immediate physical existence, nor does it lead to psychological maturity and self-mastery.

Ramana Maharshi, however, lived the truth of his teachings, completely unattached to consequences or outcomes, and acted as a catalyst to free others still enmeshed in ego identification and self-cherishing. Furthermore, he emanated love, which many of the descendants of his lineage seem lacking. He also had the ability to transmit that awareness to others. How to manifest conscious mastery in daily life, however, was beyond the scope of his teachings. Some of his followers later claimed they had attained his same level of realization, giving their lack of concern for the welfare of their families and loved ones as an example of their lack of attachment. Or they kept silence, their level of awareness remaining a matter of conjecture.

On the path of Guru yoga, it is the belief in the Guru that is essential, rather than the Guru's actual level of enlightenment. Once the Guru Principle has been invoked and the devotee has taken that being as the manifestation of God, then the universal Guru—the Higher Self—will manifest. Many have advanced far on the path with an unenlightened Guru, or even sitting before a statue to which they are committed. Whatever happens is taken as the will of the Guru, and will be a catalyst for growth.[148] Of course, that relationship can always change; when learning ceases or that manifestation is no longer seen as the Guru, then it is time to move on.

Truman spoke so effusively about Ramsuratkumar that, despite my doubts, I felt drawn to see him. Since he lived at the base of Mount Arunachala in Tiruvanamali, I could visit the sacred mountain and Ramana Maharishi's ashram at the same time. After being given a room at the ashram, I went immediately to the shrine room to begin the process of self-inquiry. As I walked up the steps I was shocked to see a large, backlit, plastic picture of Ramana Maharshi, glowing like an advertisement for beer

---

148 See the film *Kumaré: The True Story of a False Prophet* (Future Bliss Films, 2011).

in a bar, and before which people were prostrating. He would be shocked, I thought, to see that in the short time since his death, people had begun to worship him, rather than practice his teaching of self-inquiry.

Ignoring these worshippers, I went to the room where he had given daily darshan and found that at least the silence and purity of that place had been preserved. I sat before Ramana's couch and began the process of inquiry, asking

Who am I?

Within the first minute I exhausted the list of who I am not: "I am not the body, mind, emotions, name or ego, and not even the one asking the questions." Then I was at a dead end. I began to go through the list again and still arrived at the same frustrating, intellectual conclusion. After an hour of these mental gymnastics I felt a knot in my head, and I left to climb the mountain behind the ashram. I thought, "If I can find the cave where Ramana meditated I will have better results."

Taking care to avoid the cobras I had been warned about, I climbed the gentle hill and easily found his cave. Unfortunately, the view had changed since Ramana's day, and the hill now overlooked the town's bus station. The sound of the public address speakers and the incessant honking of horns filled the air. Inside, the cave was quieter, but tourists drifted in and out, taking photographs. Soon I descended to the ashram. Noting my disappointment, one of the other guests said that I should do a *Pradakshina*, circumambulate the mountain, chanting the name of Ram on the night of the full moon. Ramana used to walk around the mountain for days at a time and had said, "What better *sadhana* (spiritual practice) can there be than going round the hill?" Perhaps getting a workout before meditation was the secret that had been withheld from his teachings? Then I remembered that Ramana, himself, had not become enlightened through self-inquiry, but through an experience of spontaneous realization.

The moon was full the next night, so I bathed, put on a clean set of clothes and smeared sacred ash on my forehead, as I had been told was required. Walking barefoot, I closed my eyes and chanted "Ram" with each step, trusting that any cobras along the path would honor a pilgrimage dedicated to the realization of God. Occasionally I would open my eyes to be sure that I was not about to walk off a cliff, then return to using intuition as my guide—feeling the soft padding of my feet in the warm dust.

Although I believed that any pilgrimage done with dedication surely accrues merit, when I returned to the ashram in the early morning hours I was not aware of any change in consciousness, and fell asleep, exhausted.

When I returned to Ramana's room the next day, I sat once more before his image and repeated, "Who am I?"

Once again, I began thinking, still trapped in the mind. The process of self-analysis seemed, itself, to block finding the answer. Only later, when I stopped asking, the answer spontaneously appeared—not in words, but as a visceral experience—perhaps similar to the way it had for Ramana.

Frustrated by my lack of progress in discovering who the "I" was, I walked into town in search of Ramsuratkumar, the yogi Truman had written about.[149] If he were as great as Truman had said, perhaps he would bestow enlightenment! One never knew, for in India there are countless stories of how someone attained enlightenment when least expected, sometimes even from the touch of a Master, appearing in the form of a beggar or leper.

In the town's main square, where Truman said he hung out, I found a bedraggled man sitting on a stone, smoking a cigarette. This had to be him. When I said "Truman sent me," he nodded but continued puffing. I sat beside him for a while, waiting for some word of wisdom, but he remained silent. Finally I spoke up and said, "I just walked around Arunachala, chanting "Ram."

"Ahh, this beggar is very pleased," he exclaimed, his face brightening. Then he offered a cigarette, which I declined, and lit another for himself. He was a chain smoker, it seemed. Perhaps that was his meditation? If he were as enlightened as Truman said, one with creation, why would he smoke? He didn't even seem to enjoy it, but puffed nervously as though preoccupied with a worry.

"I will introduce my friend to you," he said suddenly, beckoning me to follow. He walked toward a huge, black water buffalo. Holding several bananas in his hand, he peeled one and inserted it halfway into his mouth. Bending over, face to face with the buffalo, he stuck the banana forward in

---

149 Yogi Ramsuratkumar (1918–2001). See *Yogi Ramsuratkumar, the Godchild, Tiruvannamalai,* by Truman Caylor Wadlington (Diocesan Press, 1972).

offering. Without hesitation, the huge beast opened its mouth and grasped the banana. For a moment their lips touched in a kiss and the banana broke in two, the animal swallowing his half in a single gulp.

"What a strange way to start the day," I was thinking, when he handed me another banana and indicated that it was my turn. I had already acquired dysentery from drinking water from the Ganges on the advice of one Guru, and was hesitant now to incur some new disease from kissing a water buffalo. I wondered, "Does this practice have some unknown significance, or is this guy simply crazy?"

I had heard that when Ramsuratkumar reached a certain level of enlightenment he began rolling on the ground in laughter, and I wondered if he had really attained enlightenment or simply had experienced a psychotic break? If he was enlightened, it seemed that he had not integrated the experience with normal reality. As if to confirm my suspicions, he said, "I acquired this Divine madness from my Guru."

Although he had sat at the feet of Ramana Maharshi, he attributed his "breakthrough" to Papaji (H. L. Poonja), both advocates of Advaita. This further aroused my suspicion that this path did not equip one with the tools necessary to function in the world.

Eating the banana, I suddenly realized that I was famished from the night's walk, and asked, "Say, would you like to have breakfast? Pick your favorite place and let me treat you."

Perhaps, over breakfast, he will transmit some of Ramana Maharshi's teachings, I thought, and guide my pursuit of non-dual consciousness. He agreed to my offer and picked up his long wooden staff, which he held above his head like an antennae as we walked down the street.

"What is that for?" I asked, unable to restrain my curiosity.

"It's an antenna, so I can feel if any of my enemies are around."

"Wow, you have enemies?" I asked, unable to imagine how someone supposedly living in non-duality could have enemies, for to recognize that there was someone other than you—other than oneness—would be a contradiction of the tenets of Advaita. I found out later that the Tamil separatists wanted to get rid of him because of his public stance for a unified India. Entering into this political conflict also seemed not in accord with the principle of oneness.

"Yes, sadly, some people wish this beggar harm," he sighed.

We ate a breakfast of *idlis* (small cakes of fermented, then steamed, rice and lentils), *sambar* (a spicy sauce), and curds, but he did not seem to enjoy himself. During the meal he kept turning around, looking at everyone coming in the door. Occasionally he would raise his stick above his head to check on the proximity of enemies. When I asked about Advaita he simply shrugged. After breakfast we returned to the street. He lit another cigarette and I bid him goodbye.

"How did this guy become recognized as a Guru?" I wondered, as I headed back toward the ashram. Years later I discovered that it was the work of my friend in New York, Hilda Charlton. After reading Truman's book, she had started sending people to see him. Years later some wealthy followers constructed a huge ashram, and people would come from the States to sit at his feet. First he protested that he did not want an ashram, but once enthroned he said, "This ashram is different from other ashrams... The whole cosmos will be controlled from *this* ashram." If not the cosmos, certainly his influence reached America.

As I walked down the street I found myself in front of the Arunachaleswara Temple, a twenty-five acre complex dedicated to Lord Shiva, and containing many other temples within its massive walls. As I sat on the steps outside the front gate, I contemplated how my search for a Guru seemed to have become clouded. There was an abundance of beggars, some of whom dressed in orange robes and called themselves sadhus, also some who were called Gurus but seemed more in search of wealth and influence than mastering the self. Then, there were those who were deluded, thinking they were more evolved than they were, many of whom also attracted followers. It seemed that most of the genuinely enlightened beings chose to remain secluded or at least silent, and the ones who did talk sent me away. A personal relationship with an enlightened being, like Ram Dass had with Maharajji, had so far been denied.

As I sat on the steps, a sadhu with a faded orange piece of cloth around his waist approached and extended his hand, which he brought to his mouth in the traditional gesture of asking for food. According to the rules of *sanyas*, sadhus were allowed to occupy a place while they prayed or recited their mantra. If no one volunteered food they were supposed to move on. Begging per se was forbidden, so when this emaciated man held out his hand I knew he had crossed the line. He looked so hungry, though, I decided to give him a rupee so he could buy food in the nearby market. As I extended the rupee note toward him he became excited and started shouting.

Attracted by the commotion, a passerby stopped to translate, "He cannot accept your money, as it is forbidden by his sect. For him to touch it would be a sin. You need to go with him to the market and buy the food for him."

I knew that if I went into the crowded market tent I would be trapped by more beggars among the narrow aisles, wanting me to buy groceries for them as well, so I sorrowfully put the money back in my pocket and rose to leave. Again the man held out his hand, bringing his closed fingers to his mouth. But, with a heavy heart I turned away, wondering how humanity had devised such complex rules about what was spiritual or not, and how people made life more painful than needed. It seemed that perhaps this beggar and I had simply agreed to play different roles in life, to learn from this play whatever our lessons might be.

I had been gone from Maharajji for close to two months now, and although I had not received any specific teachings, as I would have expected from a Guru, I had again begun to miss the love that flourished around him. Sitting at his feet and singing with Krishna Das and Jai Uttal created a sense of enchantment and I longed to return to that nurturing home— the only real family I had known.

When I heard that Maharajji was back in Vrindavan, the place where I had first tried to see him, I thought, "Maybe this time, since he at least spoke to me before I left, he will welcome me to the front row along with others."

With high hopes, I bought a ticket and prayed for the strength and patience I would need for the three-day train ride to the north. Perhaps these long train rides across India fulfilled the same purpose as Ramana Maharshi's circumambulating Mount Arunachala? The only way to survive the jostling and the sweltering heat was, I knew, in complete surrender to God in the form of the Divine Lila of the Indian railway system. During this ride I dwelled constantly on the eternal question: *Who am I?*

If I am not the ego or its attachments, not the body or its feelings, not the mind or its thoughts, not the feelings or emotions, then what am I?

After pondering this question in the spirit of a Zen *koan*, I realized that the question had no answer that could be found through rational thought. The act of questioning was merely a focus, like watching your breathing, and the answer could only be intuited; and then I wondered, "Who is asking this question?"

Listening to the click-clack of the train, I leaned back against the seat and closed my eyes. Mile after mile rolled by, day passing into night, night into day, and gradually I began to observe the mind that was asking that question, and I wondered, "Who is that? Who is that watching from the void? It is 'I,' a Self that is watching the self that has been asking all the questions"—and I began to laugh.

"How ridiculous that I had been trying so hard to find such an obvious answer. There is no question and no answer. There is only being. The void is not empty, but 'I' and the consciousness are one." That was the elusive meaning of the Sanskrit saying, *Tat Twam Asi*, and I realized[150]

I am That.

My sudden laughter in the midst of the night evoked sleepy stares from the other passengers and, unlike Ramsuratkumar, I tried to act as though nothing had happened, as though I, too, was merely a personality occupying a three-dimensional body, hurtling across the Indian subcontinent, an actor in some obscure drama.

I thought of becoming a sadhu, one of those homeless wanderers who are ubiquitous in India. I could get off the train at the next stop, leave everything and start anew. But lapsing into sleep, I remained on the train.

By the third day I was still moving in and out of this transcendent awareness, of being nothing and everything simultaneously. Few of the Gurus I encountered had produced a greater awakening than had this train

---

150 *Tat Twam Asi:* Thou Art That, from the *Chandogya Upanishad.* This expression of the oneness of individual consciousness with Divine consciousness is called a *Mahavakya* (great pronouncement) of the Sanathana Dharma.

ride across India. She was Kali, the Goddess who destroys illusion, who had danced on the prostrate form of my lower self that identified with the transitory phenomenon called reality.

The train suddenly ground to a screeching halt, and I realized with a start that we had reached Mathura and I needed to disembark. Once again there was the pressure to function in the three-dimensional world. I would have to find a rickshaw driver and haggle over his price for the ride to the hotel. Would he even go to the hotel I wanted or, as was often the case, insist on taking me to the hotel owned by his uncle or brother-in-law? I grabbed my rucksack and jumped out of the train, landing with a stiff-legged thud on the cement floor of the station platform.

CHAPTER 38

What Does God Want?

The driver threw my bag into his bicycle rickshaw and I climbed onto the seat. I was gratified that after the exhausting train ride he took me directly to the hotel where the satsang stayed. As soon as I got to the room I doused myself with a bucket of water. I put on fresh clothes, tattered after being washed on the rocks of countless rivers, and walked out the front door. Soon I found the desolate road to the Hanuman temple, where they said Neem Karoli Baba was staying. I was surprised at how eager I was to see him. There were no westerners there, and I realized that at long last I would now be alone with Maharajji. I was finally going to have the private interview I had been craving for so long. Perhaps he would say "I really am your Guru" after all? Maybe he had been ignoring me just to encourage my self-inquiry—which had worked.

Should I prostrate before Maharajji? Although that was the etiquette, it seemed ridiculous to bow before another human being. Surely, if he were enlightened, it wouldn't make the slightest difference to him. I relished the thought that finally I would be able to ask the questions that for so long had been on my mind "Why am I here, and what should I do next?"

I wanted answers not only to those immediate questions, but what to do with my life. I heard that he had been giving specific instructions, telling people where to go and what spiritual practices they should perform. He had sent devotees to many different places: Almora, Bodhgaya, even back to Nainital. Where would he send me? Since, on one level, I still regarded him as my Guru, I would go wherever he directed. Perhaps now he would also disclose why he had said to drink from the Ganges, an act o obedience that had made me deathly ill. The Ayurvedic remedies I had been taking had accomplished little.

Strolling along the dusty path through the area where Krishna had walked five thousand years before, I began to finally feel devotion to my Guru—and prepared to make whatever sacrifice he commanded, even if that meant going into a cave to perform *tapas* (austerities and meditation).

I arrived at the temple and was greeted by an attendant who said that, indeed, Maharajji was there and I could see him immediately. What fortune! My heart beat rapidly as the attendant used a huge key to open the rusty gate. Inside the compound, he locked the gate and opened a second one, admitting me to the inner court. From there I was ushered into a small room and told to sit on the stone floor before Maharajji's cot and wait.

"Maharajji will be with you shortly," the attendant whispered.

I could hardly control my eagerness to finally be alone with Neem Karoli Baba. It seemed that all the months of traveling, all the illness and hardship, had led to this moment. I would finally get to talk with the one who had called me to India.

I did not have long to wait. Neem Karoli Baba hobbled into the room, leaning on the shoulders of two attendants, and sat down on the cot. He leaned forward and glanced inscrutably at me. I wondered, nervously, "What is he going to say? Maybe he will simply put me into samadhi the way Ramamurti Mishra had!"

"Chai, chai," he shouted to the attendant, then cocked his head as though listening to far-away music. "He must be reviewing my past lives, and will soon reveal what I should do," I concluded, and leaned forward in excitement. A clay cup of tea was handed to me, but it was so hot I tried to set it on the ground.[151] Unlike all other cups I had been given, this one had a round bottom and there was no way to balance it, so I placed two fingers on its rim to keep it from falling over.

"Drink your tea," Maharajji shouted, nodding to the cup.

I tried to pick it up, passing the cup from hand to hand to keep from being burned, and then noticed it was leaking. My pants were becoming wet with the sticky liquid, which was scalding my legs. I tried to set it down, and again Maharajji commanded, "Drink your tea."

I felt desperate. This was the moment I had waited for, but it was rapidly becoming a fiasco. Maharajji did nothing to alleviate my suffering or even indicate he saw what was happening. Finally he leaned forward and spoke as to a child, "So, what do you want?"

---

151 In those days, sanitary dishwashing was not often available, so chai was served in unfinished clay cups. After use, they were smashed on the ground, where they crumbled back into the earth.

"I don't want anything," I said, stunned, "I came to ask what you wanted? Where do you want me to go? What should I do?"

"Where do you want to go?" he asked.

"I just want to go where God wants me to go."

"Yes, yes, but where is that?" he fired back.

"I don't know. You are the Guru. That is why I came to see you."

"Well," he said, scratching his head, "Where do you want to go?"

"I don't care. I will go wherever you say."

"Yes, yes, but where?" he repeated, with obvious impatience.

Couldn't he answer this simple question? Why didn't he just tell me straight out, the way he had with the others? He had told them all exactly where he wanted them to go. I was becoming more confused by the moment. The interview was not unfolding as I had anticipated. Maybe I need to say something to get him started?

"I could go to Nainital?" I finally blurted out.

"Yes, yes," he said, nodding from side to side and up and down in that unique Indian way that could mean anything. Not sure if that was his final answer, I asked, "Not Bodh Gaya?"

"Yes, go."

"Or, Almora?"

"Yes, fine," he said, impatiently, "Finish chai and go."

"But which place? I only want to go where God wants me to go."

"Don't you understand?" he shouted vehemently, as though speaking to a moron. "Don't you understand that God wants you to go where you want to go?"

With that pronouncement he waved his hand, signaling that the interview was over.[152] I tried to salvage some element of decorum by prostrating at his feet, but Maharajji waved me away, shouting, *"Jao, jao!"*

I was humiliated. I had travelled across India for this? The interview was over and I felt that I had learned nothing. Without knowing how it had happened, I had angered Maharajji and made a fool of myself. The

---

152 Krishna Das said that Maharajji told him the same thing when he said goodbye for the last time. When he asked how he should serve him when he got back to the States, Maharajji said, "Do what you want." Krishna Das was heartbroken.

attendant unlocked the gates and escorted me out. Still devastated from the interview, I was not prepared for the shock I received when I reached the street.

Sitting on a boulder across the road, and staring straight at me, was Maharajji! It was the same fat, old man wrapped in a blanket I had left thirty seconds before on the cot inside! How had this man who needed support to walk gotten out there ahead of me? The only way out was through the same gates I had used.

In a hurry to get away from this crazy magician, I mistakenly turned left, instead of turning right and walking to the main road. But this road was a dead end. I realized I would have to go back. Suddenly there was a clap of thunder. The sky became an inky black, pierced by flashes of lightning. An eerie silence filled the air, and as gusts of wind blew dust in my face, huge drops of rain began to fall. A lone shaft of sunlight pierced the black clouds and miraculously illuminated a huge tree blocking the way. In the branches were twelve peacocks illuminated by the shaft of light. Reality became transformed into the surreal landscape of a dream. The sky had been cloudless; now I was being pelted by huge raindrops. I had made a wrong turn into some alternate reality, and struggled to find a way out. My mind was numb.

Realizing that I needed to get on the main road, I turned around and headed back, but there was Neem Karoli Baba, still sitting on the boulder, scowling at me. I decided to confront him and ask what he was doing here; but he picked up a rock that he threatened to throw at me. This was the enlightened being that said we should love everyone? Not wanting to find out if he would really throw the rock, I made a wide arc around him. After passing by, I kept looking over my shoulder to see if he was sneaking up from behind—but he was still sitting on the boulder, watching. After I covered the fifty yards to the main road I relaxed, and felt normal consciousness return.

I looked back to see Maharajji still sitting there. The scowl was gone and he was now laughing. He dropped the rock, raised his hand, and waved goodbye. He seemed to be saying, "Get going—you know the way—you know where you are going!"

I began walking toward town and noticed that the rain had stopped. Once again, there wasn't a cloud in the sky, and the streets were dry and dusty. It seemed that it had not rained anywhere except at the Hanuman temple!

When I returned to the hotel, I ran into Karuna. Seeing her big smile, I said, "Wow, you look happy."

"Yes, I'm going home...I'm going to marry my sweetheart."

"Maharajji told you to go home?"

"No, I've been waiting a year for him to tell me that, but finally I realized that what I want more than anything is to marry my boyfriend, so I told Maharajji I was going home."

"Wasn't he angry?"

"Quite the contrary. He was very happy and gave his blessing. He also blessed my boyfriend and said that he was a good man. It seems that all along, Maharajji was waiting for me to tell him what I wanted!"

CHAPTER 39

Gaylord

During the six months I had been wandering around India, I had met fascinating, enlightened beings, but had not found the Guru for whom I had yearned. Although I had grown spiritually, my health had declined and my visa was expiring. It seemed that it was time to return home.

The temperature in New Delhi was one hundred and twenty degrees in the shade and I found that it would be five days before I could get a flight. The small room I had in the Palace Heights hotel was not air-conditioned, and resembled an oven. Not only was I suffering from dysentery, but I had contracted scabies, which itched intensely in the heat. There was nothing to do in this pressure cooker-like existence except to cease identification with the physical plane and continue to practice self-inquiry—to dwell on the eternal *I*.

I am not the body—I am I.

Even though I said "I am not the body," and was aware of the transcendent Self, I still observed the itching body, dripping with sweat. When I said "I am not the emotions," I observed the frustration over what I had to endure, all for the sake of the fruitless quest for the undiscovered Guru. I told myself, "God is beyond all these, beyond body, mind, and emotions," but I saw that these limitations were still a focal point of my life. I could not totally deny them. I felt that I was a failure at non-dualism because I had not totally transcended these basic elements of existence. I had experienced moments of transcendent enlightenment, but then the human world had come crashing back. Suddenly, I saw that it was a lie, that I am all these. I am the eternal, transcendent atman, but also the suffering body, the evanescent thoughts, and the tumultuous emotions. I am the heat, the scabies, and the itching they are causing. I am everything. I am the One having this experience and the One who is its Creator. I saw that as long as I was still in the world, striving for the oneness of Advaita was as much a distortion of the truth as pursuing materialism—that the pursuit of disembodied spirituality was a colossal paradox.

The last night in Delhi before my flight home, I decided to celebrate the end of my pilgrimage in India with dinner at Gaylord, the popular five-star restaurant across Connaught Circle. I thought, even if the meal goes straight through, I'll be back in the States in twenty-four hours and can go to a doctor.

After wandering like a sadhu and being accustomed to sitting on rocks, it was a welcome treat to sink into the soft cushions of the luxurious restaurant. Almost oblivious of the surroundings, I devoured a delicious meal. Not until I was almost finished did I notice with wry humor that I was the only man wearing Indian clothes. All the others were wearing dark slacks, button-down shirts and jackets, and while I had been eating with my fingers in the traditional Indian style, the Indians were using western knives and forks. The Indians had becoming westernized and I had become Indian!

While waiting for a dessert of *kheer*, a delicious rice pudding, I reflected on the fruitless quest that had consumed the last six months of my life. Despite what I had read, that everyone has a Guru, I concluded that it must be my karma not to meet him in this life. Trying to shrug off the disappointment, I paid the bill and walked outside into the street.

A few steps from the door, a street urchin in tattered shorts ran up and blocked my path. Thrusting a book into my hands, he said "Swami, this is for you," then flashed a beautiful smile.

I assumed that he wanted money, so tried to walk around him. Whichever way I turned he reappeared before me. Finally, I looked down at the book, and was startled at the title: *Be Your Own Guru.*

That was answer—the Guru is within—probably what Maharajji had been trying to teach me all along!

I pulled some rupees from my pocket to buy the book, but the little boy had disappeared. I remembered how on the way to India some boys in Istanbul had placed a silver medallion around my neck, in Rishikesh a yogi had precipitated a meal, and now this boy had given me a book whose title contained the wisdom I had been seeking.

Walking back across Connaught Circle toward the hotel, I anticipated reading the book by candlelight before bed, but when I got back to the room I fell asleep. I rose early to get to the airport on time. Later, when I reached for the book after takeoff, it seemed to have disappeared. Its message, though, was clear in my mind. It had taken six months of wandering to find what was within me all along. I did not need a Guru at all.

Part II: Being My Own Guru

CHAPTER 40

Camped in People's Park

My plane landed in San Francisco in the spring of 1972, and I relaxed into the comforting embrace of the West. Simple pleasures—breathing fresh air unpolluted by burning cow dung, and the quietude unbroken by the honking of rickshaw horns—were a relief. Still, I missed the adventure and spiritual energy of being in one of the most ancient cultures of the world—where every street vendor and rickshaw driver seemed familiar with the ancient teachings of the Vedas. To keep that spiritual connection alive I kept wearing the white kurta, drawstring pants, and Rudraksha bead mala I had been given on my first day in India.

San Francisco's Haight-Ashbury district, where the flower children gathered for the Summer of Love in 1967, had become a haven for drug pushers and other petty criminals, so I took a bus to Berkeley. As I walked down Telegraph Avenue, past the boutiques and cafes, I chanted *Om Namah Shivaya*, the Shiva mantra that dissolves illusion. Perhaps many still wanted to pursue their illusions, for many people crossed to the other side of the street at my approach. Many still felt threatened by the hippie movement and its mystique of free love, drugs, and resistance to the Vietnam War. However, many were open to the sense of freedom and spiritual expansion the hippies represented. No one was unaffected by that movement toward freedom and peace. The hippie phenomenon affected every aspect of the American culture, eventually affecting the entire world.

As I walked down the Berkeley streets, I must have appeared as a spiritual teacher to some. Much as I had been drawn to the yogis of India, some now seemed drawn to me. However, I did not feel like a teacher, nor did I want to be one. The awakening I had experienced in India had stabilized, and now I simply felt like a normal person—despite how I appeared to others.

One afternoon, without realizing that anyone had been following me, I entered the One World Family Restaurant for a cup of tea, and several young people came in and sat down at my table.[153]

---

153 The One World Family restaurant was one of the first vegan restaurants

I was shocked when the girl on my left, who was wearing bells on her ankles and many strands of beads around her neck, looked deeply into my eyes and confessed, "I think you're my Guru."

That was followed by the guy on the right, a headband restraining his long hair and holding a guitar in his lap, who said, "Yeah, man, teach us something. You look like you just dropped in from the Himalayas. Can you share some enlightenment?"

For months I had been seeking a Guru. Now that I given up that quest, these people wanted me to be their Guru! I could feel their desire to be free of the tyranny of endless sensory pursuits and see the hunger for spirit burning in their eyes. I had never thought about teaching, yet their desire for illumination touched me deeply.[154] At the same time, I saw how becoming a spiritual teacher could be a death-blow to one's own spiritual quest, for unless one was stabilized in timeless consciousness, one's attention could easily drift back into the relative world of dealing with the outer demands of egos.

Not knowing what to say to these people, I sat staring into my teacup. A few others gathered around, waiting to hear what I would say, but I was at a loss for words. I understood now why so many yogis were silent. Excusing myself, I got up and said, "I'm sorry to disappoint you, but I can't teach you anything."

I shuddered at how fast they were ready to surrender their will to someone who offered a glimmer of truth.[155] Eager to get away from these

---

in the San Francisco area, with UFOs painted on the outside wall on Haste Street. It was founded by Allan Michael (1916–2010), a painter from Iowa, who claimed that space beings from the planet Galactica revealed that he was a Cosmic Messiah, the "Comforter" spoken of in the Bible (John 14:26). The restaurant was run by members of the idealistic commune he founded.

154 When someone asked Trungpa Rinpoche about enlightenment, he said, "I really don't know anything about it." Ma Amritanandamayi (The Hugging Saint) was asked the same question, and she said, "I'm just a crazy village girl."

155 Many bogus, self-deluded teachers did not hesitate to take advantage of this willingness to surrender, and many kids were seduced by various cults from which it was later difficult to escape.

would-be followers, I hurried out the door and made a quick turn around the corner and up Haste Street. There was a grassy field with a few random trees and shrubs called People's Park, and I threw my backpack on the ground and set up camp.[156] I decided to make the park my home until I had a feeling of what to do next. The wandering life of the sadhu had become a part of me, so I just sat under a tree and meditated. I would just sit there until I had a revelation.

The next day as I walked around the park, I discovered, ironically, that across the street was the Vedanta Society. In this beautiful home they held meditations and offered the teachings Swami Vivekananda had brought from India a hundred years ago. I wondered if instead of going to India I had come here instead, would I have attained the same spiritual realization? I knew the answer, that the goal was in the journey.

Late at night after the last person had left the park, I constructed a makeshift pillow out of my extra clothes, unrolled my sleeping bag between a couple of bushes, and slept soundly. I thought it strange that I was the only one sleeping in this beautiful field, but I didn't know the park's history. I had arrived during a lull in the violent battles between the University and the community. Only a few months before, the University had erected a chain-link fence to keep out homeless people, but local activists had torn it down. Innocent of the conflicts waged for that land over the years, I was probably one of its first homeless residents.

I slept soundly until the sun appeared over the Berkeley Hills and I awakened to find I was covered in dew. Reaching over, I grabbed my shoes

---

156 People's Park is owned by the University of California, but local residents claim the right to use it for activities benefitting the community, such as a playground for children, community vegetable garden, and a place for the exercise of free-speech. In 1969, conservative private property interests invoked the use of military force to attempt to enforce legal rights. After some bloodshed an uneasy truce was worked out, allowing some community interests to prevail. As of 2013, the park is co-managed by the University and various community groups. Food Not Bombs, the all-volunteer, international organization, distributes free vegetarian meals there to anyone who is hungry. People's Park now has basketball courts at one end for university students, a stage for concerts and rallies, and has become a center for the homeless.

and walked around the corner to the One World Family Restaurant. As I had a cup of tea, a compassionate girl who worked there by the name of Una, realizing that I was homeless, offered a sofa in their communal home nearby, but I said that I preferred the freedom of the park.

One morning I awakened to find my shoes gone. Sitting up, I looked around and finally found them on the other side of a shrub. Who had taken the shoes during the night from beside my face without my waking? Was this a sign that it was time to leave? But, where should I go? I remembered that Ram Tirtha had said Mount Shasta had the same spiritual energy as the Himalayas, and wondered if I should go there? As I was pondering, a young man came and sat down nearby.

"I see you sitting here every day and wonder if there is anything I can do for you?"

"I'm thinking of going to Mount Shasta," I said, somewhat hesitantly.

"That's fantastic, I hear all kinds of amazing stories about that place, that it's the home of the Great White Brotherhood."

My heart leapt as he spoke, and I knew that feeling in my heart was the guidance I had been seeking.

"I'll go to Mount Shasta then," I said, feeling once more the energy in the words as they came out of my mouth. As I stuffed my sleeping bag into my backpack, he gave directions to the Greyhound Bus station, and I said farewell to People's Park. At least I would be going to the legendary mountain, supposed home of the Great White Brotherhood!

CHAPTER 41

Visit to Mount Shasta

My first visit to Mount Shasta did not live up to my phenomenal expectations, something I have heard from others over the years who come to the mountain expecting other-worldly things to occur. Many expect to be taken inside the mountain, meet a Master, or at least see a UFO. When that does not happen, they often find a local psychic "channel" who will conjure up an account of what happened to them on inner planes, but which they were unable to "bring through" without the channeling. In time these legends grow and spread. I discovered later that the true beneficiaries of a visit to the mountain are instead those who seek the Masters within themselves. Only then does the mountain and its brotherhood reveal its secrets.[157]

The Greyhound bus stopped in front of the Lemurian Lodge at the north end of town. I had been told to contact "Brother Charles," the owner, who would be my guide.[158] His wife, Angela, greeted me, and when she said he was not available, as he was at a meeting, I was sure the meeting must be with the Masters. Instead of waiting until the next day, as I didn't want to waste any time, I asked her where the Lemurians could be found.[159]

---

157 The first two books by Godfrey Ray King, *Unveiled Mysteries* and *The Magic Presence,* are two of the most spiritually elevating books available, and reading them invokes the consciousness of the Ascended Masters; however, not everything described takes place in the outer world—despite claims to the contrary. That they are mostly records of inner experiences was explained to me by Pearl Dorris, a personal assistant to the books' author. He felt that at that time, the 1930s, if he said these were "inner" experiences many people would think he meant dreams. Hence, he said they were "real" experiences.

158 Charles Belmont had been an assistant to Lotus, Godfre Ray King's wife.

159 Lemurians: inhabitants of the continent known as Lemuria or Mu, which supposedly sank into the Pacific eons ago. In the 1860s Philip Sclater wrote in *The Manuals of Madagascar,* "I should propose the name Lemuria," for a lost continent, which existed in the Atlantic

"I hear that people usually see them at Sand Flat," she said, as if that was a usual question.

"And what about the space brothers?" I added.

"Sand Flat is also one of the landing areas for UFOs," but you better get going because it's going to be dark soon."

I thanked Angela, and with my pack on my back began trudging up the road toward the mountain. By the time I had gone a mile and saw the sun sinking toward the hills behind me, I realized that if I didn't want to get lost in the unfamiliar terrain I had better find a place to camp. I wanted to have a good night's rest before setting out the next day to meet the Masters and the other mysterious beings that Angela implied were on the mountain.

Seeing a field behind the public library, I threw my backpack on the ground, ate a few handfuls of trail mix, and pulled out my sleeping bag. I meditated until after dark and then lay down to sleep, not realizing that I was only a hundred yards from the home of Pearl, the one to whom the Master Saint Germain would send me a year later for training. Apparently I was not ready for that apprenticeship yet, and had still more travels ahead.

Before sunrise I was up and packed, and with great anticipation was on my way up the mountain. I stuck my thumb out, and the first car that came along gave me a ride. The driver said that McGinnis Springs was a much better place to meet the Masters than where Angela had suggested, so I let him drop me off at the entrance to the dirt road that led east around the mountain. After less than an hour I arrived at a pristine mountain pond and stashed my things between two red fir trees. I explored the area for a few hours and met some of the other people camping nearby. Late in the day I came back and after I set up camp, sat to pray "Great Ascended Masters,"

---

and Indian Oceans. The first mention of a city named Telos (a Greek word) was in 1958 in George Hunt Williamson's book, *Secret Places of the Lion*, which he said existed in the Four Corners area of the Southwest. The mythical city was later relocated to Mount Shasta by Bonnie Condey (aka Bonnie Dux), who later changed her name to Princess Sharula, a name she borrowed from the romance novel *Sunrise of Splendor*. For more on Telos, see Juan Hunu's eBook, *Mount Shasta Myths Exploded* (www.smashwords.com, 2010).

I implored from my heart, "I seek your guidance. If you are real, please reveal yourselves and tell me what to do with my life."

I heard nothing but the breeze whispering in the branches of the forest, and wondered if Ram Tirtha had been right, if there really were a race of Divine beings guiding the destiny of humanity? Then I lay down and went to sleep.

Mount Shasta and lenticular clouds

I woke in the morning hungry, and realized that I had not brought any food along. I decided to follow the aphorism, "A wise man, when forced to go without food, will fast." Another camper explained that there were edible plants around, such as the young shoots of fir trees, which the deer also nibbled. They had a zingy taste, but could only be consumed in small quantities. There was also pennyroyal, a member of the mint family, which I brewed into a tea using my single burner gas stove. I felt like a yogi again, fasting, meditating, and praying high on the slopes of the mountain. As Ram Tirtha had said, Mount Shasta was truly a transmitter of great spiritual energy, so I kept silence to store that energy within myself.

I prayed that my steps be guided so I would meet a Master, and hiked up steep ravines, over boulders, and through the tangles of manzanita bushes to find a likely place, but there were no Masters in the places I searched. Amazing lenticular clouds became stacked above the mountain, looking for all the world like space ships, but no one beamed down for a rendezvous. For days I fasted and bathed naked in the icy pond every morning, shouting *Om Namah Sivaya* before the shock of each plunge.

On the morning of the fifth day, as it was turning light, I woke hearing a voice—as though someone standing behind where I lay was speaking. The voice was friendly and as I wakened I looked around to see who it was, but no one was there—no one I could see. I had never heard a "voice" like this before and lay down, perplexed. As I gazed at the evergreen branches overhead the familiar voice continued, "Peter, you have asked for guidance with such sincerity that I have come to fulfill that request, and reveal to you your coming year."

He then proceeded to demonstrate that he knew all about me, and that he had been watching over me in India. He said, "You will return to your farm, then journey again to India—this time to see Sathya Sai Baba."

"No, I'm not going back there!" I shouted, but he continued undisturbed by my rebellion.

"Then you will return to the States, sell your farm, and return to Mount Shasta, which will become your home."

"No way!" My farm was an idyllic place near Woodstock, and I intended to live there on my pastoral hilltop overlooking the Hudson Valley forever.

"One more thing, Peter...."

"What's that?"

"I want you to change your name to Mount Shasta."

"What? I can't do that!" I had met so many westerners who had taken Hindu names but had not changed inwardly. The name worked for Ram Dass, but I saw it as potentially one more ego-trip—definitely not for me.

"As I said, you will change your name," he repeated, like a patient father "You will be known by the name of the Mountain—and this is your destiny."

"Mount Shasta? I can't take the name of a mountain!"

"We shall see," he said, with a firmness that brooked no opposition, and then he was gone. I rose and looked around for the stranger, but I was alone.[160]

---

160 People often assume that when they pray for guidance or for a vision of the future, that what is revealed will always be pleasant. That is why the Masters do not often channel or reveal the future, but rather teach the

I had received the guidance for which I had prayed, but didn't like anything I had been told. Return to India? Sell my farm? Move to Mount Shasta? Change my name? What he had said was the opposite of what I wanted. I got up and walked across the meadow to take my morning plunge and clear my head. Then I pulled on my drawstring pants and had a cup of strong pennyroyal tea.

A few days later the idea for a poem began to unfold and I began to write, the first writing since I had left New York. It was an apocalyptic vision about the dawning of the Spirit in the West—an awakening of consciousness that would happen after a time of clearing. I wanted to use a pen name, and then it occurred to me that I could use "Mt. Shasta."[161] Without realizing, I had already begun to follow the Master's guidance.

I broke my fast and vow of silence that evening, and then went to a nearby campfire. Someone said, "Hey, there's going to be a Rainbow Family gathering in Colorado. It's going to be a gathering of the tribes, and people are coming from all over the country to meditate, pray, and sing together—we should all go!"

It sounded good. After weeks on the mountain I felt like going to Colorado. It would be a good change. I packed my stuff and headed down the mountain. I had blocked out of my mind the visitation from the Master I had experienced the previous morning, and as I descended the mountain I was mildly disappointed that nothing more dramatic had happened. It had been a much needed healing retreat after being a sadhu in India, but now I felt the call of Colorado and the Rocky Mountains.

The Rainbow Family Gathering took place at Table Mountain, near Granby. It was sort of a Kumbh Mela in the Rocky Mountains, with 20,000 people coming to sit around campfires, tell stories, and sing their favorite songs. There was a sense of innocence, the feeling of a new era, one of love and peace; we felt that together we could do anything, even end the war in Vietnam—and bring peace to the world.

---

lessons that will prepare us for what they know is coming.
161 In many parts of the world people are, in fact, named after mountains, gems, flowers, rivers, virtues, and even Gods.

CHAPTER 42

The Avatar Appears[162]

It was good to return to my farm and rest from traveling. Although I was glad to be back in comfortable surroundings where I could pump cool, clear water from the well and eat vegetables from the garden, I was still a sadhu in many ways. I would begin the day at dawn with Ayurvedic internal cleansing, then walk barefoot in the dew of the emerald lawn to roll out a yoga mat and do asanas with a view of the Catskill Mountains in the distance. An hour of meditation would follow.

Since *Be Your Own Guru* had been handed to me by that kid on the street in Delhi, I had not thought any more about Gurus, but put all my efforts into meditation. Deep in the silence the self would disappear; I would lose all body consciousness, and then an hour later the consciousness of self and world would reappear. But then I would not want to do anything, just sit and watch the play of light in the mountains in the distance. I vacillated between two worlds, one of the spirit, pulling upward, and one material, that wanted to be healthy and happy in my earthly body.

I even entertained the idea of relationship, and one day drove down the winding Route 9G to a bar frequented by Bard College students. After sitting on a stool for a while, listening to the inane conversation, I left and returned to my solitary hilltop.

Summer passed before I realized it, and the cool winds of fall began turning the leaves bright colors, covering the garden with frost. Then the rains began and for days on end and I paced the house, looking

---

162 *Avatar:* descent of God, an embodiment of the *Paramatman* (Godhead) who descends to Earth in times of great need. The two best-known historical Avatars are Rama, twenty thousand years ago, and Krishna, five thousand years ago. The *Puranas* say that the current *Kali Yuga* (Age of materialism and strife) began when Krishna left the Earth in 3102 BCE. Within the Kali Yuga, which lasts 432,000 years, there is a 10,000 year Golden Age, which we may now be entering.

for something to do. The cold weather quelled my desire to do yoga, and I looked out at the rain-soaked fields, yearning for change. Out of desperation, one day I decided to plan next year's garden. As I rummaged through the bookshelf for the seed catalogs, I found a picture of Sathya Sai Baba that I had stashed there and forgotten about. Months before, an acquaintance by the name of Chris Curtis had mailed it to me. It was the photo of a strange looking man in India with an Afro hairdo, who Chris said was worshipped by millions. Chris said that Baba had come to him in meditation and told him to send me the picture. As I was through with Gurus and, in any case, would not want to return to the place where I had become so sick, I had thrown the picture in the bookcase among the pile of catalogs. I had long ago banished the words of the etheric being on Mount Shasta who had said that I would return to India to meet Sai Baba.

Although I had heard of this highly popular being while in India, who supposedly had God-like powers comparable to Rama and Krishna, I had been repelled by the miracles. I dreaded the thought of the mobs that would come to see these phenomena, for I knew that real spirituality, as Ramakrishna had said, was not dependent on such seeming miracles as healing the sick or materializing objects—all of which Sai Baba performed daily. Miracles were only a diversion from the real path of inner awakening, which needed no outer demonstration. Now, as this strange looking being in an orange robe smiled radiantly from the photo, I could find no fault. He seemed the embodiment of love, standing beneath a floral archway, beaming with happiness. The photo seemed to pulse with energy, and then suddenly came to life. I thought I must have been having some kind of optical problem, for the figure began to move. His hips swayed from side to side, and then he waved his hand! I could not believe my eyes. I blinked hard and looked again, and he laughed. A wave of love washed over me and I burst into tears.

Not since childhood had I cried like that, and then only from despair. Now I was feeling tears of joy—and was filled with ineffable happiness. Over and over I repeated the word for what I had never truly felt before, "Love...Love...Love....So, *this* is unconditional love!" I had heard of that, but it was not something I had experienced.

Sathya Sai Baba

Gradually I stopped sobbing. When I finally became calm after a while, suddenly the picture came to life once more. I was shocked as a ball of orange light emerged from the picture and Sai Baba stepped into the room. I had never felt a presence as powerful as this. He was vibrant with love, joy, and even a sense of humor. It was obvious that he knew me more thoroughly than a father—and that he saw into my very soul. Images began appearing before my inner sight, revealing things that could not be expressed in words. Then I was dissolving into light. He was like a sun, illuminating the room with a dazzling light, and then changing form. He was now a large, buxom, black woman, who threw her arms around my neck. As we embraced our bodies merged. At first the union had sexual energy, but then he drew that energy upward, energizing each chakra of the body, Divine bliss permeating every cell. I saw how each chakra had its own characteristic consciousness with its own characteristic worldview; but, as the energy reached the *ajna* chakra in the forehead, duality disappeared. There was no longer self and other, spirit and matter, male and female. All polarities merged into the unity of God. I felt the bliss of pure being, free from form, space, and time.

I realized now why it is said that a yogi can only endure this state of *nirvikalpa samadhi* for a short time without leaving embodiment, for if Sai Baba had not terminated it I felt that I would have left the world of form. Gradually, as I began to re-emerge from the light, and duality began to return, I heard Baba say, "Come visit me in India!"

Again I was alone, sitting on the floor, feeling overwhelmed. I had searched India in vain for a Guru and endured all manner of hardship. Now, after giving up, it seemed that I had been visited by a Guru who was God himself. The room was filled with an exquisite fragrance that lasted for days, that I would smell again only when in Sai Baba's presence.

Next morning, instead of doing my usual yogic routine, I phoned the airline and made a reservation to fly to India. Putting aside the memories of previous hardships, I could now only think of the impending visit to see Sai Baba. I was sure that, having transmitted God consciousness from the other side of the Earth to upstate New York, meeting him would even exceed the bliss Ram Dass had experienced when he first met Maharajji. At last, I was going to meet my Guru!

CHAPTER 43

Mother Mary Comfort Me

J ust before returning to India to see Sai Baba I went to see my friend Hilda Charlton. Paramahansa Yogananda had come to visit her when she was very ill as a young girl in Los Angeles. She was healed the moment he entered the room. He later asked her to join his organization and run one of his centers but she told him, "Swamiji, I say from my heart, though you asked me to stay, I cannot. I am like the wind, which blows through the trees. The world is my home…."[163]

Later, Hilda lived in India for eighteen years and studied with many saints and gurus. "Swami Muktananda is my Guru, but Sai Baba is my God," she said one evening. Although a great spiritual being herself, she never put on airs that she was anything other than a normal person.[164] People begged her to share her wisdom, so one night a week she led a group at St. Luke's Church in the West Village, which Krishna Das, Surya Das, and others who had visited Maharajji attended.[165] Some felt that they were only able to survive the materialism of the City because of this spiritual focus.

---

163 Reported by Jan, a friend of Hilda's, at www.writespirit.net/blog/2012/01/26/hilda-charlton-a-tribute/

164 I felt the same Divine, maternal quality shining in her as I felt in Anandamayi Ma, my later teacher Pearl Dorris, and Ammachi. In addition to their expanded consciousness they were also compassionate, willing to give personal advice, and not above cooking a meal or doing whatever work was needed at the moment.

165 Krishna Das travels the world leading devotional kirtan and his album, *Live Ananda,* was nominated for a Grammy Award in 2013. He wrote a moving book about his spiritual quest with Maharajji, *Chants of a Lifetime: Searching for a Heart of Gold* (Hay House, 2010).

Surya Das later became a Lama in the Tibetan Buddhist tradition, founded the Dzogchen Foundation, and wrote a number of books for westerners about the process of spiritual awakening. See his site: www.dzogchen.org.

Hilda Charlton with Sai Baba

She had a magic ring that Sai Baba had precipitated for her, and one night she placed it in my hand. It didn't look magical, but some said it was an All Seeing Eye that would show whatever you needed to see—more specifically, it would reveal the face of your Guru. Hilda knew I was going back to India and that I had wanted to look into the ring.

236

Peering into the polished green surface of the flat stone, I saw nothing at first, but I kept moving around the room to see it in different light. No matter how I looked at the smooth stone, it remained an enigma. Just as I was about to hand the ring back I decided to try one more time. Turning my full attention inward, I talked to the ring, "All right, show me my Guru!"

I beheld what I did not want to see. There in the stone, looking back at me, was the image of my own face—and wearing a turban!

Knowing that I would be gone soon, Hilda asked one day if I would like to go on an adventure with her. She was going to Newark, New Jersey, which didn't sound like much of an adventure; but, Hilda always had such fascinating stories about India and the amazing beings she had met, that I knew the time would not be wasted. I agreed to accompany her and one of her friends. We were going to see a statue of Our Lady of Fatima that had been brought from Italy, and that supposedly shed real tears. She was going to be exhibited at the Basilica of the Sacred Heart. I was skeptical of any miracle promoted by a church, but decided to keep an open mind.

At least the Catholic Church maintained some awesomely beautiful places of worship, and this cathedral was one of them. It was one of the largest cathedrals in North American and I could feel its spiritual energy the moment I entered. The cathedral was packed with parishioners and we were fortunate to find seats in a pew halfway toward the front, but the supposedly miraculous statue of Mary was resting on a palanquin hidden from view.

After some music and an opening greeting by the priest, he said that the long anticipated statue would soon be carried around the church so everyone could see her and receive her blessings. However, they were short one bearer and requested for a volunteer to come forward and help carry the Virgin around the cathedral. No one rose, but as he scanned the audience he suddenly pointed at me and beckoned me forward. Shocked, I thought he must have been pointing at someone else, and turned around.

"Yes, you," he said, beckoning.

Trembling, I stood up. I was wearing sandals, an old flannel shirt, and jeans and felt out of place among the well-dressed Catholics and amid the splendor of the Basilica. Slowly I gathered my courage and walked up to the front of the church and stood before the white-robed priest.

"Father, I'm not a Catholic," I confessed, praying that he would return me to the obscurity of my former seat.

"I know," he smiled.

Why did he want me? Yet, he was determined and beckoned me to join him and the other three bearers in black suits. We each took an end of one of the two poles on which the palanquin rested, my position being at the rear with the statue in front on the left. Resigned to my fate, I stood ready to lift the pole. However, motivated by curiosity, I decided to check the Madonna for the tears she was rumored to shed.

There were none; but, I was shocked to see, instead of the painted eyes of a wooden face, a pair of human eyes looking back at me—looking into my soul with such deep compassion that, stunned, I took a step backward. The priest looked at me with curiosity. Then he gave the signal. All four of us bent over and lifted the platform holding the statue. With the first step forward I felt a woman's hand on my right shoulder and turned to see who it could possibly be, but there was no one there. Then I heard a gentle, comforting, feminine voice say, "My son, have no fear of returning to India, for I will be with you."

An exquisite joy went through me so that I was barely able to continue. However, we walked slowly behind the priest, who swung a censer that sent clouds of frankincense and myrrh billowing toward the vaulted ceiling as he chanted in Latin. At the back of the cathedral we turned right after the last pew, crossed the back, and then walked slowly up the far aisle toward the front again. We made three tours around the cathedral, Hilda recounted later, though I could remember only the first—so sweet was the motherly love in which I was enveloped.

CHAPTER 44

The Power of Om

What world does he who meditates on Om until the end of his life, win by That? If he meditates on the Supreme Being with the syllable Om, he becomes one with the Light, he is led to the world of Brahman [the Absolute Being].

—Prashna Upanishad

Every New Age group in the 70s seemed to incorporate somewhere in their ritual the chanting of *Om*—the primordial sound from the source of creation, which the Vedas call the *Pranava*, the life breath. Often this chanting seemed to be done more as a duty, like saying Amen after a Christian prayer. So, I cringed on the night before my flight to India when Hilda asked the group to bless me by chanting *Om*. Obediently I stood and the group formed a circle. Each held up their hands in benediction and began to chant. They all chanted at their own pace, resulting in a constant, melodious drone.

To my surprise, I was soon enveloped in white light which became brighter and brighter until I was enveloped in a luminous cloud. All I could see was a sea of hands, and from each shone a beam of light. After a while the chanting subsided and I bowed in gratitude, feeling that I had received a true blessing.

Now I could well believe what I had read in the Upanishads, that meditation on the internal sound of *Om*, alone, would lead to God Consciousness. All I wanted to do was sit immersed in *that;* however, I had to go home and pack for the next day's flight to India.[166]

---

166 Meditation on *Om* leads to God Consciousness, but also raises one out of the human world. Use "I AM" affirmations to bring that consciousness into the world in daily life. See: *"I AM" Affirmations and the Secret of their Effective Use,* by Peter Mt. Shasta (Church of the Seven Rays, 2012).

CHAPTER 45

Darshan of Sri Prabhupada

The first leg of the return to India was a stopover in Birmingham, England. I had been invited to stay at the home George Harrison gave to the Krishna Consciousness movement, now called Bhaktivedanta Manor. The monks had turned it into an Indian ashram. I was guided to my room and then escorted to the shrine room, where I was told I could have the darshan of Sri Prabhupada. I was shocked that he was in residence there, because I hadn't heard anything about him in years and hadn't thought he was still alive. The monk was so enthusiastic, however, I looked forward to receiving his blessing.

He opened the door and I followed him into the elaborate shrine to Krishna. There was Sri Prabhupada, seated in full lotus position, and apparently deep in meditation. The monk prostrated, arms stretched overhead, face down on the floor. Then he rose with his head still lowered and backed out of the room, as it was considered disrespectful to turn one's back toward a Guru. Although impressed, I had no intention of throwing myself before Sri Prabhupada, or any other Guru for that matter, so I simply offered a respectful pranam and sat back against the wall to meditate with my eyes shut.

I was surprised to see him meditating because I knew he was a *bhakta*, one who practices the path of devotion, and that his devotees danced and chanted the Maha Mantra in devotion to Krishna for hours every day. I began thinking about how simplistic that was, and that the spiritual path had to be more complicated, and then I wondered, "Can he hear my thoughts?"

I regretted being so judgmental, but if he were truly enlightened he wouldn't care, would he? Telepathically, I begged, "Forgive me."

I opened my eyes slightly to see if he was frowning in displeasure, but he seemed to still be deep in meditation and lost to the outer world. Considering it an honor and blessing to be in such close personal contact with so renowned a Guru, I threw all my effort into my own meditation.

Soon I, too, was lost to the outer world. All fatigue from the nine-hour jet flight was washed away, as was my anticipation about the upcoming

241

flight to Bombay the next day. There was only the present moment, and I lost myself within.

Eventually I returned to body consciousness and opened one eye a crack to see if Sri Prabhupada was still meditating. When I saw that he was, I turned my attention inward again—feeling blessed that the Guru was allowing me to share his meditation—something unusual for the first contact. Again, I allowed myself to let go of all concerns, stilled my mind, and tried to merge in consciousness with the Guru before me. I asked to be forgiven for any judgments I had felt toward him, and now accepted our oneness—not only with him but also with the Krishna movement, which he had brought to the West. I visualized him merging with Krishna and dissolving into a ball of golden light. That light then entered my heart and expanded throughout my being—until I too became one with Krishna, the personality of the Godhead. As the light intensified and my body became warmer, I felt that surely all my impurities were being consumed. Just as I was merging with the light, the door opened a crack and the monk stuck his head in and whispered, "Dinner."

Not wanting to be disrespectful but also not wanting to keep my host waiting, I unfolded my legs and quietly prepared to leave. With head lowered I offered pranam again, then crawled to the door. Amazingly, Sri Prabhupada was still seated in full lotus position with eyes closed, and I was glad that the slight commotion had left his meditation undisturbed. I knew that a true yogi could sit for days like that, lost in samadhi, and was glad that I had finally encountered such a being.

After dinner the lack of sleep from the past several days caught up, and I went to bed. Next morning I was up early and ready for the ride to the airport, but didn't want to leave without seeing Sri Prabhupada one more time and expressing my gratitude. The airport taxi had come, so I asked one of the monks, "Is Sri Prabhupada up yet so I can say goodbye?"

"Well, he is up. In fact, he never sleeps."

Now I was truly impressed. He was far more advanced than I had originally believed, and I thought of canceling the trip and staying here. He had surely found the inner Source, and surely there was much this Guru had to teach.

"You will have a hard time communicating with him, I'm afraid."

"Why is that?"

"Because the form you received darshan from last night in the shrine room is made of wax."

CHAPTER 46

The Abode of Everlasting Peace

Hot and exhausted after the long flight to Bombay and a connecting flight to Bangalore, I was not looking forward to a long taxi ride over bone-jarring roads to the ashram. It was the fall of 1972; only five years before there had been no road, only a rutted dirt path for bullock carts. I had prayed to Baba for help on the journey, yet was surprised when a well-dressed Indian man spoke as I was leaving the plane, "Would you be going to see Sathya Sai Baba, Sir?"

"Yes, I am."

"If you like I can give you a ride straight to Puttaparthi. I'm going there myself and my driver is waiting outside."

True enough, as soon as we descended the stairs there was a shiny black Mercedes waiting on the tarmac. His uniformed driver took my bag and opened the door. In air-conditioned comfort I was off to Puttaparthi. My excitement rose at the prospect of soon seeing the amazing being who so recently had appeared on my farm and whose love had reduced me to tears.

Watching the dusty, sweltering streets filled with water buffaloes, rickshaws, and throngs of people wandering about, I seemed to be a dream. Sooner than I imagined, we entered the archway leading into the ashram and I felt a surge of spiritual energy. I thanked the man who had provided the luxurious ride, and walked under the elaborate arch and slowly up the path to the mandir (temple). On the left was a crowd of men in white. On the right were the women in a sea of brightly colored saris. Birds of brilliant plumage chattered and fluttered in the palms overhead. Then a hushed silence fell over the crowd. On the balcony of the temple in his flaming orange robe and unmistakable bushy hair, was Sathya Sai Baba. He raised his arm and waved in welcome.

Was he waving at me? That seemed hard to believe, so I turned to see if there was someone else to whom he was waving, but no one was there. I returned his wave, and for a moment I again felt his intense gaze. He waved once more, and then walked back along the balcony to his room.

"Surely, now he will send someone out to get me," I thought, anticipating the reunion I had rehearsed over and over in my mind since the etheric union with him a few weeks before. Or, perhaps he will come out and get me himself? I sat down to wait but no one arrived, and soon I heard that we could go inside the mandir (temple). He was going to lead the evening bhajans. As soon as the doors opened, I walked into the ornately decorated shrine room and sat down on the stone floor in the front row.

Soon Baba entered and sat on his throne-like chair. He led us in *Omkar*, in which we slowly chanted *Om* twenty-one times. Then he stood and walked directly up to me, stopping with his feet almost touching my knees. I thought that surely he was going to speak, but instead he began to sing, and in a voice of such sweetness that it would have melted a rock. My heart began overflowing with such love that I had to restrain the tears. For a half hour he continued to sing, and I felt that he was singing directly to my heart. I felt old wounds enveloped in a healing balm. When his singing finally stopped, the *pujari* (temple priest) did a brief ceremony, waving burning camphor before the shrine. Then Baba left and everyone filed out. I vowed that I would sit in the same front seat the next day as well and once again allow my heart to fill with this Divine nectar; but, from then on it was difficult to squeeze into the room and I had to sit near the back. It seemed that on my first day that front row seat had been reserved.

After that, Baba seemed to ignore me. Once again, I was only one ant among tens of thousands in this anthill, all swarming around the same focus of sweetness.[167] In my dreams, however, it was a different story, for he would appear nightly. There he was the embodiment of wisdom and compassion, teaching many wonderful things. He was both the perfect father I had barely known, as well as the embodiment of the motherly love I had rarely felt. The old, seemingly imperfect parents were dissolving, and he was replacing them as a Divine father and mother.

Thousands of people were also waiting for personal contact with Swami. Everyone wanted the all-important private interview so they could ask their long-cherished questions and beg for boons.

---

167 *Puttaparthi:* anthill, the name the town was called by villagers prior to the birth of Sai Baba.

"I give you what you want, until you want what I have come to give," he said on occasion. And when asked what that was, he said sweetly, *"Prema"* (Divine love).

I became resigned to waiting, and knew that I would receive what I needed at exactly the right time. However, my heart longed for a word from him or even a glance. In the mean time I worked on myself, cutting through the illusions and attachments I hadn't perceived, and which were now bubbling to the surface. Far from being tranquil, the ashram was a pressure cooker.

CHAPTER 47

Accha!

Since Americans have never had a monarchy and not been conditioned to bow or accept anyone as superior, I was disgusted to see people bow at Sai Baba's feet. Even if he is God in human form, he says that we are all Gods—so why bow?

My foot was throbbing from an infection, shooting a red line up my leg. The nurse in the ashram infirmary had said to keep the wound dry, but that was impossible in the torrential rains. Residents of the ashram were expected to attend bhajans, but I felt weak with fever and skipped them this evening. I could hear everyone singing in the mandir, where I knew I was supposed to be. It was always the high point of the day to sit before Baba as he poured out his love and a palpable sense of grace. However, this evening I felt sad. I knew I needed more thorough medical attention than I could get here.

"What's the point?" I thought, "I have come all the way from New York to see Baba and he hasn't spoken a word to me. He's ignoring me the same as other Gurus on my previous trip to India. I know that the Guru is within, so why did I come back here? This trip has been for nothing. I'll call the airline tomorrow and book a flight."

As the sun sank into the horizon, I watched the deepening purple twilight and breathed in the refreshing cooler air of evening. The birds chattered in the trees as though they too were soothed by the bhajans. As I looked up at them perched overhead I saw the changing hues of the sky through the branches. In the distance I could hear the singing and pictured Baba leading everyone as he always did from his throne at the front of the mandir.

Oblivious to where I had wandered, I noticed that the birds had suddenly stopped singing. Since it is always significant when the wind changes directions or when noisy animals suddenly become quiet, I stood still and turned my attention inward. I felt that I was being watched and that I was not alone. I whirled around and, sure enough, there was Baba standing a short distance away. A wave of love poured through me and without thinking I dropped down on one knee and raised my hands in prayer. I was overwhelmed and remained kneeling. Like Hanuman at the feet of Rama, I wanted to continue to bask in this love.[168]

"Accha," he said tenderly, nodding his head from side to side. It was an Indian gesture that could mean anything, but which I recognized now was an expression of unconditional love and acceptance.[169] He nodded in acknowledgment of my pranam, and then walked back toward the mandir to finish leading bhajans.

"What happened?" I wondered, as I realized that I was kneeling in the sand. Spiritual pride dies a hard death, but at some point the mind submits when it recognizes its Master residing in the heart.

---

168 Hanuman: a Deity who appears to be part man, part monkey, and who is totally dedicated to Rama, the seventh Avatar of Vishnu. The *Ramayana* describes how he is offered the chance to merge with the beloved Avatar, but he chooses to stay separate in order to remain in constant love and adoration to Rama.

169 *Accha:* an expression heard all over India that can mean anything from "Good" to "All right" or "I hear what you're saying."

CHAPTER 48

Judge Not

After the one-to-one meeting with Baba I decided to stay a bit longer. At night I slept outside his door on a straw mat, making myself completely available in case he was awake at night and wanted to talk. At least I would absorb some spiritual radiation by being that close. Although the door never opened, he did come to visit in dreams— and in that plane he taught more than would be possible in a physical meeting. When he appeared in those dreams, there would be a shock of love like an explosion in the center of my being, followed by a mind-to-mind transmission of spiritual mysteries providing an illumination my soul craved.

As his birthday approached and thousands of people arrived every day for the celebration, I was told I could no longer sleep outside his door. I would have to move to the "shed," a building under construction that was presently just pillars supporting a metal roof over a sand floor. I staked out a spot and unrolled a mat, putting my backpack at the foot and cooking gear at the head. Since there were no walls, wild dogs came in at night, sniffed out food, and stole what they could. They were sickly, possibly rabid, and we were told to sleep with a stick by our sides to beat them off.

I would be awakened by people's shouts at these dogs, and occasionally hear the "thwack" of a stick hitting a dog's flank. I prayed before going to sleep that I would not be disturbed by any of these pathetic creatures, and drew a mental circle of light around my sleeping area. That visualization worked for a while, until one night I woke to find that a dog had entered the magic circle and, worse, was lying against my body. Yet, instead of repugnance, I felt bliss, every cell seeming to be illumined by an inner sun.

Gradually, as human consciousness stirred, I awoke to the realization that the head of a huge black dog was pressed against my heart, and his mouth was only a short distance from mine. As his eyes looked soulfully into mine, I raised my head and saw that his body was covered in mange and that his bare skin was pocked with open sores. In a flash, I was wide-awake and on my feet, the stick raised menacingly over my head.

"Get out, get out!" I shouted.

At my threats the thin beast rose to its feet and hobbled out of range, looking back over its shoulder with a hurt, sorrowful look. Its dark eyes penetrated my soul, and at that moment I realized the bliss was gone and the light had gone out. With a seemingly human whimper, the enigmatic creature scampered off into the night.

As the last of the adrenaline drained away, the cool, jasmine-scented night air brought me back to my senses. Still, I was haunted by the memory of those penetrating eyes and the bliss that had filled my body. I lay down again on the mat and went over what had happened. As I drifted off, I realized the fragrance in the air was not jasmine, but the unique fragrance of Sai Baba's vibhuti, the sacred ash he materializes as a sign of his grace.

In the morning I sat on a wall by the shed, eating an orange and contemplating the experience with the dog the night before. A man holding a book about Sai Baba sat down on the wall next to me and started to talk about the book's fascinating stories.

"Here's one," the stranger began. "It's about a woman who baked some sweets to take to Baba. She put them in the window to cool, but a big black dog came along and ate them. She ran outside and beat the dog with a stick. The next day when she went to see Baba she apologized.

'Baba, I made some sweets for you but a dog took them.'

'Yes, why did you beat me when I ate them?'

"Pulling up his robe, he showed the woman his side, which was black and blue. Then the woman realized that the dog had been Swami."

CHAPTER 49

Celestial Visitors

I had found a quiet place to sleep on the roof of one of the buildings, away from the teeming throng of the sheds. Early one morning before the sun rose and it was just becoming light, I lay on my back looking up at the sky. Apart from the single disk-shaped cloud directly above the mandir there was not another cloud in the sky. For some reason this cloud fascinated me, as it was low in the sky and seemed to radiate energy. I had previously seen some of these lenticular clouds over Mount Shasta. Many felt they were UFOs, cloaked to prevent panic, but I had never seen one in India. As I watched I marveled that, despite the wind, it continued to hover directly above Swami's living quarters. After about a quarter of an hour, during which I could not take my eyes from it, two beams of light shot from the side of the cloud and it began to move slowly away and finally disappear.

Lenticular cloud

Later that morning I talked to others who all said, "Did you see that amazing cloud over the mandir? It looked as though Swami was being visited by beings from space."

It was not until later that I heard of Raja Reddy's experience. He was one of Swami's attendants who performed the daily *jyoti* (light) ritual of offering burning camphor before the shrine. He had been sleeping on the veranda outside Swami's room when he awakened to a light shining between the slightly open doors. Being curious as to why there was light at this early hour, he looked in and beheld several celestial beings conferring with Swami, as well as seven great lights.

Later in the day when he asked Swami what he had seen, Swami said that the *Devathas* (celestial beings) had come for his darshan, and that the seven flames were the *Saptharishis*, the great Masters of the Seven Rays.[170] Of course, Masters can travel anywhere by the power of thought, but I was sure that these other beings had come in the cloud seen by so many that morning.

---

170 *Saptharishis*, the Seven Elohim or Seven Spirits of Creation. These aspects of Divinity manifest on many levels and are activities that are carried out at different times by different souls. In the western esoteric tradition they are sometimes called the Chohans of the Seven Rays.

CHAPTER 50

The Kalki Avatar[171]

One day I heard about Halagappa, a thief who used to steal baggage from the bus station. Now he maintained an orphanage and miraculous temple in Srirangapatna, a small town on the Kaveri River in the Mandya District, halfway between Bangalore and Mysore.

One day he had gone to Puttaparthi and Baba had asked him, "Why do you steal?"

"To support my family," the thief replied.

"Why don't you ask God for what you need?" Baba asked.

"How will God hear me?"

Baba gave the thief a photo of himself and said that whenever he needed money he should talk to the picture. Halagappa remained skeptical but said he would try. When his money ran out weeks later and he thought about returning to stealing, he looked at the picture and thought, "Well, Baba, now I need money."

Next morning as he started out the door he looked back and there, sticking out of a corner of the picture frame, was a fifty-rupee note. He then hung many more pictures of Baba on his walls, and they began to generate vibhuti. Although his fellow thieves wanted nothing more to do with him, people began showing up at his door wanting to pray before these pictures—and they would make donations. He began to maintain his home as a shrine and then an orphanage, and donations more than covered his expenses.

I decided to visit this former thief and took the bus to Bangalore. From there I shared a taxi with a group of men who wanted to go to Mysore. We should have arrived at Srirangapatna that evening, but the driver was tired and pulled over to sleep and we didn't arrive until the next morning at dawn.

It seemed as though I was expected. Wearing a white t-shirt and dhoti

---

171 *Kalki Avatar:* tenth avatar of Vishnu, whom it was prophesied would come riding a white horse.

wrapped around his waist, Halagappa offered a friendly greeting as I walked up the path. No sooner had I put down my backpack than he placed an amulet with Baba's picture on it in the palm of my hand. I stared at the smooth plastic image as a dew-like drop formed and ran off the surface onto my hand. It gave off a celestial fragrance unlike anything I had ever smelled, and that dissolved all trace of fatigue. Another drop formed and then another; soon a rivulet was running into my palm and between my fingers. To contain the liquid I put the amulet in a quart-sized can, and watched the fluid reach the brim, then stop. He removed the amulet with a spoon and poured off the *amrit* (Divine nectar) into two clean soda bottles with screw caps.[172] I had not eaten since the previous day, as I had been unable to find food that was not too spicy, and now broke my fast with this precipitated nectar. That drink was the most delicious thing I had ever tasted. Later I was told Baba said that drinking this amrit frees one from the cycle of birth and death.

The next morning I went into the shrine room to meditate. On the front wall were many pictures of Baba, all covered with thick layers of *vibhuti*.[173] This ash was said to afford protection and was credited with many healings. Yet, what attracted my attention was a striking picture of Baba riding a white horse through the sky. He held the scales of justice in his left hand and as I watched an amazing thing happened. The picture came to life and the horse galloped toward me straight out of the picture, and a sharp, two-edged sword, which I knew was Truth, emerged from his mouth. Behind him mushroom clouds of nuclear explosions blossomed terrifyingly from the desert. At the bottom of the picture I read,

---

172 *Amrit:* nectar of immortality. This liquid is symbolic of the subtle liquid secreted by the pituitary glad of yogic adepts, which is said to confer immortality. A friend told me that when he first heard of Sai Baba, a drop of amrit ran down the center of his forehead.

173 *Vibhuti:* ash symbolic of what is left of the body after cremation. As death can come at any moment, it is a constant reminder to keep one's attention on that which is permanent and eternal. It is generally produced by burning special wood in a Vedic ritual and is either consumed or applied to the body. Sai Baba frequently materializes this ash for devotees, and its use has resulted in many miraculous healings.

And I saw heaven opened and beheld a white horse, and He who sits upon it is called Faithful and True; and in righteousness He judges and wages war. And His eyes are a flame of fire, and upon His head are many crowns; and He has a name written upon Him which no one knows except Himself. And He is clothed with a robe the color as though dipped in blood; and His name is called The Word of God. And the armies which are in heaven, clothed in fine white linen, follow Him on white horses. And out of his mouth proceedeth a sharp two edged sword, so that He may smite the nations; and He will rule them with a rod of iron; and He treadeth the wine press of the fierce wrath of God, the Almighty. And on His robe and on His thigh is written, KING OF KINGS, AND LORD OF LORDS. "

—Book of Revelation 19:11-16

The horse galloped through the sky above the ruins of the world and I saw that Baba weighed the souls of human being in his scales. Then he spoke:

It is to prevent this destruction that I have come. Yet, every person must choose his own path and be judged accordingly, for everyone makes his own destiny and judges himself. There will be great changes and disasters on the Earth, but so long as you have me in your heart you will have nothing to fear. Rest assured, not even a sparrow falls to the ground of which I am not aware. Know that I am with you always.

In every age when darkness threatens to destroy humanity, a Divine being appears as a deliverer for those who will heed the call. In the past Rama came to slay certain demonic beings and restore righteousness. Later Krishna came to establish love and devotion. Other unique beings such as Jesus and Buddha have also been sent as light bearers and teachers. Now, at this crucial juncture, with humanity in danger of extinction and the forces of ego and materialism at their peak, Sai Baba has come to restore righteousness and usher humanity into an era of peace.

255

CHAPTER 51

Swami, Swami

On Baba's birthday and for days leading up to the celebration, even though it was the dry season, it rained for days. Baba said that was because he was displeased, because people came to seek "tinsel and trash" and witness miracles, rather than to obtain that which for which he had come, to give liberation. He said that he was causing this discomfort so people had to at least make some slight sacrifice to obtain the blessing he was imparting to those who attended his birthday celebration. It was obvious that this massive gathering was, for him, purely an opportunity to give blessings to the several million people who attended over the course of several days.

Sitting cross-legged on the stone floor of the mandir hour after hour, among the twenty thousand others who had come to receive blessings, eventually my knees became so sore that I could no longer remain seated. Although Baba was already displeased, I did not want to cause him any further displeasure by leaving. Nor did I want to miss out on any blessings.

A woman whose inner sight was open said that the previous day she had seen a beautiful green ball of light emerge from Baba's head. He had plucked it and thrown the ball above the audience, where it exploded in the air. A spark of that light had gone into everyone in the temple. I didn't want to miss another such blessing, but finally I could wait no longer and had to leave. Struggling over the throng of bodies, I stumbled into the rainy night. The downpour soon soaked my thin cotton clothes as I slogged barefoot through the mud toward the porch where I was staying. I apologized inwardly to Baba for leaving, but since I was only one among the millions, it seemed that he wouldn't notice that I had left, or even care.

It was a relief at first to stretch my legs and get out of the confined space, but as I walked and the rain soaked my clothes, I became sad. Again I felt, "I have come all this way to see him and am just one insignificant dot in the crowd. On top of that it's his birthday and he's displeased. Although I have done my best to send him my love and blessings, obviously that has not been good enough. Now I'm wet and cold and want to go home."

Stumbling around in the dark, I finally came to the shed where I had previously stayed, and entered to get out of the rain. Looking around, I saw it was empty. Seemingly out of nowhere, two ragged men in turbans appeared at my feet and rose from the floor. Before I knew what was happening, they threw a huge Turkish towel over my head and began drying my hair.

"Swami, Swami, you are all wet; let us dry you off," they said, lovingly, as they continued to rub the warm, dry towel from my head all the way down my body to my feet.

How strange, I thought, for them to call me "Swami," also to touch me in a country where people do not even shake hands. Where did they get this large, fluffy towel? It was warm, as if it had just come out of the dryer. Even the best store in Bangalore did not sell a towel like that.

As they worked down my body they massaged my arms and legs, and shortly I was rejuvenated and filled with love. Miraculously, I was bone dry, even my clothes. I savored the euphoria in which I was enveloped and looked around to thank the two men, but there was no one there. The shed was empty. They had simply disappeared!

CHAPTER 52

Secret Meeting

After the crowds departed, I went back to camping out in front of the mandir. I put my straw mat down under a palm tree where I could look up at Baba's window. He never slept, according to those who attended him, but would sit up in bed during the night working inwardly to help his devotees. Before lying down I would sit in meditation, trying to synchronize my intent with his. Then, as soon as my body was asleep, he appeared and taught what I was ready to learn. I would awaken in the morning with the memory of his visit and his overwhelming love. As the sun rose he would walk out on his balcony and give darshan.

One morning instead of waiting for darshan I felt a strong pull to hike up the mountain behind the ashram. Going up the trail I came to the tree Baba had planted many years before and designated as a place for meditation. Then I continued up the path that followed the ridge until I was high above the village of Puttaparthi. I could see the ashram far below and the arid valley through which the Chitravati River flowed into the distance.

Eventually I came to a tiny thatched hut without a door. Feeling hot from the climb and the intense morning sun, I sought shelter under the straw roof. The hut was no more than seven feet across and had a straw mat on the floor. It seemed an ideal bungalow for meditation, so I sat and turned my attention inward. No sooner had I shut my eyes than an overwhelming spiritual energy flooded through me. The physical world seemed to waver and turn to light. Finally, unable to withstand the pull out of the body, I lay down and immediately fell asleep.

Someone was calling, so I ventured outside. There was Swami and two beings in white robes. With a shock I realized that one was the Master Jesus. The other was the one who had visited me ethereally in Nainital during my acid experience and told me to meditate on "I AM." A few months later I would meet him in his physical form as the Master Saint Germain. He had been well-known in the courts of Europe prior to the French Revolution, the one about whom Voltaire had said, "He's the man who knows everything, and never dies."

Ignoring my shock at seeing them, they stood humbly—except for the penetrating depth of their eyes and the overwhelming love they expressed. While I wondered the occasion for this remarkable visit, Sai Baba began to speak.

"My son, you have been brought here to awaken you to your mission. You have completed the first third of your life—which has been for training and the working out of human karma. Now begins the next phase of your existence, in which your true service begins. It is time for you to remember who you are, and to awaken to your Divine nature and purpose."

As he finished speaking, he placed his hands on my head. Suddenly I was above the Earth, and in a body of a still higher frequency, and in full communion with the Source. I remembered now that these two Masters in white robes were the ones who had escorted me to Earth prior to human embodiment, who had stripped me of awareness and forced me to forget. Now they had come to help restore that awareness.

Then I was once more standing among them outside the bungalow. They bowed and disappeared. Awaking on the straw mat, I crawled outside, but the visitors were gone. My head spun as I realized that my life on Earth had been only a moment, like the nap from which I had just awakened.

As I descended the mountain I realized that my work was beginning, but I was unsure what form it would take. For the next few days I did not attend darshan, but sat under the meditation tree to assimilate the returning consciousness.

How was my work to manifest? Seeking to know the details, I once again climbed the mountain to seek that straw hut where already so much had been revealed. Starting early to avoid the heat of the day, I packed a lunch so that I could stay as long as I needed. Following the same trail, I reached the place where I had been the day before, but the hut was gone. I climbed further up the ridge and looked down. From that height I could see the whole side of the mountain and the path upward, but I could not see the hut anywhere. I sat down on an outcropping and ate lunch, continuing to scan the mountain. Finally, I started down. Again, I came to the spot where the hut had been a few days before—but there was no sign of anything ever having been there. It seemed that instead of knowing all the answers, I would have to be patient and wait for destiny to unfold, living life one moment at a time.

CHAPTER 53

The Impersonal Life

I still wanted Baba to give me a specific meditation or yogic technique that would keep me in a constant state of God conscious awareness. I heard from some that in private interviews Baba had given them mantras that had changed their lives, so I prayed that Baba would give me one also.[174] I didn't have long to wait, for the next day after lunch, as I lay on the floor looking up at the ceiling, I felt Baba's presence, and heard three Sanskrit words. As I sat up and began repeating them I felt the door of consciousness opening.

Every day I repeated the mantra as often as I could. At first the results were amazing, but after a week its magic began to wear off. By the second week it seemed to lose its power.

There were other spiritual practices that Baba gave people, and I tried them too, but each faded with time. As the departure date stamped on my return airline ticket neared, I felt frustrated that I had not found one method that worked continuously without losing its power. Then it occurred to me that I had not actually asked Baba the question, but rather had been telling him what I thought I needed. He had simply been fulfilling my requests. Now I was determined to get an answer and I sat down and wrote him a letter. I realized that he knew my thoughts and could answer them inwardly, but also that he sometimes wanted us to ask directly and to take physical action—so, I wrote him a letter.

I thanked him for his love and grace and then asked the same question

---

174 Most of the power of a Sanskrit mantra is in the vibration of the sound. These vibrations bring about a specific effect and are often appropriate only for an individual during a certain period of time. Once the energy has been assimilated or the cycle passed, the mantra is discontinued. Other mantras are general, such as the Gayatri, which can be used with great benefit by everyone. Mantras in more derivative languages derive most of their efficacy from the meaning of the words and the consciousness invoked by that meaning.

I had asked Neem Karoli Baba, "Where should I go and what should I do and, above all, what specific spiritual practice I should do?"

I folded the sheet of paper, stuffed it in an envelope, and brought it to darshan. Instead of seeming oblivious to my presence and walking by without giving any notice, as was his usual practice, today he stopped directly in front of me and began talking to the person on my left.

I have come all this way to see him, I thought, yet have had no contact. I have received many spiritual blessings but would like some outer physical recognition of our bond as well, no matter how slight, even the touch of a finger.

As he finished conversing with the person on the left he turned and started walking away, then casually extended his hand backward and closed his hand on my letter. At that moment he extended his forefinger and touched mine. For a second he paused with the tips of our first fingers touching. As he took my letter I heard him say inwardly, "Peter, take *padanamaskar.*"

This was the offer to touch his feet, considered to be the ultimate blessing, for it was said to absolve all karma and assure liberation. Without waiting for him to say the words outwardly, I placed a hand on each foot and held on to them for what seemed an age. It was a magical moment in which I felt that he and I were one. I felt complete, as though I had finally received that for which I had returned to India.

Then Swami turned and walked down the line to visit the thousands still waiting for his darshan. I sat stunned, lost in reverie, until suddenly someone I knew came up behind and thrust a small, black book, *The Impersonal Life,* into my hands.

"It's a going away present," he said.

The book was open and I read the underlined statement,

Meditate on "I Am That I Am."

I knew that was Baba's answer, for I had asked him in the letter what spiritual practice to do. Once more I was reminded of the "I Am," which I had read about in *Unveiled Mysteries.*

"What is the power in those simple words?" I wondered. People say them every day. If they were something special, wouldn't I have known it by now? Perhaps they were like a Zen koan that could not be answered directly? I vowed to meditate on "I AM," and see what would happen. It would be months before I discovered their secret power. Sitting in a living room in Northern California before a lady named Pearl, I would begin to realize,

I am God.

As I read *The Impersonal Life*, I realized how different this direct path was from the devotional path exemplified by Hanuman kneeling before Rama. Even though many worshipped Sai Baba as the Avatar, as God incarnate, he always encouraged people to seek their own Divinity.

As Christmas approached, Baba moved to Kadugodi, a small village outside Bangalore where he had founded a college, and I decided to follow in order to spend my last week in India with him. I found an empty shed where someone let me stay. Even though I could see stars through the roof and got wet when it rained, I felt lucky to be only a stone's throw from Baba's house.

On Christmas day the students at the college put on a pageant about the life of Jesus. Before it began, Baba walked onto the stage and the student actors bowed and touched his feet, as was the Hindu custom. He tried unsuccessfully to stop them, and then walked to the front of the stage and spoke words I will never forget:

Yes, it is true that I am God, but so too are you God. You are all avatars in seed form. I am only an example. What I am, you can also become. Every day, throughout the day, you should say to yourself over and over, "I Am God, I Am God, I Am God," and in that way you will become God. What your attention is on, you become. If your attention is on God within you, you will become God.

He said that Jesus was an example of a living Master, and that by meditating on the statements Jesus made in the Bible, each of us could become a Christ. Then he repeated some of Jesus' most powerful affirmations:

I Am the way, the truth and the life.

I Am the resurrection and the life.

I Am the Light of the world.

Slowly I began to feel the power in the words "I AM." As he repeated them I began to see they were not an expression of the personal ego, but an affirmation of the transcendent Self, the Paramatman. In that consciousness there is neither me/mine, nor self/other. Duality is finished, and one begins to live the impersonal life of God conscious *being*.

CHAPTER 54

Revelation

While at Puttaparthi I heard of the great sage, Bhrigu, who a thousand years before Christ had written about the future destinies of over half a million souls.[175] I had met several people who had visited various Bhrigu *shastris* (scholars), and they told of personal prophecies that had proved correct. The original book, which was written on leaves, had largely been destroyed by Muslim invaders; however, various sections had been preserved and there were specially trained readers one could consult. Since I was curious to know more about my destiny, I decided to consult the shastri in Mumbai. I had to return home through Mumbai anyway. The shastri had a collection of the palm leaves that had been in his family for generations.

Accompanied by the translator who had made the appointment, we went to the shastri's apartment. When I walked through the door, I was surprised that the first thing the shastri did was measure the length of my shadow, note the exact time, and go to his desk and scribble some calculations. With that information he knew which stack of leaves to consult. In the living room one wall was filled with shelves on which were stacked neat piles of rectangular leaves. He motioned me to sit, then went to the shelf and selected the indicated stack of about a hundred leaves, which he brought back to the desk. Each leaf told the story of past and future incarnations of a single *jiva* (soul).

He began to read the first leaf, looking at me occasionally for confirmation. That life, however, was not mine. He read through the beginnings of about twenty-five lives, but none of them described me accurately. Some lives had similar beginnings but soon digressed from

---

175 The sage Bhrigu lived in the Vedic period approximately 1,500 to 500 BCE, and is considered to be the father of *Jyotish*, predictive Indian astrology. During the Muslim invasion in the 12th and 13th centuries most of his predictive horoscopes were destroyed, with about ten percent now being scattered around India.

mine. After an hour I began to despair. Then he read a leaf that perfectly described my life up to the present moment.

It told of my birth in America, my parents divorcing when I was two, being raised by my mother and feeling like a stranger in the West. It said that I would go to college, change majors, and that after a couple of restless years would awaken spiritually and come to India in search of a Guru. I would be disappointed on the first trip, but would return to meet the Avatar, who would awaken me to my purpose. It gave my age at these turning points, and finally said that I had been in India in many previous lives and in a recent one been a spiritual teacher. I would eventually return to India and my previous ashram would be returned.[176] This prediction, written over a thousand years ago, concluded with the time at which I would come to consult this oracle—which was the present.

---

176 In the esoteric tradition an ashram is not necessarily physical but can be an etheric ashram, or even a group taught solely on spiritual planes.

CHAPTER 55

Healing by the Space Brothers

I was glad to be back on the farm. It was a good place to heal. From the time I had drunk the water from the Ganges at the Kumbh Mela, I had been plagued by dysentery, and my weight had dropped from one hundred eighty-five to one hundred nineteen pounds. I had tried all kinds of medicines and diets. I would rise before dawn and spend the next couple of hours doing various Ayurvedic cleansing practices and yoga, followed by an hour of meditation, yet my health did not improve. Feeling that I was wasting away, I prayed for guidance and heard within, "Open the Bible and read the first thing you see." I flipped it open and read words to the effect:

> *Don't kill yourself trying to be too holy. Just love God, and do the work that is at hand.*

That was exactly the permission I needed. Trying to be a yogi in the West had gotten to be a strain, so I stripped off my white clothes and mala from India and put on the old flannel shirt and blue jeans I used to wear. What a relief not to have to work so hard on being spiritual! I picked up a paintbrush and began the long deferred project of painting the house, enjoying the mindless slap...slap of the brush on the wood siding.

At the end of a hot day of painting, I walked across the field and through the woods to a roadside bar. I sucked down an ice-cold beer, as I would have done in my pre-yogi days. It felt good, but now the alcohol went to my head. As I was sitting there mindfully observing the experience, two truck drivers came in and sat down on stools, one on either side. Without seeming to see me, they began talking to each other as though talking through me. I turned from one to the other, looking at their unshaven, red faces, but neither seemed to be aware that I was sitting in the midst of their conversation. I seemed to be invisible, as though in India I had raised my vibration enough so that I was no longer visible to those on a lower frequency.[177] I said goodbye as I got up to

---

177 Eventually, I learned to invoke that Cloak of Invisibility consciously.

leave, but it seemed they still weren't aware of me, so I put my money on the bar and left.

As I walked home through the fields I realized how hungry I was, but didn't feel like cooking. Tired of the usual *kitchari,* a bland mixture of rice, lentils, and yoghurt I had learned to make in India, I drove into Hudson. There was a soul food place I had heard about, so I went there and ordered southern fried chicken, collard greens, sweet potato pie, a cup of black coffee and on the way home picked up a chocolate donut. I figured the combination would probably kill me, but was tired of being so fastidious about my diet. I had obeyed every dietary law, but nothing had helped.

When I got home I flopped face down on the futon, sure that I would probably pass away during the night. I sent out one last prayer to God just before dropping off, "I don't care if I live or die, but if you want me to live you're going to have to heal me."

Soon I found myself sitting on a white, plastic bench in what resembled a hospital waiting room. There were others on the bench but no one talked. A man in a white jacket whom I assumed was the doctor or technician approached, looked down at his clipboard, and said, "You're next."

Rising to my feet, I realized I was clad in a medical gown. The man with the clipboard guided me into a huge electrical machine with lots of dials and wires and positioned me between two rectangular, metal plates. He brought the front plate toward me so that my torso was sandwiched between the two.

"Don't move," he ordered.

There was a whirring sound and I felt a surge of energy. Looking down I saw my chakras glowing brightly, rotating in a clockwise direction. Seeing the beautiful colors and pulsating patterns, I became excited, but then the machine shut off.

"How about some more?" I called out.

"No, we have to be careful not to burn out your chakras. Now take a seat on the bench. We'll observe you for a while, then beam you back down."

"Beam me down? Who are you?"

"This is a hospital ship. We circle the planet, healing those whose karma allows us to intercede."

Shocked that the ship was not busier, I said, "Can't you heal more?

There are so many people on Earth who need your help."

"As I said, we heal those whose karma allows. Now, please sit down."

In the morning I awoke charged with vitality. Although that night had seemed like an episode of *Star Trek*, I felt fantastic, and my digestion was perfect.

CHAPTER 56

Journey West

Now that I was healthy, I felt like leaving the seclusion of my mountaintop retreat. I bought an old Dodge van for six hundred dollars, threw a futon in the back, along with a kerosene cook stove, and started west. With no destination in mind, I asked God to guide my journey. Again, I felt like a wandering sadhu and once more put on the white clothes and mala from India. In this attire I was always welcomed by other "freaks," who recognized a kindred spirit. By sunset every day I would invariably meet people who would invite me to crash at their commune or ashram. Since I was used to sleeping on the cement floors of temples and ashrams, having to sleep on an occasional sofa was a luxury. Everyone wanted to hear about India, Ram Dass, and all the other amazing beings I had met. People were kind and generous, sometimes providing me with food and money for gas along the way. In the communal spirit of those days people tended to see each other as family.

Driving through Memphis, Tennessee, I stopped and used a pay phone at a gas station to call an ashram whose number I had been given, but there was no answer. After a few rings the operator came on the phone and said, "That ashram is closed, but would you like me to connect you with other people I know who are into yoga?"

"Really?" I asked, surprised, for I had never heard of an operator volunteering to connect people before. I wondered if perhaps she was actually one of those Masters Ram Tirtha had mentioned, who intercede on special occasions and guides people's destinies.

"Sure, please connect me," I finally said, curious to see who she had in mind.

A woman with a kind voice came on the line, and after introducing herself as Lynn said, "Yoga? We don't have an ashram, but come on over." She acted as though getting a request for lodging from a total stranger at nine at night was perfectly normal. She and her boyfriend seemed like old friends who wanted to hear about my travels in India, and we talked late into the night.

The next morning as I was climbing into my van to leave, Lynn tucked an envelope containing a card and a couple of twenty dollar bills in my pocket, which the note said was to help pay for the publication of a booklet I was writing. There was also the name of a friend in Santa Fe she thought I should meet. She said she would phone him and tell him I was coming his way.

On reaching New Mexico I headed north toward Santa Fe. That was the shortened form of the original name, *La Villa Real de la Santa Fé de San Francisco de Asís*, the Royal City of the Holy Faith of Saint Francis of Assisi, and it was the end of the old Santa Fe Trail.

It was early spring, and as I left Interstate 40 and ascended from the desert lowlands toward the Sangre de Christo Mountains, I ran into a blinding snowstorm. The bald tires couldn't get traction and the van finally slid to the side of the road. There I was in the middle of nowhere wearing thin, pajama-like clothes, and nowhere near civilization. Finally I got out and started trudging through the snow toward Santa Fe. Within twenty paces a Land Rover pulled up and a man rolled down his window.

"Get in; you'll never make it to town. People freeze to death out here in the mountains. You can stay at my place."

The doors didn't lock, but as there wasn't much worth stealing, I just left the van parked on the gravel shoulder and visualized it surrounded in light. There was already about six inches of snow on the ground and I was glad to get a ride. This Good Samaritan lived nearby in the mostly adobe village of Galisteo. His wife had already prepared a dinner of hot posole and blue corn tortillas, and when I arrived she set another place at the table. After dinner I was given a warm bed upstairs under the attic and fell asleep immediately, wrapped in the blanket of silence that covered everything.

In the morning the roads had been cleared and my host gave me a ride back to my van. It seemed that my circle of light had kept it from being harmed, except on closer examination I found that my address book was missing. Instead of being upset, somehow I felt liberated. It had contained the names of people I thought I was supposed to contact, and now I was free of that obligation. There was a greater plan, I saw, one that could not be acted on in advance. I could only follow it as it unfolded, moment-by-moment. It seemed that I was being led toward the fulfillment of some higher purpose, about which I knew little.

The snow melted under the brilliant sun as I drove the remaining twenty miles to Santa Fe. Fortunately, I still had the card on which Lynn had written the address of her friend, Randy Carter, and I was soon knocking on his door. He had been a member of the spiritual group Ananda Marga, whose founder and Guru was in India.[178] Randy felt like a brother and we spent the afternoon sharing our adventures on the spiritual path. Randy truly lived the teachings, for in addition to practicing meditation he served as a doctor at the local Indian hospital in Santa Fe, where he helped many less fortunate. He was gone most of the day, often visiting the nearby pueblos, and that left me alone most of the day to meditate. I didn't want to overstay my welcome, but he said I could remain at his place as long as I needed.

---

178 *Ananda Marga:* path of bliss, founded by Ranjan Sarkar, also known as Sri Anandamurti (1921–1990). In 1971 Anandamurti had been arrested, and the members were in a state of confusion. After seven years in prison he was acquitted of all charges. There were many Ananda Marga centers throughout the US that focused not only on liberation but also practiced service to humanity.

Take Prasad

One afternoon while meditating I felt an inexplicable pull to drive downtown to the Golden Temple Conscious Cookery.[179] As I had already eaten lunch and it was the middle of the afternoon, this seemed strange. I kept resisting the urge, but finally gave in. I thought, "Well, I'll just go for a cup of tea." The restaurant was empty at that hour, and after finishing my tea I was about to leave when I heard the unmistakable, sweet voice of Sai Baba saying, "Stay! In one minute someone will come in I want you to meet."

Had I heard correctly? Could Sai Baba, who was on the other side of the world, really know what was happening in Santa Fé? I looked skeptically toward the door, then at my watch. I had heard "one minute," so I vowed to wait a minute, then leave.

Right on cue the door opened and a young woman entered. She sat at a table between where I was sitting at the window and the counter. Was this really someone Baba wanted me to meet? If so, how was I going to accomplish this? I couldn't just go up and say, "Excuse me, but a man in India just said telepathically that he wants me to meet you." She would think I was either crazy or trying to pick her up.

I watched her as unobtrusively as possible, trying to think what to say. Again I heard Baba's voice, "I told you 'one minute'; this is the one I want you to meet, now go!"

I got up and lurched nervously toward the woman.

"Excuse me, do you mind if I sit at your table while I finish my tea?"

"That's fine," she said as she shrugged, not looking up from the postcard she was writing.

"Well, what now, Baba?" I thought, staring at the table and trying to be unobtrusive.

---

179 The Golden Temple Conscious Cookery was one of several vegetarian restaurants started by Yogi Bhajan (1929–2004), founder of the 3HO (Healthy, Happy, Holy Organization), which taught kundalini yoga and at one time had over 300 centers in 35 countries.

"Show her my picture!"

"But, I don't have one with me."

"Yes you do, in your wallet."

I remembered, then, a small, ragged photo I had tucked away inside my wallet. Sure enough, after searching in all the compartments I found the photo, but should I really show her this picture of the strange looking man with bushy hair? What was the worst that could happen? She might say, "Don't bother me." If she did, I would leave.

Here goes, I thought, as I put the photo on the table in front of her and said, "Excuse me for interrupting you. I don't know why I'm doing this because you'll probably think I'm crazy, but do you know this man?"

"That's him!" she shouted, excitedly, "Who is he?"

"Sathya Sai Baba. I just returned from visiting him in India."

She looked from me to the photo and back to me again, then began talking. "A week ago I was in Los Angeles at the Bodhi Tree Bookstore, where there are pictures of holy people on the walls. I was looking around when all of a sudden I saw a picture of this man. Then the picture came to life and he talked to me! I thought I was going crazy. There I was in a bookstore with a picture talking to me! He told me to come visit him, but I didn't know his name, let alone where he lived. No one in the bookstore knew who he was, but he told me, 'In one week you will know who I am.' Now, here I am, exactly one week later to the hour, and you sit down at my table and tell me his name!"

As we sipped our tea I told her more about Baba, where he lived, and how she could visit. She said that for a long time she had been praying to be more spiritual, and that this was the answer to her prayer. I gave her the photo and she left the restaurant, clutching it between her fingers like a precious jewel.

"Well done, my son," I heard Baba say, sweetly, "Now, take *prasad!*"

Prasad is food blessed by the Guru and charged with his spiritual energy. This restaurant was famous for its cheesecake, so I sat down at the counter where I could survey the desserts. As I was eyeing the peach cheesecake with graham cracker crust, the waiter came over and cut a fat slice.

"Here, take prasad," he said, placing it before me.

Bewildered that the waiter's actions had mirrored Baba's instructions, I wondered if he had also heard Baba? I sat staring at the cheesecake, thinking to myself, "Prasad is more than a dessert; to be truly prasad it must be blessed by the Guru." In answer to my thought, a beam of light instantaneously shot down into it, and I knew that Baba was truly bestowing a blessing.

Beyond the exquisite taste, I relished the joy at being a part of Baba's Divine Lila. He had been true to the words he had spoken in my heart before I left Puttaparthi, "I will be with you always."

As I cleaned the plate one more thought came to mind; if this is truly prasad, a gift from the Guru, I shouldn't have to pay. But, would the waiter see it the same way? This was, after all, not an ashram in India, but a restaurant in America that needed to make a profit to survive. Sure that I would have to pay, yet still hoping that I wouldn't, I asked the waiter when he returned,

"How much do I owe you for the cheesecake?"

"Nothing," he said, casually. "It's prasad!"

CHAPTER 58

Dinner with Bhagavan Das

While I was in Santa Fe I looked up Bhagavan Das. He was the one who had brought Ram Dass to Maharajji, and was living there at the time.[180] Overjoyed to connect with someone who had just returned from Maharajji, he suggested we meet for dinner at Lupita's, a Mexican restaurant on the Old Santa Fe Trail.

The tall ex-surfer with blond dreadlocks strode into the small dining room. As two sadhus who looked incongruous in this Wild West town, we recognized each other immediately. Since I wasn't familiar with Mexican food, I let him order. I didn't realize what a voracious appetite he had, for in a few minutes enough food came to the table to feed a party of six. Then I watched with amazement as most of it began disappearing into his mouth, even food from my plate.

"So, how is Maharajji?" he asked, wolfing down the first taco.

"Well, nothing was really happening, except that we sang a lot of bhajans."

"Yes, you think it's *nothing*, but it isn't."

"How do you mean?"

"Well, it's a nothing that mirrors your own mind," he said cryptically.

"Yeah, like how?"

"Well, you can't be in his presence with any fixed ideas or he will destroy them," he said, decimating a burrito. "He forces you to look at your own stuff."

He went on to relate how someone in the satsang made a remark about Sai Baba, that he was only a magician. Immediately, Maharajji sent everyone on the seventeen-hour bus trip to see Baba on his upcoming visit to Delhi. Bhagavan Das had been with the group in Connaught Circle,

---

180 *Bhagavan Das:* servant of God. Ravi Das (Ron Zimardi) had in turn previously brought Bhagavan Das to India. See: *The Sacred Wanderer,* by Ravi Das (Sacred Wandered Publications, 2010); also, *It's Here Now (Are You?),* by Bhagavan Das (Three Rivers Press, 1998).

which was packed with close to a million people. Everyone wanted to get at least a glimpse of Sai Baba's orange robe, which many believed would assure their liberation.

After hours of waiting, Bhagavan Das finally saw Baba's orange robe appear on the far side of the Circle. Earlier he had bought a rose from a flower girl. Now, sitting on a wall to get a better view, he had the thought, "I wish I could give this rose to Sai Baba."

At that very moment Sai Baba turned and made his way across Connaught Circus to where Bhagavan Das was sitting. Looking at him, he said, "You wanted to give me something?"

Bhagavan Das then put the rose in Baba's hand. He smiled, and then continued on through the crowd.

On completing the story, Bhagavan Das' blue eyes suddenly opened wide with excitement, "Time for dessert, let's have *sopaipillas!*"[181]

Despite the dreadlocks of a renunciate, I was amazed at his prodigious appetite.

---

181 *Sopaipilla,* a fried pastry served with honey.

CHAPTER 59

Are You Ready to Go Up?

S anta Fe seemed to be a powerful spiritual focus, unlike the other cities I had visited on my travels across the country.[182] The native peoples said that sacred energy was due to the presence of the *Kachinas,* spiritual beings who had come to Earth to awaken sacredness in every aspect of life.[183] Others said that energy came from the Ascended Masters, who had a retreat in Truchas Peak in the Sangre de Christo Mountains. It was also regarded by some as the focus of a civilization in Atlantean times. People who slept on the Truchas Peak frequently had dreams where they went into the mountain and were taught by white-robed masters. Space ships were also seen in the area.

After a couple of weeks in Santa Fe I felt pulled to explore the desert. I didn't really know where to go, but one day I got in the van and headed north out of town. I had been meditating on the inner I AM as Sai Baba had instructed, and found that my inner guidance was becoming stronger— though it was usually not as a voice, but a feeling.

I had heard alluring stories of Black Mesa but had no idea how to get there. All I knew was that it was in the desert north of Santa Fe. Keeping my attention focused on my heart, I kept waiting for the energy that I knew would pull me in the right direction.

Passing through Española, where I had briefly been a guest at Yogi Bhajan's ashram, I soon reached Pojaque, where I saw a sign for San Ildefonso Pueblo. The name had a magic ring to it, perhaps because fifty years earlier my grandmother had visited there and bought some unique black pots from Maria Martinez, whose work later became famous. Driving along the Pojaque River toward San Ildefonso, I was happy to be in the wide-open spaces, sheltered only beneath the unlimited blue sky.

---

182 Ram Dass, Chögyam Trungpa, Allen Ginsburg, and Tsultrim Allione all showed up in Santa Fe around the same time.

183 *Kachinas:* thought to be nature spirits, ancestors from the stars, as well as objectifications of various aspects of life. Dolls are often made in their image.

Black Mesa, New Mexico

A few miles down the road I saw a sign for Black Mesa. I felt a charge of energy, which seemed to mean that I was going the right way. At a NO TRESPASSING sign I came to a stop. I wanted to respect the privacy of the pueblo and the sacredness of the land, but felt the spirit pulling me onward. I said a prayer and moved down what had now become a dirt road. The pueblo seemed deserted, and there wasn't a soul in sight. The Mesa loomed on the right and I followed a couple of tracks in the sand that led in its direction. At the end of the trail I parked in front of a sign that said NO PARKING WITHOUT PERMIT, praying to Sai Baba and whatever Masters might be watching to protect me and bring about the Divine Plan.

Stepping out of the van into the sand, I smelled the sagebrush in the air and felt the soothing stillness of the desert. Although these native people of the Pueblo had little money, a richness pervaded the land. Just being there was a meditation in which thoughts appeared with crystalline clarity, then dissolved into emptiness. In the distance a bird sang a few notes and then stopped, its message still hanging in the still air.

The path up the Mesa was steeper than I expected, and it was difficult climbing up the hillside of loose rock. The summit was farther than it appeared from below, and when I reached the top I sat in the sand and rested. It was flat and desolate, and I could see far into the distance, where the Rio Grande wound down the valley. I had reached the mesa late in the day, and the red and gold of the setting sun transformed the desert into a giant sand painting, framed by the greens and browns of the river valley.[184]

A gust of icy wind hit me in the face. It was getting colder as the sun set, so I rose and started back down. As I passed a rocky outcropping, I was startled to see a man sitting with his back to me, his legs hanging over the edge of the mesa. He beckoned for me to join him. He had found the only spot sheltered from the wind and I went and sat down next to him. He was wearing a cowboy hat with a band of silver conchos circling it and had long, black hair hanging down his back.

"Hi, my name is Quetzal," he said, offering his hand.

We sat together, not talking, watching the shadow of the mesa on the desert deepen into purple. It seemed we had met before, but I couldn't remember where that might have been. He continued to gaze into space, then after a few minutes began to talk.

"I have come here for a purpose, you know."

"Oh, really, what's that?"

"There are some people you need to meet, and I have been sent to take you there."

"What...where?" I asked, surprised at this sudden statement from a stranger.

"Up there," he nodded, pointing to the Sangre de Christo Mountains to the east.

I hesitated. Who is this guy? Who could I possibly need to meet in the mountains at night? Although this man emanated peace, people did disappear out here. I remembered stories about the people who had disappeared after being invited to a weekend in the country by the followers of Rev. Sun Myung Moon.[185]

"It's up to you," he said, somewhat allaying my doubts.

---

184 Tibetan Buddhist tantric rituals often involve the construction of a mandala made of various colored sands. After the ritual is concluded the mandala is destroyed, symbolizing impermanence.

185 The followers of the Korean, self-styled Messiah, Rev. Sun Myung Moon, were often called Moonies. Many claimed they had been held prisoner and brainwashed during weekend retreats to which they had been invited.

283

Since we seemed to have arrived here together by a sort of synchronicity, it felt right to go with him. I had been praying all day for guidance, which had brought me to Black Mesa, so it seemed now that I had to trust that guidance.

"Okay, I'll go," I said.

In the twilight we stumbled and slid down the trail to where the van was parked. The desert was still warm and smelled strongly of sage.

"Where's your car?" I asked.

"I don't have one."

"How did you get here?

"Some friends dropped me off, so we'll have to go in your car."

I didn't mind, because I was hesitant about leaving the car at the pueblo, especially right in front of the no parking sign. As night fell we drove up the winding road into the Sangre de Christo Mountains, named after the blood of Christ. A couple of hours later we arrived near Holman, then headed down a dirt road to a remote valley surrounded by National Forest. I parked and we walked uphill through a meadow that, at seven thousand feet, was still covered with snow. Although springtime, it was bitterly cold. In the thin atmosphere the stars looked closer than I had ever seen them. How could anyone think that in that vast universe there were not other beings?

I hoped that one of the stars would move and turn out to be a UFO, but they remained motionless, and my guide was silent. Finally we reached a log *kiva* built into the side of the mountain and Quetzal pushed open the door.[186]

Inside was a wood fire, which felt good after our hike up the valley. A couple dozen people greeted us, as though to have strangers walk in out of nowhere was totally normal. Perhaps the fact that we all had long hair was a sign we were family. Beneath the low roof of the kiva the warm air smelled sweetly of piñon burning in the stove, and I felt at home. Someone handed me a wooden bowl of chili and a few steaming, blue corn tortillas. Not having eaten since early in the day, I was starving. While devouring dinner

---

186 *Kiva:* Native American sacred space used for rituals, usually built partially or wholly underground.

I listened to the conversation, wondering why I had been brought here.

After everyone finished eating, there was a silence. Then a woman who was an inhabitant of the valley started to talk. Her tone was serious, different from the previous banter, and I listened spellbound as she recounted a remarkable happening.

There were three homes in different parts of the valley. Tonight they had all come together to discuss their visitations of the previous night. There had been a visit from a stranger. Some had been awakened by a humming above their roofs. Most had gone back to sleep, but one person in each house had remained awake, and now each in turn described what had happened.

The woman who was talking said she had awakened, realizing she wasn't alone. When she sat up she saw a stranger in the room wearing a white jumpsuit with elastic wrist and ankle bands. She didn't feel any fear and he spoke in a kind voice.

"You can go up now."

"What?"

"I said, you can go up now," the stranger repeated. "You are one of us and I have come here to get you. Your work here is finished."

"But, I have two small children," the woman protested.

"Yes, I know," the stranger replied, "The choice is yours. I can't wait for an answer. I need to go now."

The woman replied that she couldn't leave her husband to raise the children by himself, and that she wanted to stay. She fell back on the bed and slept undisturbed the remainder of the night. When she and her husband rose in the morning the furniture in the living room had been rearranged. She said she felt this was to show her that her experience had not been a dream.

Two others told similar stories, of being offered the opportunity to leave the Earth. None were ready, however. Each had a reason for staying. One was a musician who, after years of preparation, was finally about to produce an album. He did not want to leave until it was finished. The last man told a similar story of why he had chosen to remain. In the morning, each had found their furniture rearranged. One man, whose bed was against the wall, awoke to find it in the middle of the room. A sofa in front of the fireplace was now by the window. Wood stacked to the left of the

285

cook stove was now piled in front. None had any doubt about the reality of the visit. After the last account ended I went out into the cold night and looked up at the sky filled with stars.

"Here I am!" I shouted silently. "You asked the wrong people. Come back and get me. I am ready to go. I have nothing holding me on Earth," but not a star moved—there was only silence. I watched my breath rising skyward, but seeing no approaching craft, not even a shooting star, I shivered and went back into the warm kiva.

I looked around for Quetzal so we could head back down the mountain, but no one had seen him. After waiting for a while, he did not return, so I walked back down to the parking lot, thinking he might be waiting in the van—but he had disappeared. It was getting late, so I started back to Santa Fe. As Randy's girlfriend had come to visit, I was spending that night at Frank Waters' home, where I had been invited to stay.[187]

Although my desire to be beamed up by a space ship was not answered that night, within a few months I would meet the Ascended Master Saint Germain, who would offer an even greater opportunity.[188]

---

187 Frank Waters wrote extensively about the Native American peoples. His best-known book is *Book of the Hopi* (Penguin, 1977), which popularized the Hopi prophecies.

188 This meeting with the Ascended Master Saint Germain is recounted in the next book of this series, *Adventures of a Western Mystic: Apprentice to the Masters* by Peter Mt. Shasta (Church of the Seven Rays, 2010).

CHAPTER 60

Joseph Sunhawk at Taos Pueblo

Following the Sangre de Christo Mountains north, I soon came to the sacred Taos Mountain, where the native Tiwa tribe had been living for the past thousand years. As I neared the pueblo, a hawk swooped low by the side of the van, looked sideways at me, and then veered away. A hawk had never looked me in the eye before, and I felt blessed—as if I were entering a place of magic.

I parked on a side street near the town square and when I got out, there was a hawk sitting on a hitching post. As it looked at me I wondered if it was the same one I'd seen coming into town. Instead of walking down the boardwalk to Joe's Cafe, the local hangout where I had intended to get breakfast, I felt something pulling me into a curio shop. I resisted, as I had no inclination to buy the postcards, film, suntan lotion, or the imitation arrowheads the store advertised in the window.

However, the pull was unmistakable, so I finally entered. Inside, I was immediately attracted to an old man with braids. I thought he was a Tibetan Lama, except that he wore weathered jeans and an embroidered white shirt. Still, some Lamas in the West, like Trungpa Rinpoche, now dressed casually on occasion. As I scrutinized him I realized that he must be native. No wonder both the Tibetan and Hopi legends say that at one time they were one people.[189] He was not doing anything, just standing in the middle of the store looking straight ahead, but he had a noble tranquility

---

189 In fulfillment of a mutual prophecy of both the Hopi and Tibetan peoples, the Sixteenth Karmapa, Rangjung Rigpe Dorje (1924–1981) visited the Hopis in 1974. In the eighth century the great Tibetan Master Padmasambhava said, "When the iron bird flies and horses run on wheels, the Tibetan people will be scattered like ants across the face of the Earth, and the Dharma will go to the land of the Red Man." The Karmapa's visit was sponsored by Werner Erhard, the founder of the human growth potential organization called "est" (Erhard Seminars Training).

that drew me. Not wanting to intrude on his privacy, however, I left the store. If I ran into him again, I decided, I would speak.

That encounter took place sooner than I had anticipated. I went into a store around the corner and there he was again, standing quietly in the center of the floor. This time I used the pretext of buying a postcard to draw close, but he still did not speak. He had a similar energy to Trungpa Rinpoche—luminous awareness, yet rooted in the earth. Again, I refrained from speaking. Although he wore no feathers or ritual objects that would betray his status, he emanated a nobility that indicated he must be a chief or shaman. Out of respect, I again did not speak, and walked past him to the door.

Continuing down the dirt street, I began to think that it would be nice to have a piece of local turquoise, so I went into a shop that had some beautiful green turquoise stones in the window. Yet, I could not get the image of the beautiful native man out of my mind, and felt sad that I had not spoken up. I thought of going back, but was sure he would no longer be there. Feeling that I had missed a great opportunity, I entered the store.

Once again, there he was. I knew now that I could not avoid speaking, as three was the magic number granting permission. But, how had he flown here ahead of me? There was no shortcut and he was an old man. It was as though he had simply materialized. When I approached, he cocked his head, as though listening to words as yet unspoken.

"Hello, my name is Peter Mount Shasta."

"Joseph Sunhawk," he said, extending a soft yet leathery hand. "I was wondering when you were going to speak to me. You know, it's not good to make an old man run around so much."

I apologized, and told him I hadn't wanted to intrude on his space.

"My space?" he asked, smiling, and I realized how strange it sounded to imply that one could own space. "You know, we were meant to meet. This is why I came into town."

"Really?"

"Yes, I saw you coming into town."

"You did?" I asked, startled, not sure if he had literally seen me, or if he had seen me with his inner sight. My rational mind went numb as I felt myself shifting into a state of expanded awareness, and I realized that I was in the presence of one of those Great Ones. It seemed he could be

288

wherever he wished, or disappear into thin air. Yet, he was not aloof, and I felt warmth, compassion, and deep wisdom emanating from him.

"Do you live in the pueblo?" I asked.

"Yes."

"May I come visit you there?"

"No, not in the pueblo. Visit me in the mountain behind," he said, enigmatically.

"In the sacred Mountain?"

"Yes."

Looking at me with penetrating eyes, he said, "We will see each other again."

Sensing that our meeting was over, I bowed and walked out the door. I had completely forgotten about buying the turquoise.

That evening I drove north to where there was a dirt road leading into the mountains, and followed it to a flat place looking out on the sacred mountain. I unrolled my sleeping bag in the back of the van and went to sleep. Soon I was in a council chamber within the Mountain and there beside me was Joseph Sunhawk, just as I had seen him earlier that day.

"Welcome to the sacred chamber. We are all here now, representatives of the Native Peoples," he said, pointing around the circle. I saw the proud, earthen faces of the tribes of the Americas, the Hopi, the nomadic peoples of Asia and the dark skinned Africans, all looking back as they nodded in greeting. I was the only white-skinned person there.

"We are gathered here to discuss what is happening to our Mother, the Earth, why the white men want to destroy Her, and what we can do to help.

"Why is the white man doing such terrible things?" Joseph said, turning to me. But, before I could answer he went on, "It is because he is cut off from the feminine. He trusts in the logic of the mind alone, and does not know the truth of the heart. Because he is separate from his own feminine nature he does not know that everything is alive, that the Earth itself is alive, that the Earth is his mother, and that without the Earth he is nothing. He does not know this, so for him life is about power and greed. Because he has no roots in the Earth, he feels cut off from life. He thinks that by acquiring more things, by controlling the world, he will be more alive; but, instead, he is more dead. The more he acquires, the less he is in touch with the Earth and with himself, the less he knows who he is, and the less he has happiness.

"What can we do to awaken the white man before he destroys our home, the planet on which we live?" Joseph asked, looking me in the eye, and then looking at the faces around the circle.

We turned our attention within for a solution. When I opened my eyes, the council chamber was filled with light, and I began to think that perhaps the prayer itself was the solution. In releasing that light we were sending out into the world what people needed to heal their hearts. It was this light that would help humanity awaken. After that I remembered no more.

I awakened in the middle of the night and sat upright. Was the van surrounded by moonlight, or had I brought back the light of the council chamber? In the morning, as the sun rose over the Sangre de Christo Mountains I stepped outside and surveyed the turquoise sky. The sage-scented air made me hungry, and I drove into town to eat at Joe's Café.

I hoped to see Joseph Sunhawk again, so after I had eaten I walked to the same stores where I had seen him the day before, but he was nowhere. In the plaza there was an old Indian man sitting on a wall rolling a cigarette and I asked him if he knew Joseph Sunhawk, but he just shook his head. As I walked away he shouted, "Hey, he died last year."

I drove north out of Taos feeling my heart full. I felt I had received the gift Spirit had wanted to give. Reaching the highway, a hawk swooped down like the one that had looked into my eyes on the way into town. For a moment it flew in front the van like a sentinel, then veered off into space.[190]

---

190 A few years later, Taos was chosen as the location for a temple dedicated to Maharajji, who left his physical body in 1973. Ashes from his cremation were installed there. See: www.maharajji.com/Taos/taos-ashram.html.

CHAPTER 61

Surprise Meeting at Lama Foundation

I drove north out of Taos on Highway 64 and soon passed the fabled New Buffalo Commune in Arroyo Hondo.[191] They were trying to incorporate Native American values into their commune life, but the local Pueblo natives still regarded them as way too hippie to feel allied with them. I thought of hanging out with them for a while and pulled into their driveway, but there were a bunch of naked children playing in a mud puddle out front, and I decided that it was not my style either. So, I kept going.

Less than a half hour later I came to the turnoff for the Lama Foundation, and turned up the dirt road. It was a commune up in the mountains that had been started by friends of Ram Dass. He had stayed there after his first return from India and given them the manuscript for *Be Here Now*. The commune residents had helped design and publish the book that, with his personal story and illustrated introduction to Vedic philosophy, rapidly became the book many hippies had in their backpacks or vans. Invariably I found copies on the tables of commune and ashrams across America.

On arrival, I left the van in the lot. Walking toward the dome that was the main structure, I was greeted by a girl in a straw hat and overalls who said, "Oh, you want to stay? Far out. You can put your stuff in that building up the hill."

There was no mention of money, but it was assumed that everyone would pitch in with gardening and other work. I was assigned the job of carrying food and supplies to the people staying in retreat cabins up the mountain. These people were on solitary retreat and not allowed to have human contact, so I had to make deliveries when everyone was inside. They would leave lists outside of anything they wanted and the commune

---

191 For more on Taos at that time and the New Buffalo Commune see *Scrapbook of a Taos Hippie: Tribal Tales from the Heart of a Cultural Revolution*, by Iris Keltz, Ed Sanders (Ibid).

would try to supply their needs, even if it was some rare translation of the *I Ching*. I hoped someday to return and do a retreat there.

Later in the afternoon I walked down to the main building, which was still under construction, in search of the library. Inside, there was a man wearing an old flannel shirt and jeans, just standing in the middle of the floor. At first I thought he was one of the Mexicans who was there to make adobe for construction, but he wasn't doing anything, just standing there, staring at the bookshelves as though waiting for something—radiating a sense of calm, abiding peace.

I had gone into the building to donate a booklet I had written on Mount Shasta; but, instead of putting the booklet on the shelf, I handed it to him.

"You might like this," I said, placing the white pamphlet with a gold stamped title in his hand. I hadn't wanted the book to be commercialized, so had printed "Free" on the cover. Without looking up, he stared at the cover for what seemed a long time, and then made a shocking, single word comment, "Free!"

He handed the booklet back and looked me in the eye with the sweetest smile. Suddenly, we were interrupted by an intent young man who strode into the room and announced, "Rinpoche, we can go now; the car is ready." The two then walked out, with the man to whom I had shown the pamphlet leaning on the young man's shoulder.

Rinpoche? Who was that? Although this was the Lama Foundation, it was not affiliated with Buddhism. I was later to learn that "lama" was colloquial Spanish for "mud," the name of the mountain on which the commune was situated. Nonetheless, the fact that the man had been addressed as Rinpoche meant he was a Tibetan Buddhist Lama. Going in search of an answer, I found someone whom I asked, "Who was that guy in the flannel shirt who just left?"

"Oh, that was Trungpa Rinpoche."

He was the one who had written *Meditation in Action*, the book that had been dropped in front of me on the houseboat in Varanasi, and the Lama I had vowed to look up someday.

"What was he doing here?"

"Oh, yesterday he came down from Boulder and gave a talk to the community and stayed overnight. Now he's heading home."

Even though he had said only that one word, "Free!" it carried such a field of awareness that it has stayed in my mind ever since. I realized that a highly conscious person does not need to say or do anything, for their simplest act, even if silence, can contain a transmission.

Trungpa Rinpoche

293

Trungpa Rinpoche

CHAPTER 62

The Crazy Wisdom of Trungpa Rinpoche[192]

W anting more contact with this enigmatic Guru, I left the Lama Foundation the next day and drove north into Colorado. Soon I was in Boulder, sitting in a park a block south of Pearl Street, wondering where Trungpa Rinpoche hung out and how I could meet him again. At that moment a guy I had last seen in India, Dinabandhu, appeared. We had shared a house on the beach in Jagannath Puri. He was sort of a cosmic messenger, always appearing at a moment when some sort of catalyst was needed. Now he lived up to his reputation and blurted out, "Trungpa Rinpoche is having a meeting tonight at Karma Dzong, and you're invited."

"Really? You're not a member, so how can you invite me?"

"One of Rinpoche's top people told me that it's an open meeting, and that I could invite anyone. So, I'm inviting you. It's at seven o'clock. Rinpoche will blow your mind."[193]

I stood in the entrance to the shrine room with about a dozen others

---

192 This chapter previously published as "A Trungpa Rinpoche Crazy Wisdom Teaching," in *Elephant Journal* (www.elephantjournal.com, April 5, 2012). Crazy wisdom is a concept common to many spiritual traditions, including the Tibetan, Sufi, and Native American, where the *Heyokha* (trickster) shocks the student out of conventional dogma into genuine, spontaneous realization. In response to some hippies who simply acted crazy or tried to be outlandish, Trungpa Rinpoche said, "The wisdom comes first, then the crazy."

193 Ösel Tendzin, born Thomas Rich (1943–1990), was appointed by Trungpa Rinpoche to be Vajra Regent in 1976. Rinpoche said on his deathbed that this had been a "terrible mistake...I've created a monster." Both Trungpa Rinpoche and Ösel Tendzin had personal lives involving abusive relationships, which brought about the disillusionment of many followers. Students and teachers who become intimately involved do so at their own peril.

that Dinabandhu had invited, waiting for the arrival of this Lama who had already had such an influence on me—little suspecting the nature of the curious lesson he was about to impart.

On arrival at Karma Dzong, I was met by a tense young man by the name Ösel, who took his role as chief organizer very seriously. He announced, "This is a closed meeting, and you're all going to have to leave."

"Closed?"

"Yes, closed, it's for members of Karma Dzong only, so all of you will have to leave."

Most everyone left, but a few of us continued to hang on, perhaps hoping just for a glimpse of the Lama renowned for bringing Vajrayana (tantric) teachings to the West. As with any teacher embodying truth, even a glance can impart an energy that can be life changing. I expect some stayed, hoping for just such a catalyst.

"I thought I told you to leave," Ösel said, condescendingly, after the first group had left.

I had been painfully shy since childhood and normally would have fled a scene where I wasn't wanted, but a heaviness rooted me to the spot. Although my mind echoed the command to leave, my heart felt at peace with staying. I felt that an authentic teacher, which I felt Trungpa to be, would not deny a sincere seeker access to his teachings.

Gradually, Ösel intimidated the few remaining seekers into leaving, and I was the only non-member left. Brazenly, when the doors to the shrine room opened, I walked in first, marched up the aisle, and sat on the cushion directly in front of the Lama's chair, which rested on a low platform.

"When Rinpoche comes in I'm going to tell him you don't belong here," Ösel said, returning in a rage.

"OK, fine, tell him," I said, feeling strangely calm.

Suddenly everyone stood as Rinpoche entered. This time, instead of jeans and a flannel shirt, he was wearing a three-piece suit. He limped to the front of the room, leaning on Ösel's arm (he had been injured in a car crash in Scotland after his escape from Tibet). As Rinpoche sat down, true to his promise, Ösel pointed finger at me and said to the Lama, "That guy doesn't belong here; he's not a member of our community."

As I had hoped, Rinpoche did not react, but simply smiled and beckoned me to sit. Then he drew a bottle of sake from his pocket and handed it to me. From the other pocket he produced a glass and handed that over also. With a fatherly smile, he said, "Stay…you pour. Keep the glass full."

Trembling with confusion, Ösel beat a hasty retreat to the back of the room. I filled Rinpoche's glass with the clear alcohol and sat on the cushion beside him—an honor, I later discovered, only accorded to the privileged few.

His words came from his heart, without pretense. For the first time I understood Buddhist compassion, why they stressed this quality of the heart—for here is where heaven and earth unite. Charged into his words was an electricity—the energy of truth—that can be felt during an authentic transmission. This electricity filled the room.

At one point Rinpoche stopped and look at me with an amused smile. With a shock I realized that his glass was empty. After I replenished it with sake he took a long drink and continued. However, soon I was distracted by the precarious situation of his chair. Gradually he was pushing it toward the back of the platform, inching toward a backward flip into annihilation. Affected by the flowing sake, I thought he must have lost awareness of the edge. Was a Lama more conscious than someone else who was drunk? Did he realize the danger of his situation?

My anxiety increased as I refilled his glass once more, and again he shoved his chair backward a few more inches. To my horror, the right, rear chair leg was overhanging the platform. The slightest backward movement would now flip him over, so I moved directly behind the chair, ready to catch him—which I was sure would happen any moment. Yet, it was a moment that never came. Despite drinking two-thirds of a bottle of sake, he kept talking with great lucidity and eloquence. I wondered if perhaps he was totally lucid, and only doing this to test me?

"Any questions?" he finally asked at the end of his talk. After a long silence a man asked, "Rinpoche, I have a question. Didn't you tell me that this was an open meeting and that I should invite anyone I wanted?"

"Yes, that's right," Rinpoche nodded.

Frowning perplexedly, the man sat down. Then Ösel raised his hand and whined, "But, Rinpoche, didn't you tell me it was a closed meeting, and not to let anyone in who's not a member?"

"Yes, that's right."

His refusal to comment seemed to convey, "So, what's your problem? What could be simpler than my giving each of you contradictory requests?" His answer had the absurd simplicity of a Zen koan. There was a stunned silence. I sensed that most of the audience missed the brilliance of this profound teaching. I discovered later that this was a traditional practice, which translated from the Tibetan as,

> *Invite everyone, but station a lion at door.*
> *Only those truly called will be able to enter.*

CHAPTER 63

Who Is Watching the Movie?

After experiencing the crazy wisdom of Trungpa Rinpoche, I decided to stay in Boulder and seriously practice the Buddha Dharma. One of his students gave me a place to stay and every morning I walked down Spruce Street to *Karma Dzong*, then up the stairs to the exquisitely decorated shrine room.[194] The space was charged with the consciousness established by thousands of meditators and the enlightened intent of many high Lamas. In one corner was a sand mandala that had been created by the 16th *Karmapa*.[195] These two-dimensional blueprints of etheric temples were normally destroyed at the conclusion of a ritual as a reminder of impermanence, but this one had been preserved here at the request of the sangha. Their presence, and the consciousness they embody, provide constant impetus to realize the nature of basic emptiness.

I arrived every morning around nine and practiced Vipassana until noon, then came back in the afternoon and stayed until five. No one asked who I was, pressured me to join the organization, or pay any fees. Most of the time I was alone, completely undisturbed. On leaving I always stopped to read the sign outside the shrine room door, "All dharmas should be seen as dreams, including this one."

This statement about one's attitude toward spiritual practice was reminiscent of what my Hungarian fencing coach in college had said about hold one's sword, "It is like a bird. Hold it too tightly and you will crush it, but too loosely and it will fly away." One needs to be serious about the path, but if you grasp the rules too tightly then realization is blocked.

---

194 *Karma Dzong:* (Tibetan) Fortress of Karma. Karma means action, and since all actions have consequences, the name implies a place where people attempt to practice conscious thought and action.

195 *Karmapa:* head of the *Kagyu* lineage, which descended from the Buddha Vajradhara to Tilopa, Naropa, Marpa, and Milarepa. This Gyalwang Karmapa (1924–1981), the 16th dharma holder in this lineage, was regarded as a living Buddha.

I went to this shrine room every day for months to sit in meditation. Using the Vipassana method that Buddha had used, I observed the feeling of breath going in and out, allowing the mind to expand naturally as the duality of the breath merged into unity. If a thought arose I labeled it "thinking," and returned to feeling the rise and fall of my chest. Sometimes it seemed maddeningly painful and I wanted to run. Other times I would feel charged with energy, as if my body were going to burst into flame, and other times I would have to fight against sleep. No matter what happened, I kept labeling each phenomenon as merely *thought*. Becoming a silent witness, I watched the flow of thoughts and feelings passing on the screen of consciousness. Yet a part of me still identified with those phenomena. There was the fear, "If I let go of *me*, then who is there? It was the ego's fear of death. The ego had taken a lifetime to build up its control, and it wanted to hold on. I prayed to subdue this domination of the limited self.

One evening I decided to take a break from this austerity and went for a walk down Pearl Street. Coming to a cinema, I went in. I had not been to a movie in over a year and welcomed the break. As I sat in the dark watching the mediocre film, suddenly the realization came over me that I had no idea who I was, who the being was occupying the seat. I looked back and forth from the images on the screen to the body in the seat, but did not know whose body it was. There was no sense of identity. I looked around for someone to ask who I was, perhaps a friend or acquaintance, but I was alone.

"If I just sit here until the movie ends, then I will remember who I am," I thought. But the film ended, and I could still not remember. The body got up and walked outside. On Pearl Street I stood looking for a sign, hoping that I would see something familiar to jar my sense of identity, but there was nothing. I felt in my pocket for a wallet that might contain an ID, but I hadn't carried a wallet in years.

In a sense, it was refreshing to have no concerns, but gradually I realized that I needed to take care of this body, that I was responsible for its safety. It was getting cold, the air from the Rocky Mountains descending upon the city, and I knew that I needed to find a place for the body to spend the night. But where? Perhaps if I just start walking it will have the instinct of a horse, and find its way home?

"I am going where I belong," I affirmed, planting the seed of action, and began to walk. The body turned left and continued down the street. A sign on the corner said Pearl Street. On the front of a newspaper I read "Boulder, Colorado," but that did not tell me where to go, why I was here—or, more importantly, *who* was here.

After a while I found myself standing in front of a house, staring at the steps leading up to the front door. It had a warm, inviting feeling, and I hoped it was the right one. I had no idea who lived there, but finally got up the courage to open the door and walk upstairs. There were two apartment doors at the top. Without knocking, I entered. No one was home, so I walked around. Finding a blue sleeping bag on the floor, I suddenly knew I was in the right place. I undressed and climbed into the warm, downfilled bag and went to sleep.

In the morning I again remembered who I was, and what I was doing there. Walking toward *Karma Dzong*, I stopped for a cup of coffee, the first I had had in years. It shocked me back into my body. The word "Free," which Trungpa Rinpoche had said to me at Lama Foundation, came suddenly to mind. I realized that freedom also had its limitations. For it to be real it had to be balanced with responsibility. The work was not to dissolve the ego, but to purify it so that it was obedient to the Higher Self.

Instead of continuing down Spruce Street to Karma Dzong as I had done every morning for the past few months, I realized that my time in Boulder was finished. I reversed direction and went back to the house to get my things and say goodbye. I had learned what I needed, and it was time to continue on the westward journey.

301

First Mesa (Waipi Village), Arizona

CHAPTER 64

Meeting the Hopi

After leaving Boulder I went south to Albuquerque, then again west. In Gallup, New Mexico, the center of Navajo country, I stopped to get something to eat. As I walked down the main street I was shocked by the lines of native men leaning against saloon fronts, many staggering down the sidewalk, drunk at mid-day. I could not help thinking that perhaps these were the souls of the cavalry who had destroyed the native way of life, now come back in these bodies to reap their karma. I was glad to leave and was soon sailing past Window Rock, the giant red formation in which the wind had carved a window. It seemed to mark a dimensional doorway, opening into a more expanded sense of being.

A sign announced that I was entering Arizona, and an hour later when I saw a mesa in the distance, I knew I was entering the land of the Hopi. Many of them had broken away from the traditional ways to embrace the white man's life of promised ease and comfort. Those who adhered to the old ways remained on the heights of the mesa. After my experience with Joseph Sunhawk in Taos, I wanted to connect with the Hopi elders; but a sign along the road said that visiting First Mesa was prohibited. If it's meant to, it will happen, I thought, and drove with my heart open to the possibility of ascending those cliffs and visiting the ancient keepers of the land.

It was after three o'clock, and I saw a group of young native kids walking along the highway on their way home from school. Although I rarely picked up hitchhikers, when one of them stuck out his thumb I stopped and three smiling kids piled in.

"Where are you going?" I asked.

"Up there," one of them said, pointing to the mesa.

"But I can't go up there."

"With us you can!"

I wasn't sure they were right and thought I might get in trouble. I had heard stories of whites being beaten or disappearing in this part of the country, but it was an opportunity I couldn't ignore. I left the main road and began ascending the dirt road that led up the cliff to the village of adobe homes on the flat summit. The place seemed almost deserted, with only an occasional pick-up truck parked in a desolate street.

After the kids piled out, I shut off the engine, and the quiet and peace were overwhelming. In this silence I could really experience my true self, undisturbed by the extraneous intrusion of other people thoughts and noise. This was where I had longed to be, so I got out and walked down the rutted dirt road.

At the end of the road the faded blue door of an adobe house pulled me like a magnet. I didn't want to intrude, but I felt I had been brought here for a purpose. As I approached, I heard a few voices inside. The door was open, so I entered the weathered wooden frame and looked into a dim kitchen. Seated around a table were a number of old men with dark, sun-wrinkled faces looking at me. On the table were coffee cups, a tin of tobacco, and rolling papers. It was a moment that lasted a long time, as we exchanged looks. There seemed to be nothing to say, but I felt an understanding pass between us. Some of these men I seemed to recognize from the meeting inside the sacred mountain of Taos Pueblo. We had already communicated on that inner level, and now there was nothing more to say. I nodded and clasped my hands in pranam. They nodded, and I turned and left.

As I neared the van, a pickup truck with three men in the back, holding rifles, sped down the road toward me in a cloud of dust. When they were alongside they shot angry glances, but continued on their way. I realized that I had made the contact I had come here for, and that there was no longer a reason to stay. These people had been so abused over the past century that their suspicion of strangers was warranted. I closed the door and drove back down the edge of the mesa to the main road. Continuing west, I realized that it must have been along this road that the Hopi, White Feather, had been walking when he had been given a ride by the missionary that had led to the Hopi prophecies being made public.

The prophecies said to watch for signs that would indicate the approaching end of the Fourth World, triggered by an apocalyptic war against the United States.[196] This world war would be initiated by peoples

---

196 *Book of the Hopi*, by Frank Waters (Ballantine Books, 1963), containing

of distant lands long abused by the United States. It said that gourd-shaped clouds in the sky would rain ash on the ground, causing much death and making the growing of crops impossible. At that time many will journey to the stars in "birds without wings." Only those who adhere to the ancient law will survive. Then the lost white brother from the stars, the *Pahana*, will return to establish order and help those who remain enter the Fifth World. Then peace will prevail.

I watched the stark desert flashing past the window and remembered the eighth prophecy, "You will see many youth, who wear their hair long like my people, come and join the tribal nations to learn their ways and wisdom," so even the visits to the mesa by my generation was part of that progression toward this coming time of transition. I remembered standing before the picture of Sai Baba in Srirangapatna, where he was riding a white horse through the clouds with atomic explosions in the distance, and I had heard him say, "I have come to avert this catastrophe or all humanity will perish."

I realized that prophecy is simply a warning of what will happen if people do not change their ways. Years later Baba announced that the Golden Age was beginning. One of his students asked, "Why, then, is there still so much darkness?"

His reply was, "How long it takes for the light to fully manifest is up to you!"

---

prophecies given by White Feather in 1958 to David Young, a Christian missionary. The last of the nine prophecies was likely fulfilled 36 years later in 2003 when the space shuttle Columbia, containing nine astronauts, burned up on reentry to the atmosphere, giving off a bright, blue light: "You will hear of a dwelling-place in the heavens, above the Earth, that shall fall with a great crash. It will appear as a blue star."

CHAPTER 65

The Goddess of Phoenix

The further west I drove the stronger became the pull to visit Phoenix, Arizona—like the pull of a strong magnet on iron filings. I interpreted this attraction as a sign that I was following the plan. The thought of Phoenix had fascinated me from childhood, named after the mythical bird that bursts into flame every five hundred years and is then reborn. Perhaps this city in the desert held the secret of my own resurrection?

Late that day, driving into Phoenix, I turned here and there, continuing to follow the magnetic pull and watching for a sign that would indicate a destination. Seeing a white building with a sign that said 3HO Ashram, I felt a surge of energy that meant I had found the place. It was another one of Yogi Bhajan's ashrams, whose satsang ran the Golden Temple Conscious Cookery in Santa Fe.

I parked the van and went in, not knowing what to expect. A girl completely in white with a turban on her head rose from a desk and introduced herself as Isha Kaur, which she said meant Goddess. When she asked if she could be of service, I explained that I had just returned from India and was interested in seeing the ashram. She gladly offered a tour of the shrine room, where daily meditation and yoga classes were held, and soon we were back at the reception area. I was about to thank her for the tour and head out the door when she said, "Don't go yet, I'm coming with you."

"What?"

"Spirit told me to go with you."

"Spirit told you that?"

I was speechless as I tried to grasp that this girl wanted to come along.

"Wait here while I say goodbye," she said.

A few minutes later she emerged with a bag of belongings and we walked out the door. Pulling out of the parking lot, she gave driving instructions. As we sailed down the highway I kept glancing at her, wondering again who she was and what was happening.

Seeming to read my mind, she explained that she came from a wealthy Jewish family in New Jersey. When they had pressured her to get married, she ran off and became a yogini.

"Do you do this often?" I asked.

"Do what?"

"Run off with a total stranger?"

"You're not a stranger."

"I'm not?"

"No, I've been seeing you in dreams for weeks, and been waiting for you. When you walked through the door I recognized you immediately."

"Really?" I was in shock.

I wondered what our purpose together was, and where it was going to lead. She was so straightforward and guileless that I believed her. It seemed that her presence in my life was part of a plan, but what plan?

"Don't you have any fears?" I asked.

"About what?"

"Well, about me, for example."

"You're not the least bit scary, but you need to let go of your fear of me."

She was right. I had not been alone with a woman in a long time. Since I had left Colette a year before, to embark on a journey to the East, I had not thought about relationship. Is that what Isha had on her mind? Once she took off her turban and let her curly, auburn hair flow over her shoulders she was quite beautiful. However, she didn't even hint at intimacy. In fact, she closed her eyes and began singing a beautiful Jewish lullaby. Finally we were on the freeway, cruising along like old friends.

"I'm taking you to Picacho," she said out of the blue.

"Where's that?"

"It's in the desert on the Colorado River, twenty miles north of Yuma. It's a very magical, spiritual place. You'll like it. We can spend the night there."

I wondered again what she had in mind by "spend the night." Did she mean together? I tried not to think about it and to concentrate on the driving. After a while she had me turn off I-10 onto Highway 95, headed south. It was dry and scorching hot. The name Picacho rang a bell. I remembered it was the place that Eric had told me about, a guy I had seen doing Tai Chi on Mount Shasta the year before. He told me he spent winters there when it got too cold on the mountain. He lived there in a cave like a real yogi, and had invited me to visit him. When I'd asked for directions he'd said, "It's impossible to give directions; if you're meant to find me you will."

In Yuma we reached the Colorado River, which was on the Arizona-California border, and turned onto a dirt road. We headed north into the boulder-strewn desert. After an hour on the dusty road we emerged again at a bend of the Colorado River. After the long, hot drive we decided to go for a swim. Walking down to the riverbank, we had to push aside the reeds until we came to the water's edge. Isha shocked me by stripping off her clothes and wading naked into the river. I was amazed that hidden within the baggy yoga outfit was the body of an exquisite woman. Waist deep in the river, she resembled an Egyptian princess I had once seen in an art book.

I soon accompanied her in the swiftly moving river. After being refreshed, I came back to shore, where Isha was already on the riverbank, drying her long hair. As I sat beside her I wondered what bizarre destiny had brought us together and what our relationship was meant to be.

As a man growing up in the West, I had been programmed with two conflicting standards of behavior. Even though church taught abstinence prior to marriage, the culture was permeated with the desirability of romantic encounters. Men were raised to believe that women's motivating drive was sexual and that it was their duty to satisfy that desire. Now I was in a situation where, even though I felt no lust, the momentum of cultural conditioning was carrying me forward. I leaned over and gave Isha a kiss, and as my lips brushed hers I noticed a rivulet run from her wet hair down her breasts. Yet, she seemed unmoved and did not kiss back. Looking me straight in the eye she said, "You can have me, but is that really what you want?"

I was startled, for isn't that what I was supposed to want? What she wanted? Isn't that why she had brought me to this secluded location?

"Well, isn't that what you want?"

"No, that is not why I brought you here."

"Oh?"

"I brought you here to give you an initiation."

"An initiation? What kind?"

"I can't tell you until you give me your answer."

This is not what I had been expecting. Here we were, a man and woman, naked as Adam and Eve, alone in the wilderness, and we were not going to have sex? In one sense I was relieved. Or, was this just a feminine wile? Perhaps she secretly wanted to be overwhelmed and would be angry if I did not?

As we sat there looking into each other's eyes, our consciousness suddenly returned to ancient Egypt on the banks of the Nile. We were young lovers, who frequently slipped out of the palace to meet at the river. She had become pregnant, which caused a scandal, and the baby died of a fever soon after birth. After that heartbreak she had become a religious renunciate, and I had never seen her again.

Now, as we sat in the reeds and looked out at the river, we both saw only the reeds growing along the Nile.

"Yes, Egypt, we knew each other then," Isha said, confirming that she had been seeing the same vision.

I felt overwhelming love for her, and she leaned over and placed her lips on my forehead. She already knew my answer, but I said it anyway, "I want the initiation."

Without hesitation she assumed the cross-legged *padmasana* pose, and I saw the temptress dissolve into Kali, the Divine Mother—the ancient initiator of yogis, who destroys illusion in those she loves.

"Assume this asana, and follow me," she said.

Raising her arms skyward, she began a bellows-like breathing process. Then she lowered her arms parallel to the horizon, with her hands in a special mudra, and guided me in a visualization. Suddenly, in my inner sight a rainbow appeared overhead.

"You've got it," she said, seeing what I was experiencing.

Energy ran up my spine and into my crown chakra, suffusing itself through my body, putting me into euphoria. Here, on the border of two states, I felt transported to another world, sitting there in bliss.

After the ecstasy subsided and I returned to a more normal state, we dressed and walked silently back to the van. Isha had brought along some tabouli from the ashram, which we now ate for dinner. We talked for a while, and then spread a blanket and our sleeping bags on the ground. Isha sat up for a while singing another Jewish lullaby, which was so soothing I was soon out of my body and soaring among the stars. Twice during the night I awakened. The first time Isha was still sitting up singing, her eyes closed, the second time she was sitting in full lotus pose, deep in meditation. In the morning she was already dressed and had packed her few things.

"I'm leaving now," she announced.

"What, leaving to go where?"

"Phoenix."

I felt heartbroken, as though we were a couple and breaking up. I had never met a woman like this—so loving and self-contained, yet also such a spiritual warrior. I had thought we were going to be partners, that our relationship was just beginning, and we would travel west together.

"I have fulfilled my assignment. While I was meditating last night I saw that I have done what I was sent to do."

Can a Goddess do that, I wondered, open you up and then abandon you?

"But, we're in the middle of nowhere, and I don't want to leave now. After all, we just got here," I protested, hoping she would change her mind.

"Don't worry, you don't need to do anything, you can stay here. A ride is being sent for me."

"Oh, sure, not in this remote place," I thought. We hadn't seen another car since we had left Yuma. But, she was right, for a minute later a black Mercedes-Benz came slowly around the bend. Isha flagged it down and asked, "Going to Phoenix?"

"Yes."

"Can I have a ride?"

"Sure, get in."

The door opened and she slid in, then it shut, and she was gone. The Goddess Kali left me standing in the middle of the road. No wonder Maharajji had not told me where to go and what to do. Even if he could have told me, it was not something I would have wanted to hear. Anyway, life was so complex that it could only unfold spontaneously in the moment, as we follow our hearts. Despondent, I got into the van and headed down the road.

Now that I'm here, why not explore the area?" I thought. Making a sudden left turn, I headed up a dirt road that became narrower the further

I went. Finally it ended at a trailhead. Leaving the van I walked uphill, following the trail until I came to a small lake. On the left was a cliff, and at its base was the opening of a huge cave. Standing in the entrance, to my great surprise, was the man from Mount Shasta, Eric, who had said there was no way he could give me directions to find him. He was right; it seemed that only destiny and following my heart could have brought me here. He didn't seem surprised, as though he had been expecting me, and he invited me into the cave for tea. "I was expecting you," he said.

We drank our tea but didn't seem to have much to say. I couldn't talk about Isha and the initiation she had just put me through, and Eric seemed satisfied to sit in silence. We were like a couple of yogis, and perhaps we had been yogis together in ages past.

"Are you going back to Mount Shasta?" he asked.

"What for? I have no idea where I'm going."

Chapter 66

Seven Sacred Falls

I continued driving west until I reached San Diego, where I drove straight to the ocean. I kicked off my sandals and walked down to the beach to the Pacific. After years of travel and weeks of driving, the sun-warmed sand felt good. Sandpipers danced in and out of the waves and I inhaled the salt air. I scooped water from an incoming wave and splashed it on my face. The goddess of the Pacific seemed to offer her blessings, so I stripped off my clothes and threw myself into her warm, churning waters.

Rejuvenated by the ocean's embrace, I drove up the coast, enjoying the warm air blowing off the Pacific. With no plans in mind, I prayed for guidance and let the car go where it wanted. By the end of the day I was in Isla Vista, west of Santa Barbara, high on the cliffs watching the sun set into the ocean. After eating a local avocado for dinner, I lay my pad and sleeping bag down at the base of a tree whose spreading branches made a canopy. This particular tree seemed welcoming. Although I had never seen a nature spirit, I prayed to the spirit of this tree and asked it to watch over me while I slept.

During the night I awakened, enfolded in a shimmering light descending from the leaves and branches above. Each leaf seemed to be sending down a ray in blessing. Looking backward over my head, there in the trunk was a young girl with arms spread, extending her hands as if in protection. She smiled as she looked down with tenderness.

"Thank you," I sighed, feeling enfolded in her love, and fell once again to sleep.

Awakening with the sun's rays in my eyes, I rose and looked at the tree trunk, searching for the girlish spirit I had seen watching over me during the night. "I know you're in there, even though I can't see you," I said, hoping that she would once again appear. When all I could see was the tree's rough bark, I felt sad and tried to communicate: "Thank you for your protection, for showing that you are real. I will always love you."

I envied the tree. She didn't need to go anywhere, for everything she needed was provided. She didn't need to exhaust herself traveling the world on a quest, for she knew who she was and her purpose in life. Sensing she was in communication with all the other trees on the planet, I put my hands on her trunk and sent love to the forests of the Earth, and apologized for how arrogantly men were decimating them. I sensed the trees were intermediaries between Earth and other worlds of being, holding together the web of life.

A girl by the name Tanya, who owned a nearby metaphysical bookstore, gave me a morning welcome with a cup of hot tea. She had copies in her store of the booklet I had written the year before, which she gave out to special customers. She told me of a sacred spot in the nearby Santa Ynez Mountains called the Seven Sacred Falls. This sounded like a good place to fast and meditate, so I asked for directions.

After fasting for two days I felt that I had purified myself sufficiently to ascend the Seven Sacred Falls, and to ask for initiation into whatever mystery I was ready to receive. Following Mission Creek into the mountains, I climbed over boulders in the riverbed and up through the pools at the base of each waterfall. Tanya had said that you needed to ascend through all seven pools, each of which corresponded to a chakra, to receive the initiation. As I climbed, I prayed to be worthy.

It had been a wet winter, and the stream was running swiftly. After the third pool I ran into an overwhelming torrent and had to detour up the side of the ravine. The cliff became steep, and I soon found myself a hundred feet in the air, looking down on the boulders in the stream. I looked up the increasingly steep cliff and wondered by which route to ascend.

Clinging desperately to the rock face, I suddenly felt weak, probably as much from fear as not having eaten. I couldn't feel any handholds in the rock. There was nothing but smooth sandstone. Below, I could no longer find the toeholds, so going down was impossible. With endurance waning, I began to feel the moment of truth had arrived, that I would soon plunge to my death, and I called out for help.

"Dear God, if you don't want me to die, please help me now!"

There was no response. I tried again, calling this time to Jesus, Sai Baba, Maharajji, the Ascended Masters, and every saint and Guru that came to mind. My legs began to tremble and my fingers weaken. I knew that I had only seconds before the inevitable plunge. Then I remembered, I had heard that your last thought determines where you go after death, so you should die with the name of God on your lips. With that realization, I began to chant *Om*, the primordial sound from which all creation originates and to which it will return. The sound began spontaneously in my abdomen and rose upward. It became louder and louder as it ascended through each chakra, until *Om* vibrated in every cell and I merged with the power of its resonance.

Suddenly I was charged with seemingly limitless energy, and I was scrambling effortlessly up the face of the cliff. Straight up, free of fear, unconscious of hand or footholds in the rock, I shot straight up the rock face. At the top I flew into space and crashed onto my back on the forest floor. I didn't know what had happened. I was looking up at emerald leaves and through them saw the azure sky. Panting with euphoria, I lay there feeling the grace by which I had been saved.

What had happened? I sat up and looked over the edge. Far below, the river coursed around massive boulders. Scanning the face of the cliff, I could not find a single crevice that might have assisted my ascent. Pushing through the dense underbrush, I finally found a path leading back down the mountain. As I walked toward camp I regretted that I had not made it through all seven pools. Nevertheless, it seemed that I had received some sort of initiation. I reflected that, after all, initiation means being led within to greater awareness and power. It had not been through any external Guru, but through the power of my own true Self, the vibration of Brahman vibrating through my body, that I was still alive.[197] Who knows the meaning of every experience, and in what form an initiation might arise?

197 *Brahman:* universal consciousness, which gives rise to *Om* as the first act of creation. All else manifests from that. So, in chanting Om one opens the doorway back into the infinite, and has access to unlimited power. The great secret is *Tat Tvam Asi,* Thou art That.

CHAPTER 67

Vajrasattva

D escending the trail down the Santa Ynez Mountains, I realized that my search for a Guru had been destined to failure from the inception. For two years I had been traveling, trying to be something I was not. I could not be someone's devotee for long. My destiny was not to find another self, but my own Self. Although the ancient teachings said that the purpose of the Guru was to empower you to realize *that,* many seekers became addicted to being in relationship with an external person. For those people, whatever happens in life is perceived as the grace of the Guru, a view that ultimately is transcended in the achievement of self-realization and mastery.

When I sat at Sai Baba's feet and felt his love, I understood how addictive that relationship with the Guru could become. But, I could not spend eternity at his feet, and knew that I also needed to see him as a reflection of my inner Self. Once you have seen that Source, the path becomes one of turning inward and realizing *I Am That.*

Couldn't I have both, love of the other as well as the realization of the basic emptiness of all phenomena? Even the great Masters, who are fully enlightened, feel limitless love and devotion for each other. I loved the devotional singing of the Maharajji satsang, but I had begun to feel like a teenager waiting to leave home.

Tibetan Buddhism seemed to offer a solution. Its tantric rituals combined devotion to the Guru with self-awareness. Ever since that copy of Trungpa Rinpoche's book, *Meditation in Action,* had been dropped in front of me, I had increasingly felt drawn to these teachings. After experiencing the transformative presence of Trungpa Rinpoche, the pull had become stronger.

Rather than deny the world as an illusion and sit singing endless bhajans to illusory Gods, I wanted to learn how to manifest enlightenment in daily life in the world.[198] India had denied the importance of mundane

---

198 Tantric Buddhism also invokes many Gods; however, they are usually

reality for centuries, building temples before water and sewage treatment plants, and so the infrastructure was crumbling. As long as I was in the human world I wanted a spiritual path that embraced all aspects of life, from earning a living to being in relationship. It was at this point that Chagdud Rinpoche appeared in my life. He was one of the last great Tibetan tantric masters.[199]

Rinpoche came in a dream in which he revealed a past life in which I had been a teacher in Tibet. "You have been reborn now to continue that work. However, first you need to finish your training. Come see me and I will initiate you."

I had just seen his picture on a flyer in a natural food store, advertising the Red Vajrasattva *Drubchen.* This nine day tantric practice was said to bestow greater benefit than a year of solitary practice. I phoned the *gonpa* (ashram) and made plans to attend.

Chagdud Gonpa was in the Trinity Mountains of Northern California, west of Weaverville, and as soon as I arrived I set up camp in the nearby forest. Next morning as I emerged from the trees and stood on the hill overlooking the gonpa, I saw the snow-covered Trinity Alps, like jagged, white teeth in the distance. Below was the ornate temple bordered by *stupas* and prayer flags flapping in the breeze.[200] With Rinpoche's revelation of the lifetime in Tibet still vivid in my memory, I felt that lifetime telescoping into the present one.

Descending the path, I waited outside the temple with the other retreat participants, many of whom were long time practitioners. Inside, Rinpoche conducted a ritual to establish the sacred *mandala.*[201] During the practice

---

seen as *yidams*, aspects of oneself to be invoked in meditation, and then dissolved.

199 Chagdud Tulku Rinpoche (1930–2002), author of *Lord of the Dance: Autobiography of a Tibetan Lama* (Padma Publishing, 1992). For more information see: www.ChagdudGonpa.org.

200 *Stupa:* rounded structure representing various aspects of the mind of the Buddha, usually containing various sacred relics and used as a place of meditation.

201 *Mandala:* two-dimensional pattern used during tantric ritual, and which becomes a three-dimensional etheric reality, invoking a specific aspect of consciousness.

we would become part of that mandala, the etheric temple of Vajrasattva, the Deity who manifested the consciousness of all the Buddhas, female as well as male.

After being purified with consecrated water and incense at the entrance of the temple, we took our seats on floor cushions before rows of benches. Our piles of lengthy texts were placed on the benches. Then began an empowerment unlike anything I had experienced. Although I had attended Tibetan rituals before that were called empowerments, the transmission of consciousness had been absent.

Now a pristine energy filled the room like waves of shimmering light, waves that emanated from the Guru. He sat motionless on a raised, throne-like platform, maintaining the equipoise of multi-dimensional awareness. Immersed in the consciousness of Vajrasattva, he maintained the view that all beings are manifestations of the Deity. Each practitioner, in turn, visualizes the Guru as the Deity. Soon I found myself chanting in Tibetan,

Sovereign Lord, grant me the supreme empowerment of your enlightened intent. Grant me the dynamic energy of intrinsic awareness and the ripening and freeing into true reality.[202]

After this empowerment we progressed to the actual practice, but I lost my place in the Tibetan text. There were several complementary texts printed on loose, unbound, rectangular pages, each one for different parts of the ritual. As we moved back and forth between texts, the pages gradually fell out of order. In addition, we each had a bell to ring and *damaru* to beat at appropriate places, while simultaneously visualizing the mandala in multiple dimensions.[203]

Skilled practitioners sitting nearby tried to point out the current location in the text, but by noon I had little conception where we were or what was happening, and fell into despair. Not only was I lost, but I had

---

202 *Red Vajrasattva*, from the *Padma Sangwai T'higle Cycle* of Padgyal Lingpa, translated by Chagdud Rinpoche and Richard Barron (Chagdud Gonpa).

203 *Damaru*: double-headed drum with a clapper attached to a thong that is rotated back and forth with the wrist. Originally they were made of two human skulls, serving as a reminder of impermanence.

trouble ringing the bell in my left hand while simultaneously shaking the drum in my right hand. During the break I asked several of the old time students about the significance of the practice, but was shocked to find that they had little understanding. Trying to reassure me, one said, "If the Lama wants us to do it, then it must be good for us. Just have faith in the Lama."

This was no better than blind devotion. Here I am again, sitting at the feet of a Guru, I thought, chanting in a language I don't understand— participating in another meaningless ritual like the countless *pujas* I had seen enacted in temples all over India.[204]

During the lunch break I confronted the administrative head of the gonpa, Candace, with whom I had spoken on the phone to reserve a place at the drubchen.

"I came to tell you that I'm leaving," I blurted out.

"Why, what on earth for?" she asked, taken aback.

"I have no idea what's going on. I don't understand Tibetan, and don't know where we are in the text, or what it all means."

"Look, you can't leave!" she said, planting herself directly before me with a fist on each hip.

"Oh, yeah?" I fired back, wondering if I was going to have to make a break for it—remembering an old movie where hippies were held captive by a bunch of psychos in a California ashram.

"If you try to leave, I will throw my body down in front of your car!"

I was dumbfounded. Not since I had tried to walk out of a similarly confusing *Yom Kippur* service at a synagogue in Chicago had anyone tried to force me to participate in a religious service. Then the door had been locked and guarded by two burly men. Now this crazy woman was going to risk death to get me to stay. The thought of being trapped here was a nightmare.

"I will only let you leave after you talk to the Lama. Then you can go. In the meantime, forget the Tibetan. Just read the English words below the Tibetan. Will you agree?"

"Well, OK," I said, grudgingly. "I've been wanting to talk to the Lama anyway. But, if he can't tell me what's going on by tomorrow, I'm leaving."

---

204 *Puja:* a tantric ritual used to invoke the Gods and their consciousness.

Chagdud Rinpoche

Candace said she would put in the request for me to see the Lama. When the ritual resumed in the afternoon, I explained to the practitioners nearby, who had been supervising my clumsy attempts at Tibetan Buddhism, that I would not be chanting. Instead, I would silently be reading the English. They looked shocked, as though my words were blasphemy.

"You won't get any benefit if you don't chant in Tibetan," they exclaimed in disgust.[205]

This time as the ritual began I read the English description, and saw that through the union of our focused intent we were creating an etheric temple. In that ornate structure, encrusted with jewels, the Deity sat on a throne that rested on the sun and moon, and united within a lotus. Billowing clouds of incense smoke carried our prayers for the liberation of humanity skyward. As the Deity became ever more luminous, rays of light streamed from its heart to ours, and to the hearts of all sentient beings— and to every atom in creation. Vajrasattva dissolved into pure light and reappeared in our hearts. All beings were transformed into Vajrasattva, the mother of all the Buddhas. At that point, to my utter amazement, the text said, "Realize yourself as the Deity, and repeat inwardly, 'I AM Vajrasattva!'"

Once again, I AM! Those enigmatic words had appeared again where I least expected, in the midst of a Buddhist ritual. It was the same simple teaching I had rejected at the Theosophical Society, the truth of which I now perceived with utter lucidity. It was the same koan-like statement on which Sai Baba had asked me to meditate. The truth was inescapable: The Self is God. What your attention is on, you become. Focus on God and you become God.

Even Jesus had said, "Before Abraham was born, I AM!"

He also quoted the ancient prophets: "Thou shalt love the Lord thy God with all thy heart, with all thy soul, and with all thy mind." Giving what he said was the greatest of all the commandments, he added, "Love thy neighbor as thyself."[206]

This was the essence of all religion. What could be simpler? But, who

---

205 Years later I had a talk with Dzongsar Khyentse Rinpoche (Lama and filmmaker who also uses the name Khyentse Norbu; born: Bhutan, 1961), and he said that every Lama takes a vow to teach the dharma in the language of the local people, that in America the teachings, except for the Sanskrit mantras, should be given in English. Trungpa Rinpoche, who had attended Oxford University, was a master of the English language and fulfilled this dictate.

206 Luke 10:27.

could accomplish this? Could this purity of intent be practiced in daily life? It was much easier to chant a foreign language and do rituals to external Gods.

At the afternoon break Candace came up and apologized that she had not been able to arrange a meeting with the Lama.

"It's not necessary anymore. Now I understand what's going on."

"Really?" she inquired, a look of awe on her face, "Maybe you can tell me later."

For the next eight days I repeated the ritual, visualizing myself as the Deity, and moving in and out of timeless awareness. I felt like a Jack-in-the-Box that had sprung from the confines of the illusory self, and knew that I would never fit back into that confining box. Once free, who would want to go back to prison? Why pursue the worldly dharmas, the pursuits of the transitory world that bring you back into embodiment lifetime after lifetime?[207]

At the conclusion of the ritual on the ninth day, we lined up to present our *katas,* traditional silk scarfs, to Rinpoche. It was at this time that he bestowed his personal blessing by tapping each of us on the head with his *dorje.* This is a metal, double-headed instrument, symbolic of a thunderbolt, that can awaken intrinsic awareness.[208] When it was my turn, I looked into his face and tried to make eye contact; however, he kept his eyes down.

"Remember me? You appeared in a dream, and I'm here as you requested," I wanted to say.

However, he acted no differently toward me than he had toward everyone, and accepted the kata I held out on my outstretched arms. He returned it, placing it around my neck, then tapped the top of my head with the dorje. I lingered before his throne, wanting to talk to him and establish a personal relationship, but another Lama, who was supervising the process, gave me a shove. Disappointed, I continued along with the others toward the temple door.

---

207 The Eight Worldly Dharmas are polarities: fame and disgrace, gain and loss, praise and blame, and pleasure and pain.

208 *Dorje:* (Tibetan; *Vajra,* Sanskrit) literally thunderbolt, a double-headed, metal instrument, symbolizing instantaneous awakening.

Running into Candace outside, I thanked her profusely for her dramatic insistence that I stay, and not bolt on the first day. As I was about to express my sorrow that I couldn't meet Rinpoche personally, I suddenly realized that I had encountered him in the dream state in a far more intimate way than any physical meeting could have accomplished. We had encountered each other mind to mind, and I saw now that there was no separation. On the highest level, his mind, my mind, and the Buddha mind were one.

A year later Chagdud Rinpoche left his body while at his ashram in Brazil. He was found seated in Lotus posture. His heart area remained warm for days.[209] It is said that the soul of a liberated being ascends to the Buddha realm of enlightened intent during the forty-nine days after leaving the physical form. On the final day of this interval, while in deep meditation, I received a transmission of consciousness from him. Many others with whom he had a bond experienced a similar blessing. He was a true Guru, unconcerned with self or attracting a following, whose only desire was the liberation of all sentient beings.[210]

---

209 Before Rinpoche left his body, he named an American as dharma heir to carry on his work. This ex-hippie, Lama Drimed, had in a past life reportedly been a disciple of Padmasambhava, who brought Buddhism to Tibet.

210 I heard someone ask Ram Dass how they could tell if they were becoming enlightened or simply going crazy. He said that if you feel increasingly like helping others you are on the way to enlightenment, but if you find you are becoming increasingly preoccupied with yourself, that is insanity.

Chapter 68

Back in People's Park

Once again I found myself in Berkeley, camped in People's Park. It had been a year since I had been there after returning from my first trip to India. It had been a haven then; however, now the energy had changed. There were continuing battles over the park, one of the last remaining gathering places for free expression near the university. After spending a sleepless night in the park, I decided to look up a few of the Maharajji satsang who lived in Berkeley. Jai Uttal kindly gave me a space on his floor. However, bhajans no longer seemed to move me as deeply as they had sitting at Maharajji's feet. I could no longer sit adoringly for hours before pictures and statues of Gods. Once I had found the Inner Deity, I no longer felt so much outer devotion. Rather than sit at the feet of a God-realized being or worship a God, I wanted to *be That*.

Berkeley was a cauldron of worldly pursuits, and feeling that I was being cooked, I yearned for escape, for immersion in Spirit. I felt trapped between two worlds, one promising comfort and pleasure, and another offering escape into bliss. I had already drunk from the cup of materialism and found its pleasures fleeting, and the thought of leaving the world using the method of the Himalayan yogis was become increasingly appealing.

I had lived a full life. I had experienced all the pleasures the West could offer, and found them ultimately unsatisfying. In the East I had learned the path to liberation, so why not complete the process and leave the Earth with all its sorrows? I prayed for guidance before going to sleep that night.

At dawn I sat up to meditate, wondering what the day had in store. Suddenly, a dazzling ball of light appeared, and while trying to focus on it I heard a voice from within the light say, "Go to Muir Woods, and I will meet you there...."

"Who is that?" I wondered. Without hesitation, I gathered my belongings and was soon driving across the Golden Gate Bridge. The sun was rising over the Bay, and I remembered another sunrise I'd watched from the Brooklyn Bridge three years before. The epiphany then had been a turning point in my life. Soon after, I'd left for India. Now, I felt a similar change was coming. I had just finished a long journey, yet felt that a new one was about to begin. I did not realize that on the other side of the bridge, among the redwood trees of Muir Woods, I was about to meet the Master who had been guiding me inwardly over the past year—and that for this meeting he would appear in physical form. He would offer the freedom I sought, to leave the Earth, but would also offer another option—one that would change my life forever.

Ascended Master Saint Germain

Afterword

Born into materialism, I began a quest for that which, I discovered, did not exist in the material world—lasting happiness. How could it? Everything material has a beginning and end, but the happiness I sought did not have an end.

After seeing glimmerings of that happiness in a higher world, I embarked on the quest for enlightenment—to become one with the light. As it seemed necessary to have a teacher, known in the East as a Guru, I traveled to India to find the one who would show me the way. After many adventures and frustrations, I discovered what I sought—but which had been with me all along—the inner God Presence. But, what should I do with That?

I was drawn to leave my body and return to the universal Source, a transition that yogis in India learn to accomplish. My meeting with the Ascended Master Saint Germain, which I recount in my next book, *Adventures of a Western Mystic: Apprentice to the Masters*, altered that desire, and I saw another option—to remain on the Earth and share the love and wisdom I had gained with others.

Read the continuation of this autobiography in

Adventures of a Western Mystic: Apprentice to the Masters.

Glossary

Ashram: Place where spiritual aspirants meet or reside to do spiritual practice.

Atman: Soul, individualized Divine self.

Avatar: A descent of God in human form.

Advaita: Non-dualism, the philosophy that there is no difference between the individual soul and God.

Ayurveda: Traditional Indian medical system passed down from ancient Vedic times.

Baba: Endearing form of address for father, or holy man.

Babaji: Highly respected father.

Bhajan: Devotional singing.

Bhakti: Path of devotional worship of the Divine.

Brahman: The supreme and formless, eternal consciousness from which everything originates.

Buddha: One who is spiritually awake, enlightened.

Chakra: Wheel-like energy center of the body.

Chela: Disciple.

Deva: Celestial being, God.

Dharma: Practice of righteousness in accord with the laws of the universe.

Guru: Teacher, especially someone who reveals divinity within oneself.

Kirtan: Devotional singing in the form of call and response.

Kali: Goddess who rules the darkness, time and death, the consort of Shiva, destroyer of illusion.

Kurta: Collarless, loose fitting shirt that can extend as low as the knees.

Mala: Rosary-like string of beads on which to count mantras.

Maharajji: Respected great ruler.

Mahatma: Great soul.

Moksha: Liberation from the cycle of repetitive birth.

Mudra: Symbolic hand gesture.

Pandit: Pundit, Brahman scholar learned in the scriptures.

Paramatman: Brahman, the primordial self.

Prana: Life force, believed to originate in the sun.

Prema: Divine love.

Pranam: Sign of respect in which one bows with hands clasped, acknowledging the divinity of the other. There are seven types, ranging from simple bow to full prostration with arms outstretched.

Prasad: Food blessed by the Guru.

Puja: Spiritual ritual invoking consciousness.

Sadhana: Spiritual practice.

Sadhu: Wandering ascetic pursuing the path of liberation.

Samadhi: Union of individual consciousness with absolute consciousness. There are various stages, levels and durations.

Sathya: Truth.

Shanti: Peace.

Siddhi: Power attained through mastery of the self. One who has attained those powers is a **Siddha**.

Samsara: Repetitive cycle of birth and death due to ignorance of one's true nature, ending with moksha (liberation).

Samskara: Impression of past lives still embedded in the subconscious mind. Second meaning: Stages of life called *ashramas,* marked by rites of passage such as attending school, pursuit of career, marriage and the spiritual quest for liberation. There are from twelve to eighteen rituals performed at various stages to mark one's progress in life.

Shakti: Primordial life energy, the Divine feminine, consort of Shiva.

Swami: Spiritual seeker who has taken vows and been initiated into a particular order.

Sanatana dharma: Path of righteousness leading to liberation. The ancient teachings of India.

Satsang: Group that follows the same Guru.

Upanishads: Revealed teachings on the nature of reality, passed down orally from ancient times prior to the current era. There are over 200 that have been written down, of which about a dozen contain the core teachings of what has come to be known as **Vedanta.**

Vedas: Directly revealed knowledge from enlightened beings of ancient times.

Vipassana: Meditation leading to insight, attained by initial observation of the breath.

Yoga: Practice of uniting duality within the individual for the purpose of attaining enlightenment. Hatha (Sun-Moon) is the most basic form, whose purpose is to prepare the body for the more intense energies of higher consciousness.

Other Books and DVDs by the Same Author

Adventures of a Western Mystic: Apprentice to the Masters, Peter Mt. Shasta (Church of the Seven Rays, 2010)

"I AM" the Open Door, Peter Mt. Shasta, editor (Pearl Publishing, 1978)

"I AM" Affirmations and the Secret of their Effective Use, Peter Mt. Shasta (Church of the Seven Rays, 2012)

Becoming a Master, 2–disc DVD Series, Peter Mt. Shasta and Aralyn Rose (Siskiyou TV, 2011)

Peter Mt. Shasta, 2013